The Gift of Tongues

Christine F. Cooper-Rompato

The Gift of Tongues

WOMEN'S XENOGLOSSIA IN THE LATER MIDDLE AGES

THE PENNSYLVANIA STATE UNIVERSITY PRESS
UNIVERSITY PARK, PENNSYLVANIA

Library of Congress Cataloging-in-Publication Data

Cooper-Rompato, Christine F., 1970– .
The gift of tongues : women's xenoglossia in the later middle ages /
Christine F. Cooper-Rompato.
p.   cm.
Includes bibliographical references and index.
Summary: "Explores the phenomenon of xenoglossia, the sudden,
miraculous ability to speak, understand, read, or write a foreign language,
as it appears in the later medieval hagiographic record
and in English literature. Includes discussion of the late medieval
English writers Geoffrey Chaucer and Margery Kempe"—
Provided by publisher.
ISBN 978-0-271-03616-8 (cloth : alk. paper)
1. Glossolalia.
2. Xenoglossy.
3. Women in Christianity—History—Middle Ages, 600–1500.
4. Women in literature—History—To 1500.
I. Title.

BT122.5.C66 2010
234'.1320820940902—dc22
2009028044

It is the policy of
The Pennsylvania State University Press
to use acid-free paper. Publications on uncoated stock
satisfy the minimum requirements of American National
Standard for Information Sciences—Permanence of
Paper for Printed Library Material,
ANSI Z39.48-1992.

This book is printed on Natures Natural,
which contains 50% post-consumer waste.

FOR MY PARENTS,

Ruth and Ronald Cooper

Contents

Acknowledgments

I owe a debt of gratitude to many who have assisted me throughout this project. Many thanks to colleagues, friends, and students at Utah State University, including Alice Chapman, Lawrence Culver, Scarlet M. Fronk, Anne Cecile Martin, Phebe Jensen, Alexa Sand, Jamie Sanders, Steve Shively, Steve Siporin, and Amy Wilde Taylor for their ongoing support. My research has been funded in part by Utah State University's Department of English, the Office of Research, and the Women and Gender Research Institute. Many thanks also to Harvard University's Department of English and to the Huntington Library for their support of this project.

I was very fortunate to have extraordinary professors in the Medieval Studies Program at the University of Connecticut. I must express my deepest thanks to my advisor, C. David Benson, for his unfailing encouragement and mentorship, both when I was a student and now as a faculty member. Without his help I could not have finished this book. I am also grateful to other professors at the University of Connecticut, including Robert Hasenfratz, Benjamin Liu, Thomas J. Jambeck, Sherri Olson, Frederick M. Biggs, Sarah R. Johnson, and Jean Givens, all of whom have contributed in many ways to this project. I owe special thanks to Thomas A. Suits for his suggestions regarding my Latin translations; all errors that remain, however, are strictly my own. I must also thank a number of fellow English and Medieval Studies graduate students at the University of Connecticut, especially Will Eggers, John Sexton, and Chandra Wells, as well as others who read and commented on drafts in various forms. I would also like to thank Diana R. Uhlman, who first introduced me to the wonders of Margery Kempe and medieval studies when I was a creative writing student at Bowling Green State University.

I owe many thanks to other scholars who have discussed this project with me, including Pamela Benson, Nicola Bradbury, Ruth Evans, Andrew J. Furer, Joseph Harris, William Marx, Iris Müller, Rosemary O'Day, James Simpson, and Robert Stanton. This book would not have been possible without the help of many librarians at Utah State University, the University of Connecticut, Harvard University, and the Huntington Library, in particular Steven Batt, Richard Bleiler, Denis Brunke, Jennifer Duncan, Steven R. Harris, and Cynthia Nordgren. Special thanks also are due to the interlibrary loan staff at Utah State University and the University of Connecticut.

I am especially grateful to the Pennsylvania State University Press, in particular Eleanor Goodman, Executive Editor for Arts and Humanities, Laura Reed-Morrisson, Managing Editor, Patricia A. Mitchell, Production Coordinator, and Danny Bellet, Editorial Assistant, for their guidance and support, as well as Andre Barnett for her copyediting. I also owe special thanks to the critiques of the readers for the press, who offered many helpful suggestions for improvement. I am particularly grateful to Rebecca Krug for her revision suggestions and advice. Any deficiencies in the text or errors, however, are entirely my own.

Material from Chapter 3 has appeared as "Miraculous Translation in *The Book of Margery Kempe*," in *Studies in Philology* 101 (2004): 270–98, and an earlier version of part of Chapter 4 has appeared in the *Yearbook of English Studies* as " 'But algates therby was she understonde': Translating Custance in Chaucer's *Man of Law's Tale*," 36 (2006): 27–38. Revised versions appear here by kind permission of *Studies in Philology* and the *Yearbook of English Studies*.

I am profoundly grateful to my parents, Ruth and Ronald Cooper, for their continued support, as well as to my husband, Giovanni, and daughter, Francesca.

INTRODUCTION

According to the Acts of the Apostles, on the day of Pentecost, the Holy Spirit descended upon the apostles, and they began to speak in languages that they did not know. The Pentecost narrative is an important model for holy men and women in the later Middle Ages, many of whom were said to have experienced what is known today as *xenoglossia*, or the sudden, miraculous ability to speak, to understand, to read, or to write a foreign language.[1] Medieval miracle accounts, however, describe men and women as performing their miraculous tongues in remarkably gendered ways. For example, the early fourteenth-century Latin text *Actus Beati Francisci et Sociorum Eius* and its Italian translation and adaptation, *I Fioretti di San Francesco d'Assisi*, report that St. Anthony of Padua (d. 1231) was called to preach before a papal audience that included many men of different nationalities. Although he spoke

---

1. Although the term *glossolalia* has been used in a number of studies to indicate any kind of speaking in tongues, it usually has a more specific usage meaning speaking in tongues incomprehensible to humans. In this study, I use the term *xenoglossia* (variantly *xenoglossy*, *xenoglossa*, *xenolalia*, *zenolalia*, and *xenoglossolalia*) to refer to both speaking and being understood in a human language previously unknown to the recipient, as well as reading and writing in that language. In some critical literature, *xenoglossia* is used to refer only to the miraculous ability to speak a foreign language, while *heteroglossolalia* refers to those miraculous instances in which the foreign language of the speaker is understood by the listener. See Stanley M. Burgess, "Medieval Examples of Charismatic Piety in the Roman Catholic Church," in *Perspectives on the New Pentecostalism*, ed. Russell P. Spittler (Grand Rapids, MI: Baker Book House, 1976), 14–26, at p. 19. For further discussion of terms, see Stanley M. Burgess and Eduard M. van der Maas, eds., *The New International Dictionary of Pentecostal and Charismatic Movements*, rev. ed. (Grand Rapids, MI: Zondervan, 2002), 670.

his native tongue, he was miraculously understood in the diverse languages of his listeners, who reportedly asked in amazement, "Is he not a Spaniard? How then are we all hearing him in the language of the country where we were born—we Greeks and Latins, French and Germans, Slavs and English, Lombards and foreigners?"[2] Over one century later, the English visionary text *The Book of Margery Kempe* records a much more modest gift of xenoglossia. After two weeks of intense prayer, the monolingual Margery, while on pilgrimage to Rome, was gifted with the ability to communicate with one German priest who did not know English.

Many today consider the gift of tongues, either xenoglossia or *glossolalia* (speaking in an incomprehensible language), to be a long-dormant biblical experience revived in the modern period by the Pentecostal and Charismatic churches. Scholarly studies describe the medieval occurrences of xenoglossia as sporadic and isolated at best. My book challenges this perception by arguing that xenoglossia forms a vital part of later medieval religious culture. The purpose of this book is to examine medieval accounts of xenoglossia in both the hagiographic record and later medieval English literature to discover what the accounts reveal about gendered experiences of language and translation in the Middle Ages. In this book, I first examine the prevalence of xenoglossia in medieval vitae, canonization records, and miracle accounts, with particular focus on the lives of women. I then explore how the later medieval English writers Margery Kempe and Geoffrey Chaucer adapt the hagiographic model of xenoglossia in their own texts as a way of exploring issues of writerly control and authority. Saints' lives imagine men and women as practicing their xenoglossia quite differently from one another; women's miraculous experiences of translation are much more limited in scope and duration than men's, to the point that they often appear almost "mundane," or nonmiraculous. I argue that it is this "feminine" model of xenoglossia that Kempe and Chaucer adopt and develop to help them forge their identities as writers and translators.

Modern Experiences of Xenoglossia

The term xenoglossia or xenoglossy (French *xenoglossie*) was first used in print in 1905 by Charles Richet, a French physiologist (and future Nobel Prize laure-

---

2. "The Little Flowers of St. Francis," trans. Raphael Brown, in *St. Francis of Assisi: Writings and Early Biographies; English Omnibus of the Sources for the Life of St. Francis*, ed. Marion A. Habig, 3rd ed. (Chicago: Franciscan Herald Press, 1973), 1267–530, at pp. 1390–91. "Nonne iste Hispanus est? Et quomodo nos omnes audimus per eam linguam nostram in qua nati sumus,

ate), who investigated the case of a medium named Madame X. While in a trance, Madame X suddenly wrote long sentences in Greek, although she reportedly never studied or learned the Greek language.[3] Since the mid-nineteenth century, a number of Spiritualists had claimed they spoke in foreign tongues while in trances.[4] Richet was particularly fascinated by the errors in Madame X's Greek and concluded it was as if she had seen the letters and copied them without understanding what they signified. He eventually discovered that the sentences had come from a rare Greek-French dictionary housed in the French National Library. Richet suggested three theories to explain the event: first, fraud; second, an unconscious memory of something Madame X had seen at an earlier date; and third, a spirit intelligence working through her. Each of these theories he denied, finally, concluding that the event was "inexplicable."[5]

Richet's second theory, forgotten memories that are stored subconsciously and arise later in life, had long been recognized as a possible explanation for the apparent miraculous speaking of foreign languages. A notable literary reference to this occurs in Herman Melville's novel *Moby-Dick*. Reflecting on Queenqueg as he lies dying, Starbuck muses to Pip how feverish men who are "all ignorance" can suddenly start speaking ancient languages. He explains, "when the mystery is probed, it turns out always that in their wholly forgotten childhood those ancient tongues had been really spoken in their hearing by some lofty scholars."[6] In 1900, Théodore Flournoy labeled this phenomenon *cryptomnesia* in his study *From India to the Planet Mars: A Study of a Case of*

Graeci et Latini, Francigenae et Teutonici, Sclavi et Anglici, Lombardi et Barbari?" (146) in Paul Sabatier, ed., *Actus Beati Francisci et Sociorum Ejus,* Collection d'études et de documents, vol. 4 (Paris: Librairie Fischbacher, 1902), and *Floretum S. Francisci Assisiensis, Liber aureus qui italice dicitur I Fioretti di San Francesco,* ed. Paul Sabatier (Paris: Librairie Fischbacher, 1902), 159–60.

3. Charles Richet, "Xenoglossie: L'Écriture automatique en langues étrangères," *Proceedings of the Society for Psychical Research* 19 (1905–1907): 162–94. More recent studies often employ the term *xenography* for the apparent miraculous writing of a foreign language.

4. According to Rosemary E. Guiley in *Harper's Encyclopedia of Mystical and Paranormal Experience* (San Francisco: HarperSanFrancisco, 1991), "One of the earliest recorded cases of responsive xenoglossy was reported in 1862 by Prince Galitzin, a mesmerist who magnetized an uneducated German woman. The woman told of a life in eighteenth-century France, and spoke French fluently" until she awoke (655).

5. Richet's study of Madame X provoked much commentary, beginning with Sir Oliver Lodge's response to Richet in "Discussion of Professor Richet's Case of Automatic Writing in a Language Unknown to the Writer," in *Proceedings of the Society for Psychical Research* 19 (1905–1907): 195–204. Lodge argues that what Richet witnessed could not be fraud but rather a "crystal vision," in which the subject sees something clearly in front of him/her and writes it down without understanding it (204).

6. Herman Melville, *Moby-Dick; or, the White Whale,* Everyman's Library Classics (New York: Alfred A. Knopf, 1991; originally published New York: Harper, 1851), 479.

Somnambulism with Glossolalia, which explores the famous case of Hélène Smith and her various earlier incarnations, as well as her "travel" to Mars where she spoke with intelligent beings in a Martian language. Flournoy attributes Smith's ability to write several words in Sanskrit to her subconscious internalization of some of the grammar of a Sanskrit book that may have been shown to her after a séance.[7]

Paranormal explanations for xenoglossia have also continued to attract attention throughout the past century. Popular studies include Ernesto Bozzano's 1932 *Polyglot Mediumship (Xenoglossy)*, which describes thirty-five cases of xenoglossia that he attributes to spiritual possession, and Frederic Herbert Wood's *This Egyptian Miracle; or, The Restoration of the Lost Speech of Ancient Egypt by Supernormal Means* (1939), which explores the famous "Rosemary Case" and suggests that the female subject was a reincarnation of a Syrian woman named Vola who lived approximately 1400 B.C.E.[8] More recent studies have also attempted to link xenoglossia to reincarnation, particularly the work of the late Dr. Ian Stevenson, professor in the Department of Psychiatric Medicine at the University of Virginia. Celebrated cases described by Stevenson include T.E., an American woman who, under hypnosis, spoke in Swedish of her life as a peasant farmer named Jensen Jacoby, and Dolores Jay, an American who, also under hypnosis, began to speak in German and claimed her name was Gretchen Gottlieb.[9] Interest in the paranormal and xenoglossia continues today; a quick search of these two terms on the Internet yields numerous sites for people to write in about their own paranormal xenoglossic experiences.

7. Théodore Flournoy, *From India to the Planet Mars: A Study of a Case of Somnambulism with Glossolalia* (New York: University Books, 1963; originally published New York: Harper and Brothers, 1900), 332–36; for "cryptomnesia," see 276.

8. Frederic Herbert Wood, *This Egyptian Miracle; or, The Restoration of the Lost Speech of Ancient Egypt by Supernormal Means* (Philadelphia: David Mckay Co., 1939), 38. Rosemary's spirit-guide was a woman named Nona, who was Vola's contemporary and a reincarnation of a Pharaoh's wife (21). Other popular studies of paranormal activity and xenoglossia include A. Neville J. Whymant's *Psychic Adventures in New York* (London: Morley & M. Kennerley, Jr., 1931), and Florizel von Reuter's *Psychical Experiences of a Musician (in Search of Truth)* (London: Simpkin, Marshall and the Psychic Press, 1928) and *The Consoling Angel* (London: s.n., 1930).

9. For Ian Stevenson's study on Jensen, see *Xenoglossy: A Review and Report of a Case* (Charlottesville: University of Virginia Press, 1974); Stevenson argues that Jensen's vocabulary and familiarity with certain objects such as the potato suggest that he lived in the seventeenth century (29–37). For the case of Gretchen, see Stevenson, *Unlearned Language: New Studies in Xenoglossy* (Charlottesville: University of Virginia Press, 1984); on the basis of her vocabulary and her references to specific cultural and political references, Stevensen dates her life to the late nineteenth century (18–25). In his work, Stevenson distinguishes between "responsive xenoglossy" (when a person both understands and responds intelligibly in the foreign language) and "recitative xenoglossy" (when a person speaks in a foreign language by rote). Stevenson, *Xenoglossy*, 2–8.

Perhaps the gift of tongues is best known today as a religious phenomenon, specifically as a spiritual practice of the Pentecostal and Charismatic churches.[10] Whereas contemporary tongue-speakers usually give voice to language that is incomprehensible to other listeners without the gift of interpretation (*glossolalia*), accounts from the very early Pentecostal movement often claimed that the recipients were speaking in human tongues. The many followers of Charles Fox Parham, who is credited with spearheading the development of Pentecostalism in America at the turn of the twentieth century, believed that their glossolalic utterances were actually human tongues.[11] Gary B. McGee writes of those present at Parham's Topeka, Kansas, Bethel College meetings in 1901: "Participants testified, as others did at later Pentecostal revivals (e.g., the Azusa Street revival of 1906–9), that God had given them the languages of the world, including Greek, Latin, Hebrew, French, Spanish, Italian, German, Hungarian, Norwegian, Swedish, Bulgarian, Russian, Syrian, Zulu, Swahili, Hindi, Marathi, Bengali, Tibetan, Mandarin, Japanese, Chippewa, 'Esquimaux,' and even sign language for the deaf."[12]

Parham imagined that "mission tongues" would enable his followers to evangelize throughout the world.[13] He argued, "If Balaam's mule could stop in the middle of the road and give the first preacher that went out for money a bawling out in Arabic . . . anyone today ought to be able to speak in any language of the world if they had horse sense enough to let God use their tongue and throat."[14] Missionaries in the field would soon realize, however, that the gift of tongues could not replace intensive language study. Even so,

10. For the distinction between Pentecostal and Charismatic or Neo-Pentecostal churches, see Allan Anderson, *An Introduction to Pentecostalism: Global Charismatic Christianity* (Cambridge: Cambridge University Press, 2004), esp. chap. 8, 144–65. In sum, *Pentecostal* usually refers to "classical Pentecostalism," which developed after the turn of the twentieth century. The *Charismatic Movement* once referred to the practice of spiritual gifts that developed in the 1960s in the older "historic," or "mainline," churches, including Catholic and Protestant churches. With the development of a number of charismatic nondenominational churches in the later twentieth century, the term *Charismatic* was also applied to them (144).

11. James R. Goff Jr, *Fields White unto Harvest: Charles F. Parham and the Missionary Origins of Pentecostalism* (Fayetteville: University of Arkansas Press, 1988), 72. According to Goff, Parham formulated "the theological definition of Pentecostalism by linking tongues with the Holy Spirit baptism" (11).

12. Gary B. McGee, "Shortcut to Language Preparation? Radical Evangelicals, Missions, and the Gift of Tongues," *International Bulletin of Missionary Research* 25 (2001): 118–23, at p. 122.

13. According to Grant Wacker in *Heaven Below: Early Pentecostals and American Culture* (Cambridge: Harvard University Press, 2001), "belief in missionary tongues dated from the 1830s in Scotland" (45). Parham "taught his followers that *all* authentic tongues involved extant foreign languages" (45) and believed this until he died in 1928 (287n70). The term *missionary tongues* is Wacker's (287n68).

14. *Apostolic Faith Report* Editorial Files (Baxter Springs, Kansas) 2 (July, 1926): 2. Quoted in Goff, *Fields White unto Harvest*, 75.

tales of xenoglossia received by missionaries continued to circulate well into the twentieth century.[15]

With so much popular and scholarly interest focused on the Pentecostal and Charismatic experiences of tongues, earlier xenoglossic occurrences have received much less attention. Many scholars exhibit little awareness of the long tradition of xenoglossia in the Middle Ages, arguing that it ceased almost entirely after the apostolic age until it was revived in the modern age. There has been no book-length study of medieval accounts of xenoglossia to date, a gap this book hopes to remedy.

Early Experiences of Tongues

Medieval Christian manifestations of xenoglossia arise from the New Testament's depiction of the gift of tongues. Over thirty references to tongues appear in Acts and 1 Corinthians.[16] Acts 2 offers the most detailed description of the gift. Fifty days after the resurrection of Jesus Christ on the Day of Pentecost, the Holy Spirit descended on the apostles in Jerusalem, and they began to speak in languages that they previously did not know:[17]

15. Wacker suggests, "For the first five or six years most saints likely shared his view" that tongues were extant foreign languages (45). For the resulting difficulties for missionaries, see Wacker, *Heaven Below*, 45–51.

16. According to Roy Harrisville, twenty-eight of these references are in 1 Corinthians; see Harrisville, "Speaking in Tongues: A Lexicographical Study," *Catholic Bible Quarterly* 38 (1976): 35–48, cited in Burgess and van der Maas, *New International Dictionary*, 671. There is one reference in Mark 16:17, which reads, "And these signs will accompany those who believe: in my name they will cast out demons; they will speak in new tongues." *The New Oxford Annotated Bible with the Apocrypha: Revised Standard Version*, expanded ed., ed. Herbert G. May and Bruce M. Metzger (New York: Oxford University Press, 1977).
The *Vulgate* records, "signa autem eos qui crediderint haec sequentur in nomine meo daemonia eicient linguis loquentur novis." *Biblia Sacra iuxta Vulgatem Versionem*, ed. Bonifatius Fischer et al., rev. Robertus Weber, 4th ed. (Stuttgart: Deutsche Bibelgesellschaft, 1994). Biblical scholars have argued that verses 9–20 of Mark 16 were added at the earliest in the second century. See Frank W. Beare, "Speaking with Tongues: A Critical Survey of the New Testament Evidence," in *Speaking in Tongues: A Guide to Research on Glossolalia*, ed. Watson E. Mills (Grand Rapids, MI: W. B. Eerdmans, 1986), 107–26, at p. 108.

17. There is some debate over whether this was a miracle bestowed on the apostles, the disciples, or both. While the apostles are specifically mentioned in Acts 1:16–20 and 2:14, Acts 1:15 refers to the 120 disciples. See Beare, "Speaking with Tongues," 115. Carolyn Valone has argued that, in Renaissance Italy in the late sixteenth century, the traditional image of the descent of the Holy Spirit on the twelve apostles and Mary was expanded to include the 120 disciples who are mentioned in Acts 1:15. See Valone, "The Pentecost: Image and Experience in Late Sixteenth-Century Rome," *Sixteenth Century Journal* 24 (1993): 801–28, at p. 801.

And they were all filled with the Holy Spirit and began to speak in other tongues, as the Spirit gave them utterance. Now there were dwelling in Jerusalem Jews, devout men from every nation under heaven. And at this sound the multitude came together, and they were bewildered, because each one heard them speaking in his own language. And they were amazed and wondered, saying, "Are not all these who are speaking Galileans?" And how is it that we hear, each of us in our own native language?[18]

Acts 2:4–8

Acts also records that years later, the Holy Spirit descended on a group of Jews and gentiles who were gathered to hear Peter preaching in the house of the Roman centurion Cornelius; the participants began to speak in tongues (Acts 10:44–46). Furthermore, in Ephesus, the Holy Spirit descended on twelve disciples when Paul laid hands on them, and "they spoke with tongues and prophesied" (Acts 19:1–7).[19]

18. Translation from May and Metzger, *The New Oxford Annotated Bible with the Apocrypha*. The *New Revised Standard Version* translates 2:4 as, "All of them were filled with the Holy Spirit and began to speak in other languages, as the Spirit gave them ability." *The New Oxford Annotated Bible: New Revised Standard Version*, ed. Michael D. Coogan, 3rd ed. (New York: Oxford University Press, 2001). To replace "tongues" with "languages" suggests that the NRSV is clearly asserting that the apostles received human language, not incomprehensible language, as some scholars have suggested. In "Tongues or Languages? Contextual Consistency in the Translation of Acts 2," Jenny Everts argues that the NRSV has been influenced by Dynamic Equivalence Theory, which emphasizes contextual meaning over the retaining of original language. *Journal of Pentecostal Theology* 4 (1994): 71–80. The Douay-Rheims Bible, an English translation of the Latin Vulgate, states, "And they were all filled with the Holy Ghost, and they began to speak with divers tongues, according as the Holy Ghost gave them to speak." *The Holy Bible: Translated from the Latin Vulgate, diligently compared with the Hebrew, Greek, and other editions in divers languages. The Old Testament first published by the English College at Douay, A.D. 1609, and the New Testament first published by the English College at Rheims, A.D. 1582* (Rockford, IL: Tan Books, 1971). The *Vulgate* reads:

> 4. et repleti sunt omnes Spiritu Sancto et coeperunt loqui aliis linguis prout Spiritus Sanctus dabat eloqui illis
> 5. erant autem in Hierusalem habitantes Iudaei viri religiosi ex omni natione quae sub caelo sunt
> 6. facta autem hac voce convenit multitudo et mente confusa est quoniam audiebat unusquisque lingua sua illos loquentes
> 7. stupebant autem omnes et mirabantur dicentes nonne omnes ecce isti qui loquuntur Galilaei sunt
> 8. et quomodo nos audivimus unusquisque lingua nostra in qua nati sumus.
>
> *Biblia Sacra 2:4–8*

See also *Acts* 2:9–21, 10:44–46, and 19:6.

19. Commentators have suggested the presence of tongues in Acts 4:31 and 8:14–24. Burgess and van der Maas, *New International Dictionary*, 672.

The gift of tongues finds a more extended discussion in 1 Corinthians, which was written by Paul in part to correct the errors and abuses that had arisen in the Church at Corinth. Paul stresses the importance of all the *charismata*, or gifts, of the Holy Spirit and warns the congregation that its focus on the gift of tongues creates disunity within the church. According to Stanley Burgess, Paul advises not that the Corinthian Church should cease speaking tongues completely but that their experience should be governed by the following guidelines: first, "recognition of the diversity of charismata graciously given by the triune God"; second, "the supremacy of love, without which no charisma counts," and third, "the priority of congregational edification over personal benefit."[20] Paul emphasizes that the gift of tongues must be accompanied by the gift of interpretation, so that the entire congregation may come together and grow from the experience.

Whether these passages in the New Testament indicate comprehensible or incomprehensible language has inspired great scholarly debate. To summarize briefly, it is generally assumed that the gift described in Acts concerning the Day of Pentecost refers to recognizable human tongues, or xenoglossia.[21] The experiences in 1 Corinthians, however, are usually understood to indicate the speaking of unintelligible or incomprehensible tongues (glossolalia), although there is much disagreement over this point.[22] Some have argued that because Paul speaks in 1 Corinthians of tongues needing interpretation, this would seem to indicate that what Paul was describing was not a known human language; others insist that prophecy always needs interpretation, regardless of the language it is voiced in.[23]

Many of the early Christian theologians, however, seem to have believed that the descriptions of tongues in both Acts and Corinthians referred to human language, although scholars do debate this.[24] The Church Fathers also

20. Ibid.

21. According to Watson E. Mills, "Almost all interpreters recognize that Luke represents the tongues on the day of Pentecost as understandable language of some kind" (14), in "Glossolalia: A Survey of the Literature," in *Speaking in Tongues*, 13–31.

22. See Beare, "Speaking with Tongues," and Bob Zerhusen, "The Problem Tongues in 1 Cor 14: A Reexamination," *Biblical Theology Bulletin* 27 (1997): 139–52. For a discussion of scholarship on this debate, see J. Massyngbaerde Ford, "Toward a Theology of 'Speaking in Tongues,'" in Mills, *Speaking in Tongues*, 263–94. Many have weighed in on this debate; Cyril G. Williams, for example, in "Glossolalia as a Religious Phenomenon: 'Tongues' at Corinth and Pentecost," *Religion* 5 (1975): 16–32, argues that the descriptions in both Acts and Corinthians are of glossolalia, not xenoglossia, whereas Vern S. Poythress, in "The Nature of Corinthian Glossolalia: Possible Options," *Westminster Theological Journal* 40 (1977): 130–35, argues that we can draw no firm conclusions about the nature of glossolalia in Corinthians.

23. It has also been suggested by Pentecostal church members that the gift of a foreign human tongue requires interpretation if no one in the congregation is familiar with the language.

24. Nathan Busenitz, for example, has argued that early writers undoubtedly understood the

appear to agree that the gift aided the growth of the early church by enabling the apostles and disciples to preach to and to convert those who spoke other languages. For example, in his *Homily 35 on 1st Corinthians*, John Chrysostom asserts, "Wherefore then did the Apostles receive it [the gift] before the rest? Because they were to go abroad every where."[25] Several early theologians noted that the gift of tongues served an important part of the missionary movement but that it was no longer necessary.[26] St. Augustine writes in his *Homily 6 on the First Epistle of John* that the tongues in Acts "were signs adapted to the time. For there behooved to be that betokening of the Holy Spirit in all tongues, to shew [*sic*] that the Gospel of God was to run through all tongues over the whole earth. That thing was done for a betokening, and it passed away."[27] Similarly, Chrysostom suggests that gifts of tongues "used to occur but now no longer take place."[28] Although it is not part of my current project to explore these very early attitudes toward tongues, it is important to recognize that statements like these have been taken as evidence that experiences of glossolalia and xenoglossia in the late antique period had waned, not to be revived until the modern period.[29]

---

gift in Corinthians as human tongues. See Busenitz, "The Gift of Tongues: Comparing the Church Fathers with Contemporary Pentecostalism," *The Master's Seminary Journal* 17 (2006): 61–78.

25. John Chrysostom, *Nicene and Post-Nicene Fathers, First Series*, vol. 12, *Saint Chrysostom: Homilies on the Epistles of Paul to the Corinthians*, ed. Philip Schaff (New York: Christian Literature Company, 1899; reprinted Peabody, MA: Hendrickson, 1995), 209. Other writers who commented on tongues include Origen, Tertullian, Iraneaus, Hilary of Poitiers, Jerome, Ambrose, Leo I, Gregory the Great, and Bede. See Ford, "Toward a Theology"; E. Glenn Hinson, "The Significance of Glossolalia in the History of Christianity," in Mills, *Speaking in Tongues*, 181–203; and Kenneth Bruce Welliver, "Pentecost and the Early Church: Patristic Interpretation of Acts 2" (Ph.D. diss., Yale University, 1961), for discussions of these writers.

26. See Hinson, "The Significance of Glossolalia," 187.

27. Augustine of Hippo, *Nicene and Post-Nicene Fathers, First Series*, vol. 7, *Augustin: Homilies on the Gospel of John, Homilies on the First Epistle of John, Soliloquies*, ed. Philip Schaff (New York: Christian Literature Company, 1888; reprinted Peabody, MA: Hendrickson, 1995), 497–98. In "Tractate 32 on the Gospel According to St. John," Augustine suggests that tongues are no longer necessary because the church has spread through many languages. "Why is it that no man speaks in the tongues of all nations? Because the Church itself now speaks in the tongues of all nations. Before, the Church was in one nation, where it spoke in the tongues of all. By speaking then in the tongues of all, it signified what was to come to pass; that by growing among the nations, it would speak in the tongues of all" (195). In *Augustin: Homilies on the Gospel of John, Homilies on the First Epistle of John, Soliloquies*, 7:195.

28. According to Chrysostom, "The obscurity is produced by our ignorance of the facts referred to and by their cessation, being such as then used to occur but now no longer take place." "Homily XXIX," in *Chrysostom: Homilies on the Epistles of Paul to the Corinthians*, vol. 12, *Nicene and Post-Nicene Fathers, First Series*, 168.

29. "It was Augustine who established the belief, deeply held by many to the present day, that the charismata ended with the days of the apostles," assert Burgess and van der Maas, *New International Dictionary*, 674.

Medieval Experiences of Xenoglossia

The past fifty years have witnessed a tremendous number of studies published on glossolalia. Many of these studies discuss xenoglossia as a subcategory of glossolalia or simply do not distinguish between the two and treat them as similar phenomena.[30] The gift of tongues has been approached from a variety of perspectives and fields, including anthropology, sociology, psychology, and linguistics. Tongue-speaking is now recognized to comprise many kinds of linguistic experiences practiced by a variety of cultures.

Unfortunately, most of the historical studies on speaking in tongues in the Christian tradition either gloss over or completely ignore medieval occurrences, mentioning that tongues were claimed by some but that it was not a widespread phenomenon. In fact, in his essay "The Significance of Glossolalia in the History of Christianity," the historian E. Glenn Hinson has characterized this early period (250 C.E. and onward) to 1650 C.E. as a "Long Drought" of tongues.[31] This perception is repeated in a number of other studies; George H. Williams and Edith Waldvogel's essay, "A History of Speaking in Tongues and Related Gifts," for example, devotes less than three pages to medieval tongues before turning to early modern Protestant examples.[32] These are typical of the many studies that quickly pass over the Middle Ages as if they had little of importance to offer.

When studies do mention medieval xenoglossia, George B. Cutten's important 1927 work, *Speaking with Tongues, Historically and Psychologically Considered*, is frequently cited. Cutten, a minister and president of Colgate University, devoted almost an entire chapter to a number of medieval holy men and women who received linguistic gifts. Cutten associated speaking in

---

30. Two important early works not translated into English are Eddison Mosiman, *Das Zungenreden, geschichtlich und psychologisch untersucht* (Tübingen: J. C. B. Mohr, 1911), and Émile Lombard, *De la Glossolalie chez les premiers chrétiens et des phénomènes similaires, étude d'exégèse et de psychologie* (Lausanne: G. Bridel, 1910). In addition, Arno Borst's multivolume *Der Turmbau von Babel: Geschichte der Meinungen über Ursprung und Vielfalt der Sprachen und Völker* (Stuttgart: A. Hiersemann, 1957–1963) is an invaluable source for medieval linguistic miracles of all kinds. For extensive bibliography on glossolalia, see Mills, "Glossolalia: A Survey of the Literature," in Mills, *Speaking in Tongues*, 13–31, and Burgess and van der Maas, *New International Dictionary*.

31. Hinson, "The Significance of Glossolalia," 197. He notes, "Those who have been sharply critical of glossolalia have made much of the paucity of evidence of tongue-speaking from about A. D. 100–1900" (182).

32. George H. Williams and Edith Waldvogel, "A History of Speaking in Tongues and Related Gifts," in *The Charismatic Movement*, ed. Michael Pollock Hamilton (Grand Rapids, MI: W. B. Eerdmans, 1975), 61–113.

tongues with hysteria and women, and his elitism is quite evident when he writes that tongues were experienced by Christians who were "ignorant" and of a lower economic class.[33] Fifty years later Stanley Burgess's short essay, "Medieval Examples of Charismatic Piety in the Roman Catholic Church," heavily criticized Cutten's work for its blatant inaccuracies and vague, undocumented references, which Cutten had pulled from an earlier study by Joseph van Görres.[34] Burgess corrects several of Cutten's errors and cites the following male religious who received the gift of tongues: SS. Pachomius, Dominic, Vincent Ferrer, Anthony of Padua, Louis Bertrand, Francis Xavier, Stephen, and Bl. Angelo Clareno. Regarding religious women who receive the gift of tongues, his findings are limited to SS. Clare of Montefalco, Colette, Hildegard of Bingen, and the sixteenth-century Spanish nun, Joan of the Cross.[35] In this work and others, Burgess calls for more extensive research on the medieval primary documents describing glossolalia and xenoglossia, although his interest lies in determining which were legitimate experiences and which can be attributed to "stylized encomium."[36] My interest lies not so much in determining whether the events "really happened" (although I do suggest that some may reflect lived experience) but rather in examining how the accounts craft the presentation of the miraculous event. In essence, it is just this encomium, or praise, that most interests this project.

I have located a number of examples of medieval xenoglossic experiences not included in the studies of either Cutten or Burgess, which lead me to argue that reports of this miracle were more widespread and indeed more important to medieval piety, in particular women's piety, than previously recognized. To Burgess's list of xenoglossic holy men must be added a number

---

33. For Cutten's medieval examples, see chap. 3, "Fathers and Saints," in *Speaking with Tongues, Historically and Psychologically Considered* (New Haven: Yale University Press, 1927), 32–47. Cutten writes, "Those who speak with tongues are almost without exception devout, but ignorant and illiterate people" (168); for his association of tongues with women and hysteria, see 158–59.

34. Cutten quotes in English translation from the French edition of Joseph von Görres, *La Mystique Divine, Naturelle, et Diabolique*, trans. C. Sainté-Foi (Paris: Poussielgue-Rusand, 1st ed., 1854–1855; 2nd ed., 1862), 1:451ff originally published as *Die Christliche Mystik*, 4 vols. (Regensburg: G. J. Manz, 1836–42; 2nd ed., 5 vols., 1879) Cutten, *Speaking with Tongues*, 37–40. Burgess asserts, "Cutten, who was hostile to tongue-speaking, did not bother to search out the primary sources used by the erudite German scholar. Pentecostal historians have shown the same aversion to the primary records, with the result that the same stories are repeated again and again—usually without question—and mistakes once made are perpetuated and often compounded." Burgess, "Medieval Examples," 16.

35. Regarding St. Hildegard's miraculous ability to write in Latin, "a language completely unknown to her," Burgess asserts, "this must stand as the most unusual claim made on behalf of a medieval charismatic." Burgess, "Medieval Examples," 20.

36. Burgess and van der Maas, *New International Dictionary*, 674.

of male saints, including SS. Christopher, Patiens, Basil the Great, Ephrem, Teilo, Padarn, David, Cadoc, Andrew the Fool for Christ, Norbert, Francis of Assisi, and Bernard of Siena. To his list of holy women, St. Lutgard of Aywières, St. Bridget of Sweden, and the fifteenth-century English mystic Margery Kempe must be included for their gifts of vernacular xenoglossia. When we consider the gift of Latin for holy women as a variation of xenoglossia, the list becomes much longer, including, for example, SS. Catherine of Siena, Elisabeth of Schönau, Bridget of Sweden, Umiltà of Faenza, Bl. Ida of Louvain, and Christina Mirabilis, in addition to a number of other women.[37]

My premise in this book is that xenoglossia is much more popular in medieval hagiographical texts than previously realized. It is not an isolated or sporadic experience for the few, as has been claimed; rather, xenoglossia is intimately linked with perceptions of holiness and inspiration in the Midde Ages.[38] This is particularly so for women, who are imagined to experience miraculous Latinity much more frequently than vernacular xenoglossia. Several scholars in the past two decades have explored how medieval women's vitae and visionary texts rely on claims of miraculous Latinity to support holy women's spiritual and textual authority. Notable studies include Anne Clark Bartlett and Barbara Newman on Hildegard of Bingen, Ann L. Clark on Elisabeth of Schönau, Alexandra Barratt on Lutgard of Aywières, Catherine Mooney on Umiltà of Faenza, and Carolyn Muessig on the gift of Latin song in the vitae of medieval holy women from the Low Countries. Recently, Anneke Mulder-Bakker and Katrien Heene have examined how claims of miraculous Latinity function in the vitae of a number of women from the later Middle Ages.[39]

37. Elisabeth of Schönau is discussed in Lombard, *De la Glossolalie*, 66–67. Bridget of Sweden and Catherine of Siena are also mentioned in Anderson, *An Introduction to Pentecostalism*, 22.

38. Hinson refers to instances of medieval tongues as "isolated, spasmodic experiences." Hinson, "The Significance of Glossolalia," 197. A much more recent study, Anderson's *An Introduction to Pentecostalism*, refers to the instances of xenoglossia in the Middle Ages as "isolated reports" (22).

39. Anne Clark Bartlett, "Miraculous Literacy and Textual Communities in Hildegard of Bingen's *Scivias*," *Mystics Quarterly* 18 (1992): 43–55; Barbara Newman, *Sister of Wisdom: St. Hildegard's Theology of the Feminine* (Berkeley and Los Angeles: University of California Press, 1987); Anne L. Clark, *Elisabeth of Schönau: A Twelfth-Century Visionary* (Philadelphia: University of Pennsylvania Press, 1992); Alexander Barratt, "Language and the Body in Thomas of Cantimpré's *Life* of Lutgard of Aywières," *Cistercian Studies Quarterly* 30 (1995): 339–47; Catherine M. Mooney, "Authority and Inspiration in the *Vitae* and Sermons of Humility of Faenza," *Medieval Monastic Preaching*, ed. Carolyn A. Muessig, Brill's Studies in Intellectual History 90 (Leiden: Brill, 1998), 123–43; Carolyn Muessig, "Prophecy and Song: Teaching and Preaching by Medieval Women," in *Women Preachers and Prophets Through Two Millennia of Christianity*, ed. Beverly Mayne Kienzle and Pamela J. Walker (Berkeley and Los Angeles: University of California Press, 1998), 146–58. See also the introduction, trans. Myra Scholz (1–19) in Anneke Mulder-Bakker, ed.,

These remarkable studies offer ways of understanding women's relationships to language, literacy, and authority, and they have greatly influenced my own work and consideration of xenoglossia. What this book contributes to this scholarship on miraculous language is twofold: first, it considers how vernacular and Latinate xenoglossia function in a variety of medieval hagiographic sources; in doing so, I demonstrate that this is a much more widespread phenomenon than previously recognized, one that it indeed central to the medieval religious experiences of many. My book therefore places cases previously considered on an individual basis in a wider context. Furthermore, my book also focuses on how the hagiographic model of xenoglossia is carried over and adapted into Middle English literature, an important literary motif that for the most part has been overlooked in scholarship.

Xenoglossia in the Medieval Hagiographic Record

The popularity of the miracle of xenoglossia during the twelfth to fifteenth centuries can be attributed to several factors. First, we must acknowledge that miracle accounts were more frequently recorded, and with much greater detail, as the Middle Ages progressed; the work of both Michael Goodich and André Vauchez attests to the developing documentation of miracle accounts in the later Middle Ages.[40] Moreover, an increasing number of miracle "genres" reflected the apostolic model of Christ and his followers in the New Testament, including miracles featuring curing mutes and the paralyzed, exorcising demons, and even resurrecting the dead. It should not be surprising, therefore, that the description of tongues in Acts would inspire many similar accounts in later medieval saints' lives. Certainly, the popularity of the xenoglossic miracle parallels developments in the perception of sanctity in the later Middle Ages, in particular the increased emphasis on the imitation of the life of Christ and on following the *vita apostolica*.[41]

Seeing and Knowing: Women and Learning in Medieval Europe, 1200–1550, Medieval Women: Texts and Contexts 11 (Turnhout: Brepols, 2004), and Katrien Heene, "'*De litterali et morali earum instruccione*': Women's Literacy in Thirteenth-Century Latin Agogic Texts," in *The Voice of Silence: Women's Literacy in a Men's Church*, ed. Thérèse de Hemptinne and María Eugenia Góngora (Turnhout: Brepols, 2004), 145–66.

40. See Michael Goodich, *Miracles and Wonders: The Development of the Concept of Miracle, 1150–1350* (Aldershot, UK: Ashgate, 2007), and André Vauchez, *Sainthood in the Later Middle Ages*, trans. Jean Birrell (Cambridge: Cambridge University Press, 1997).

41. On changing perceptions of sanctity, see Vauchez, *Sainthood in the Later Middle Ages*, and Renate Blumenfeld-Kosinski and Timea Klara Szell, eds., *Images of Sainthood in Medieval Europe* (Ithaca: Cornell University Press, 1991).

Second, it has been noted that the occurences of vernacular xenoglossia increased as orders dedicated to missionary work developed. Many of the religious who experienced the xenoglossic gift belonged to the mendicant orders. Dominicans and Franciscans championed the apostolic model, and these friars focused their efforts on public preaching and missionary efforts, devoting themselves to ministering to urban populations with diverse linguistic backgrounds as well as to foreign evangelizing. Thus, hagiographic literature seems to privilege xenoglossic miracles because the miracles emphasize the commitment of prominent preachers to teaching and preaching to diverse populations.

Third, it is also reasonable to assume that descriptions of the xenoglossic gift became more popular in the later Middle Ages because there occurred an "expectation of tongues"; once the miracle entered the horizon of expectation of audiences, the miracle propagated itself. The miracle also became an important proof of sanctity. By the early modern period, we see an example explaining why a holy person did not have the gift of tongues: the vita of the Franciscan St. Peter of Alcántara (d. 1562) states quite emphatically that Peter did not receive the gift because he did not need it since he preached only in Iberia.[42] To call attention to the lack of xenoglossia in the life of a popular holy preacher would seem to indicate that by this period the gift of tongues was almost expected in the vitae of famous preachers, and that if a prominent preacher perceived as blessed did not receive it, an explanation was deemed necessary.

Fourth, it must be noted that later medieval religious culture grew increasingly concerned with the power of the tongue in both extremes, the miraculous and the sinful. Indeed, the miracle increased in popularity either in tandem with or in response to the emerging emphasis on the "Sins of the Tongue" and "errant speech" in late medieval popular preaching. Edwin D. Craun has traced the development of the "Sins of the Tongue" and demonstrates that the discourse on the abuse of speech gained prominence during

---

42. "Cum igitur Apostolis annuntiandum incumberet Evangelium toti orbi, tot immerso vitiis et peccatis, tantaque in medio idololatriae laboranti caecitate; necesse fuit, ut non minus hac gratia donarentur quam caeteris omnibus. Aliud erat de Sancto nostro, qui praedicationis munus extra Hispaniarum limites non obivit, nec proinde occasionem est nactus, qua dono linguarum ad aliorum salutem uteretur" (Oct., VIII, 687) in *Acta sanctorum quotquot toto orbe coluntur* (Antwerp and Brussels: Société des Bollandistes, 1643–1940), hereafter abbreviated *AASS.* All references to the *Acta Sanctorum* are by month, volume number, and page. Unless otherwise indicated, all references refer to the *AASS* database, which states that the source text is "that of the original edition, recomended by the Société des Bollandistes, and not the later incomplete editions published in Venice in 1734–1760 and by Palme in Paris in 1863–1870." See "About Acta Sanctorum," http://acta.chadwyck.co.uk/moreinfo/aboutacta2.htm (accessed August 18, 2008).

the thirteenth century, which saw an intense focus on pastoral care.[43] Perhaps it is not a coincidence then that the corresponding "miracles of the tongue" became so visible in mendicant vitae during this period. Moreover, as Sandy Bardsley has noted, fourteenth- and fifteenth-century art and literature is deeply interested "both with speech in general and the instruments of speech, the mouth and the tongue, in particular."[44] Medieval hagiographic accounts of xenoglossia demonstrate remarkable extremes in their desire to explore the specific mechanics of the miracle. Whereas some accounts focus on how or where the miracle takes place (in the saint's mouth or in the ears of the listener), others completely gloss over the specific instruments involved, preferring to focus on the power of the xenoglossic speech on the listeners.

Last, one of the main reasons the Latinate version of the xenoglossic gift became so important in the later Middle Ages is because of an increased amount of attention paid to literary and scriptural translation during this period. In response to a growing demand for religious literature in the vernacular, a number of texts were translated from Latin into the emerging vernaculars, as well as between vernaculars. Intense debate ensued over the proper translation of religious texts, in particular Scripture, and many fears were voiced that biblical and other religious texts would be mistranslated or misinterpreted by the laity.[45] Xenoglossia alleviates these fears, for what lies behind the idea of miraculous translation is the promise of complete equivalence between languages and a desire for "pure translation" that does not mutate, manipulate, or alter the text in any way.[46] This longing for purity in translation increased in tandem with the realization and acknowledgment that, in practice, translation necessarily shapes and rewrites.

Argument of the Book

The main question this study investigates is how the gift of xenoglossia, or miraculous translation, is imagined in later medieval literature and culture.

43. Edwin D. Craun, *Lies, Slander, and Obscenity in Medieval English Literature: Pastoral Rhetoric and the Deviant Speaker* (Cambridge: Cambridge University Press, 1997), esp. chap. 1, 10–24. See also Thelma Fenster and Daniel Lord Smail, eds., *Fama: The Politics of Talk and Reputation in Medieval Europe* (Ithaca: Cornell University Press, 2003).

44. Sandy Bardsley, "Sin, Speech, and Scolding in Late Medieval England," in Fenster and Smail, *Fama: The Politics of Talk*, 145–64, at p. 147.

45. For a discussion of the difficulties in translating holy texts, see Lynne Long, ed., *Translation and Religion: Holy Untranslatable?* (Clevedon: Multilingual Matters, 2005).

46. *Equivalence* refers to the correlation(s) of statement and meaning between source and translated text. Definitions of equivalence are relative, for understandings of source and target text meaning and expectations of target text form are culturally determined. According to Law-

In developing this book, I have found translation theory a useful tool for exploring how these narratives stage and describe acts of xenoglossia. Theorists, including Susan Bassnett and André Lefevere, have encouraged the study of the "idea of translation" throughout history to understand how translation has been both enacted and conceptualized.[47] When medieval people describe translation in its ideal state, they imagine xenoglossia, a miraculous process that effortlessly erases all linguistic and cultural borders. The xenoglossic holy person becomes the locus of desire for perfect, equivalent translation, as well as the locus of anxiety about imperfect, asymmetrical, problematic translation (the lived experience of translation). This becomes particularly evident when examining women's experiences of xenoglossia, as a number of questions are exposed concerning women's "appropriate" language acquisition, usage, and access to translation, questions that hide behind xenoglossia's "illusory effect of transparency," the assertion that languages and texts (oral or written) are perfectly translatable and leave no record or mark of their transferal.[48]

This book, therefore, discovers what kind of translators medieval xenoglossic women are imagined to be. More specifically, it looks closely at both the hagiographic record and late medieval English writings to explore both what the gift "does" (the access to language afforded the xenoglossic person), and how the gift is "used" (the practice and performance of that language). To explore these questions, the book is divided into two parts. Chapter 1 examines the more familiar model of xenoglossia as a vernacular gift granted to facilitate conversion and strengthening of the faith. Whereas men receive vernacular xenoglossia for the sake of wide-scale preaching efforts, women receive a gift that is much more narrow in scope, for the purpose of semiprivate spiritual conversation and counseling. Chapter 2 explores an important variant of xenoglossia for women, gifts of Latinity. I argue that women receive strikingly limited gifts of the Latin language, which may reflect either the "lived experience" of women's nontraditionally acquired literacy or a desire on the hagiographers' part to curtail women's access to, and practice and performance of, Latinity. By the end of the Middle Ages, however, the hagiographic record has developed to include several accounts of xenoglossia af-

rence Venuti, *The Translation Studies Reader* (New York: Routledge, 2000), *equivalence* has been defined as "accuracy," "adequacy," "correctness," "correspondence," and "fidelity" (5).

47. Susan Bassnett and André Lefevere include this direction as one of their ten suggestions for further research in, "Introduction: Where Are We in Translation Studies?" in *Constructing Cultures: Essays on Literary Translation*, Topics in Translation 11, ed. Bassnett and Lefevere (Clevedon: Multilingual Matters, 1998), 1–11, at pp. 10–11.

48. For "the illusory effect of transparency" in translation, see Lawrence Venuti, *The Scandals of Translation: Towards an Ethics of Difference* (London: Routledge, 1998), 12.

fording actual literate practices for women. The vitae and canonization process of St. Bridget of Sweden claim that she was miraculously tutored in Latin by the Virgin Mary and St. Anne so that Bridget could oversee the translation of her *Revelations* from Swedish into Latin. Xenoglossia, therefore, becomes a metaphor for authorizing textual practices.

The second half of the book turns to discovering how the hagiographic tropes of xenoglossia are carried over into late medieval literature. The third and fourth chapters discuss how the English writers Margery Kempe and Geoffrey Chaucer develop the model of xenoglossia in their texts as a way to explore their own identities as writers. For the visionary Kempe, whose *Book* is closely modeled on hagiographic sources, miraculous and mundane (or everyday, nonmiraculous) translation become two of the most important means Margery has for ensuring access to religious and devotional practices. The *Book* uses successful acts of miraculous and mundane translation as a way both to attempt to control Margery's reception as a holy woman and to support Kempe's own claims of writerly authority. The final chapter turns to a male literary author creating xenoglossic female characters and using them as metaphors for the writing process. In the *Canterbury Tales*, Chaucer explores the intersections between mundane and miraculous translation in the *Prioress's Prologue* and *Tale*, the *Man of Law's Tale*, and the *Squire's Tale*. Imagining xenoglossic women in several related genres (the vita, romance, chronicle history, and miracle of the Virgin) allows Chaucer to examine the ways in which claims of miraculous translation are used to legitimate the role of the translator.

ONE

According to the thirteenth-century *Chronicle* of Jordan of Giano, the first Franciscan mission to Germany was a dismal failure, in large part because of a problem of translation. In 1219, a group of more than sixty Franciscans set off for Germany to begin a new foundation there. None of them spoke German, and they brought along no translator. When first greeted by the Germans and asked whether they needed food and shelter, not understanding the question, the Franciscans answered the only word of German they knew, "Ja." Having been treated very well, they imagined that they should answer all questions with such a useful word. The plan backfired, however, when they were asked if they were heretics. After answering, "Ja," the friars were variously beaten, imprisoned, or mocked by being paraded nude throughout the town. Understanding that they would not have any success in Germany, they returned to Italy and, learning from their mistake, reorganized the mission two years later with a German speaker as the head.[1]

---

1. "In Theutoniam vero missi sunt fratres . . . Johannes de Penna cum fratribus fere 60 vel pluribus. Hii cum partes Teutonie introissent et lingwam [*sic*] ignorantes interrogati, si vellent hospitari, comedere vel huiusmodi, responderunt 'ia' et sic a quibusdam benigne sunt recepti. Et videntes quod per hoc verbum 'ia' humane tractarentur, ad quelibet interrogata 'ia' debere respondere decreverunt. Unde accidit, ut interrogati, si essent heretici et si ad hoc venissent ut Teutoniam inficerent sicut et Lombardiam pervertissent et respondissent 'ia,' quidam ex ipsis plagati, quidam incarcerati et quidam denudati nudi ad choream sunt ducti et spectaculum ludecre [*sic*] hominibus sunt effecti. Videntes ergo fratres, quod fructum in Theutonia facere non possent, in Ytaliam sunt reversi" (5–6), in *Chronica Fratris Jordani*, ed. H. Boehmer, *Collection d'études et de documents sur l'histoire religieuse et littéraire du moyen âge*, vol. 6 (Paris: Librairie

More than forty years later, when Jordan (who was a member of the second, much more successful mission) recorded this event in his *Chronicle*, the situation regarding linguistic preparation for foreign missionaries had changed considerably. During the rapid growth of their orders in the thirteenth and fourteenth centuries, both Franciscans and Dominicans focused their efforts on preaching across Europe and the Near East.[2] An important part of this effort included the study of foreign languages, or at the least the acquisition of proficient translators, to ensure that their proselytizing could be more effectively communicated. A number of Dominican and Franciscan accounts contain descriptions of friars' arduous language study.[3] Some religious ventured even further in their attempts to facilitate foreign conversions: for example, the Tertian friar Raymond Lull attempted to devise in his *Ars magna* "a system for a perfect language with which to convert the infidels."[4] One could imagine that by the time Jordan composed his account, looking back on the early friars' complete lack of linguistic preparation, it surely must have seemed like an incredible account of linguistic and cultural naiveté.

Or perhaps their lack of linguistic preparation was understood by Jordan to be a desire on the friars' part for divine intervention in the form of a miraculous, Pentecostal gift. In tandem with the recognition of the importance of learning foreign languages to be effective missionaries, there persisted the belief and hope that "God would provide" for preachers and other religious in linguistic need. Stories of just such a sort circulated in hagiographic accounts, for during the later Middle Ages, a number of holy men and women

---

Fischbacher, 1908). Jordan records that the friars from the first mission thought Germany was only suited to those religious who desired martyrdom. John Moorman dates the chronicle to about 1262 (67n4) in *A History of the Franciscan Order, from Its Origins to the Year 1517* (Oxford: Clarendon, 1968), 67–69.

2. For a discussion of mendicant missions in the Near East, see Andrew Jotischky, "The Mendicants as Missionaries and Travellers in the Near East in the Thirteenth and Fourteenth Centuries," in *Eastward Bound: Travel and Travellers, 1050–1500*, ed. Rosamund Allen (Manchester: Manchester University Press, 2004), 88–106.

3. For Dominicans studying foreign languages, see Pierre Mandonnet, *St. Dominic and His Work*, trans. Mary Benedicta Larkin (St. Louis: B. Herder, 1944), 78–79. In the *Summa Theologiae*, St. Thomas Aquinas writes that man can approximate the gift of tongues by studying language: "Thus, for instance, he [God] gave the Apostles knowledge of the Scriptures and of all languages, which men may acquire by study and custom, though not in so perfect a manner" (Sicut Apostolis dedit scientiam Scripturarum et omnium linguarum, quam homines per studium vel consuetudinem acquirere possunt, licet non ita perfecte), ed. Anthony Kenny, Part 1, Q. 51, Art IV, vol. 22 (New York: McGraw-Hill, 1964), 64–65. According to Umberto Eco, Roger Bacon, a Franciscan, "foresaw that contact with the infidels (not merely Arabs, but also Tartars) would require study of foreign languages" (53), in *The Search for the Perfect Language*, trans. James Fentress (Oxford: Blackwell, 1995).

4. For a discussion of this "universal language," see Eco, *Search for the Perfect Language*, 53–72.

were reported to have experienced a type of miracle that both drew attention to and erased linguistic difference. This was afforded by the divine gift of xenoglossia, the sudden, miraculous ability to speak, to understand, to read, or to write a foreign language previously unknown to the recipient. These men and women could do what the first Franciscan missionary movement in Germany only imagined was possible: they could ignore language difference simply by opening their mouths and be understood by (or understand) foreign speakers, without years of study and toil or, indeed, any preparation at all.

Medieval accounts of xenoglossia are modeled on the New Testament's description of the gift of tongues bestowed on the apostles (or disciples) to facilitate the growth of Christianity through evangelizing. The accounts emphasize the saints' similarities with the apostles and demonstrate the importance of the theme of conversion in hagiographic literature. For medieval vitae, this includes the conversion not only of non-Christians to Christianity but also of Christians to a more penitent lifestyle, or even the "conversion" of a layperson to the joining of a religious order. The xenoglossic experiences of medieval men and women range from male missionary saints, who are engaged in large-scale preaching efforts and who receive the ability to speak the many languages of their listeners, to small-scale, more private linguistic miracles experienced by holy women for the sake of one-on-one spiritual guidance and conversation.

Although at first glance many of these accounts seem quite similar, what each chooses to emphasize can differ greatly. Some focus on the nature of the miracle (does it occur in the mouth of the speaker or the ears of the listener, for example), others on why the miracle occurs (the purpose of miraculous translation), or the manner or means in which the miracle is bestowed. Many direct their attention to the audience of the miracle, the translation "receivers" (those who directly receive the miraculous translation) and the larger community of translation "users," those who observe the miracle or even hear or read about it later, thereby benefiting indirectly from the event.

More important, the accounts imagine the experiences of miraculous translation as remarkably gendered. Whereas xenoglossic men often receive the full command of the language for their use in the company of many (lasting a particular evening, several days, or even a lifetime), no women receive these wide-scale preaching miracles. Women typically experience vernacular xenoglossia for briefer periods (one conversation) in one-on-one situations of counseling and spiritual conversation, when approached by another in need. Unlike their male counterparts, vernacularly xenoglossic women generally do not seek out the gift, and whereas holy men appear to gain fame and positions of responsibility because of their xenoglossia, women's xenoglossia does not tend to lead them directly to positions of power. This suggests that when hagiographers imagined xenoglossia they imagined experiences that were highly gendered and reflected their expectations of men's and women's appropriate social behavior. In some cases, the more modest scope of the miracle might also reflect actual lived experiences.

In the following discussion, I have grouped the medieval examples of xenoglossia into two types of experiences: (1) large-scale preaching and (2) smaller, semiprivate miracles. I refer to the small-scale experiences as "semiprivate" rather than "private" because even when miracles are shared by only two people in intimate conversation, the miraculous events do not happen in isolation without witnesses, for they are a kind of "sacred performance" that is observed, commented on, and documented.[5] It is of course important that the miracle is observed, or else it could not be used as formal evidence of blessedness. If the purpose of reporting instances of xenoglossia is to strengthen the faith of the larger Christian community, then audiences of the vitae become a larger circle of users of that miraculous translation. In many xenoglossic narratives, therefore, what is most important is not necessarily the actual words of what is translated (xenoglossia as the *medium*) but rather xenoglossia as the *message* itself: that this person is so holy that God has rendered his/her language transparent and translated it.

Part 1: Vernacular Xenoglossia in the Lives of Men

The Apostolic Model

The most common and widely recognized form of xenoglossia is that attributed to a number of holy men: it is the large-scale preaching miracle, modeled on the description of the Pentecostal gift in Acts, in which the apostles (or disciples) preached, and their words were either translated in the ears of their listeners (hence, a gift of aurality), or they were enabled to speak the foreign languages of their listeners (hence, a gift of orality). These prominent medieval holy men were reported in vitae to have experienced the gift of vernacular tongues for the purpose of preaching to the masses or for sustaining them-

5. For the concept of witnessing performance, see Mary A. Suydam and Joanna E. Zeigler, eds., *Performance and Transformation: New Approaches to Late Medieval Spirituality* (New York: St. Martin's Press, 1999), esp. chaps. 1 (pp. 1–25) and 7 (pp. 169–210), both by Suydam.

selves while engaged in missionary activities. The narratives therefore emphasize how their linguistic gifts facilitated the growth of the church. It is
important to note that only men receive this large-scale preaching miracle;
no medieval woman is granted xenoglossia with this kind of scope, reflecting
the Pauline edict that women must not preach.[6]

Xenoglossia is reported in several later medieval lives of the apostles. For
example, the immensely popular thirteenth-century *Legenda aurea* (*Golden
Legend*) by the Dominican Jacobus de Voragine records that the apostle Matthew used his gift of tongues while preaching in Ethiopia. While Matthew was
staying with a eunuch who had been baptized by Philip,

> the eunuch asked Matthew how he happened to speak and under-
> stand so many languages, and he explained that after the descent of
> the Holy Spirit upon the apostles, he found that he possessed knowl-
> edge of all languages. Thereafter, whereas those whose pride had
> made them want to build a tower reaching to heaven had to stop
> building because of the confusion of languages, so the apostles, by
> their knowledge of all languages, were able to build a tower not of
> stones but of virtues, by which all who believed could ascend to
> heaven.[7]

Matthew's gift is described as the direct remedy of the confusion of tongues
resulting from the fall of the tower of Babel, which medieval people believed
had divided a monolingual world into seventy or more separate languages.
Medieval xenoglossia fosters a temporary healing of the divisions, or
"wounds," caused by the fall of the tower of Babel and allows the saints to

---

6. Despite injunctions against women preaching, a number of medieval women did preach
and teach; see Beverly Mayne Kienzle and Pamela J. Walker, eds., *Women Preachers and Prophets
Through Two Millennia of Christianity* (Berkeley and Los Angeles: University of California Press,
1998).

7. Jacobus de Voragine, *The Golden Legend: Readings on the Saints*, trans. William Granger
Ryan (Princeton: Princeton University Press, 1993), 2:184. Ryan made his translation from the
Latin second edition of Th. Graesse, Jacobus de Voragine, *Legenda aurea vulgo historia lombardica
dicta* (Leipzig, 1850). All Latin quotations from the *Legenda aurea* are from the authoritative Latin
edition edited by Giovanni Paolo Maggioni, 2nd ed., 2 vols. (Tavarnuzze-Firenze: Sismel, Edizioni
del Galluzzo, 1998). "Eunucho autem sanctum Matheum interrogante quomodo tot linguas loqueretur et intelligeret, exposuit ei Matheus quomodo spiritu sancto descendente omnium linguarum scientiam recepisset ut, sicut illi qui per superbiam turrim usque in celum edificare
uolebant pre confusione linguarum ab edificio cessauerunt, sic apostoli per omium linguarum
scientiam turrim non de lapidibus, sed de uirtutibus construant, per quam omnes qui crediderint
in celum ascendant." Jacobus de Voragine, *Legenda aurea*, 2:958.

take part in their own miracle of Pentecost.[8] This miraculous language acquisition erases all linguistic differences and creates a wider Christian community forged outside of linguistic divisions.

We find similar references to Pentecost in accounts of xenoglossia occurring in the lives of medieval saints who follow in the apostles' footsteps. For example, the later medieval life of St. Patiens, the fourth bishop of Metz, emphasizes this connection by describing how a gift of tongues enabled him to function in a new land and to demand "the things necessary to him" when he entered the land of Gaul after a difficult sea voyage: "This was the miraculous token in the Church of the first men (i.e., the Apostles), that those whom the Apostles anointed, or ordained for preaching to the nations, on the spot plainly received the knowledge of tongues, just as the Acts of the Apostles tell of Cornelius. And so with this certain sign Blessed Patiens came to the city of Metz."[9] Similarly, St. Norbert of Xanten (d. 1134), the founder of the Premonstratensians, was attributed a miracle of vernacular speech in a land in which he would start his religious community. Clearly linking Norbert with his apostolic models, the vita of the German saint records how, on the day after he arrived at Valenciennes with three companions, "he delivered a sermon to the people scarcely yet knowing or understanding anything of their language, that is 'Romana' [French] since he had never learned it. But he did not doubt that, if he attempted to speak the word of God in his mother tongue, the Holy Spirit, which once had taught [the apostles] 120 diverse tongues, would make the foreign rudeness of the German language, and the difficulty of Latin eloquence, easy for the listeners to understand."[10]

8. The concept of "healing the wound of Babel" can be found in Eco, *Search for the Perfect Language*, 351. For a discussion of the gift of tongues in relation to Babel, see Frank D. Macchia, "Babel and the Tongues of Pentecost: Reversal or Fulfillment? A Theological Perspective," in *Speaking in Tongues: Multi-Disciplinary Perspectives*, ed., Mark J. Cartledge (Bletchley, UK, and Waynesboro, GA: Paternoster, 2006), 34–51.

9. "Gallorum fines intrauit. Mirare! Linguam Barbarorum, quam pridem ignorabat, intelligebat, & respondebat, necessariaque requirebat. Fuit hoc insigne miraculum in Ecclesia primitiuorum, vt quos Apostoli chrismate praesignabant, vel ad praedicandum gentibus ordinabant, illico manifeste scientiam linguarum accipiebant, sicut de Cornelio Actus Apostolorum narrant. Itaque certo indicio B. Patiens Metim ciuitatem deuenit." *AASS*, Jan., I, 470. Tradition also says that Patiens was a disciple of St. John the Evangelist. See *AASS*, Jan., I, 469–70.

10. "In crastinum ergo fecit sermonem ad populum vix adhuc aliquid sciens vel intelligens de lingua illa, Romana videlicet, quia numquam eam didicerat: sed non diffidebat, quin, si materna lingua verbum Dei adoriretur, Spiritus sanctus, qui quondam centum viginti linguarum erudierat diversitatem; linguae Teutonicae barbariem, vel Latinae eloquentiae difficultatem, auditoribus habilem ad intelligendum faceret." *AASS*, June, I, 827. The *Acta Sanctorum*'s editorial note to this passage states, "He [Norbert] understands poor men, uneducated men, illiterate men, and countrymen." It is also suggested that the "Romana" language was that which is called "Gallicana," or "Frankish." "*Pauperes, rudes, ineruditos & rusticos intelligit*. Romana lingua *erat, quae modo Gallicana seu Francica dicitur*." *AASS*, June, I, 828 note k. Whereas the vita suggests

After pursuing itinerant preaching throughout the regions of modern-day Belgium and France, Norbert founded his religious community in Prémontré; the attribution of the xenoglossic gift therefore emphasizes his apostolic undertaking and his success, both spiritual and linguistic, in the "Romano"-speaking community. Many medieval accounts draw out the similarities with the apostles, asserting how their holy subjects remedy the divisions caused by Babel, be those languages that were miraculously translated deemed a "foreign rudeness" or a "difficult eloquence."

Large-Scale Preaching Enterprises

Similar to Norbert's account, many anecdotes of medieval xenoglossia describe the gift of tongues granted to holy men for wide-scale preaching efforts. The gift enables holy men to travel through foreign lands and to achieve recognition through evangelizing. Three sixth-century Welsh saints, David (the patron saint of Wales), Teilo, and Padarn are all said to have experienced the gift of tongues on their journey to Jerusalem in later medieval versions of their vitae. Xenoglossia is clearly a significant sign of blessedness in these vitae, for what emerges is a situation of "dueling tongues" in which each saint appears to be asserted by its cult to be the more gifted.[11] These three lives alone suggest that the gift of tongues in the Middle Ages is not "occasional" or "sporadic," for claims of xenoglossia in David's *Life* appear to have influenced similar claims in the vitae of Teilo and Padarn.

The *Lives* of David, Teilo, and Padarn emphasize the holy men's connection to the apostles on the Day of Pentecost. An account in the vita of David records his own reception of the gift when he crossed from Britain into Gaul on his way to Jerusalem: "When, however, they traveled to Gaul, having sailed across the British sea, and heard the foreign languages of the different peoples, Father David was enriched with the gift of tongues, just as that renowned

---

that Norbert's Latin and German were translated in the ears of the listeners, the commentators in the *Acta Sanctorum* suggest that Norbert understood the language of his listeners.

11. According to G. H. Doble and D. Simon Evans, ed., *The Lives of the Welsh Saints* (Cardiff: University of Wales Press, 1971), "inspired by the conflicting interests of the three principal churches of South Wales, represented by David, Teilo and Padarn," three variations of the story of the saints' journey to Jerusalem developed; Doble asserts that the story of the three saints' journey "must have been invented at St. David's" (176). Rhigyfarch's *Vita David* (c. 1090) records that only David received the gift of tongues in Gaul (177); the *Lives* of Padarn and Teilo came after and were heavily influenced by the *Life* of David. See also J. W. James, ed. and trans., *Rhigyfarch's Life of St. David: The Basic Mid Twelfth-Century Latin Text* (Cardiff: University of Wales Press, 1967); D. Simon Evans, *The Welsh Life of St. David* (Cardiff: University of Wales Press, 1988); and Elissa R. Henken, *Traditions of the Welsh Saints* (Cambridge: D. S. Brewer, 1987).

Apostolic assembly had been, so that they did not need an interpreter while spending time among foreign peoples."[12] Similarly, the vita of Padarn in the fifteenth-century *Nova Legenda Anglie*, which is based on the fourteenth-century *Sanctilogium Angliae, Walliae, Scotiae, et Hiberniae* by John of Tynemouth, asserts that the saints, while traveling in foreign lands, received the gift of tongues so that each person understood their words in his/her own tongue.[13]

The three experience the gift again in Jerusalem, further emphasizing their apostolic similarities and the effect of their wide-scale preaching. The *Life* of Teilo records:

> In order that he might satisfy the wishes of the imploring people, he began to lay open sacred Scripture, and each one of those standing near him heard him speaking in his own tongue. And when all had been affected by the sweetness of his sermon to such a degree that the longer they listened to him, the more they desired to hear him, in order that he might not seem to appropriate the office of preacher, if he alone had preached, he said to the people: "Listen now to the words of life from my brothers, who are more perfect than I in their lives, and more diligent in their learning." SS. David and Paternus arose therefore and preached to the people, with all understanding them perfectly in their own tongue.[14]

Teilo's account calls attention to the effect of his sweet speech on the audience and focuses on his humility in turning over the role of preacher to his companions. The account of David, however, focuses on the conversion of non-

12. "Cum autem trans mare Britannicum vecti, Gallias adirent, ac alienas diuersarum gentium linguas audirent; linguarum gratia, sicut Apostolicus ille coetus, ditatus est Dauid Pater: vt ne in extraneis degentes gentibus, interprete egerent." *AASS*, Mar., I, 44. See also *Rhigyfarch's Life of St. David*, ed. James, 20.

13. "Per barbaras enim nationes iter agentes, gratiam linguarum a domino acceperunt, vnumquemque hominem propria lingua in qua natus fuerat alloquentes." John of Tynemouth, *Nova Legenda Anglie*, ed. Carl Horstmann, 2 vols. (Oxford: Clarendon, 1901), 2:276; see also *AASS*, Apr., II, 380.

14. Translation mine. "Vt tamen populo supplicanti et illorum voto satisfaceret, sacras scripturas exponere cepit: et vnusquisque astantium illum sua lingua loquentem audiuit. Cumque omnes tanta dulcedine sermonis illius essent affecti, vt quanto eum diutius audirent, magis illum audire desiderarent; ne predicandi officium videretur presumere si solus predicasset, populo dixit: 'Audite iam a fratribus meis verba vite, qui me perfectiores in vita sunt, et diligentiores in doctrina.' Surrexerunt ergo sanctus Dauid et Paternus, et predicauerunt populo, omnibusque in sua lingua perfecte intelligentibus eos." *Nova Legenda Anglie*, 2:365–66. See also *AASS*, Feb., II, 309.

Christians to Christianity through the saints' preaching.[15] Doble has noted that Celtic hagiography of this time period often includes the motif of a journey to Jerusalem;[16] another prominent sixth-century Welsh saint, Cadoc, was also reported to have experienced xenoglossia while in Jerusalem, no doubt reflecting the emphasis on tongues in the the medieval Welsh tradition.[17]

In the later Middle Ages, a number of Dominicans and Franciscans, famed for their preaching efforts, were credited with large-scale xenoglossic preaching miracles. The mid-fifteenth-century canonization process of the Dominican St. Vincent Ferrer (d. 1419), who is reported to have converted tens of thousands of Jews and Muslims to Christianity, imagines his xenoglossia occurring in a mixed linguistic community of Christians and possibly non-Christians. The vita emphasizes how Ferrer's audience responds to and benefits from the miracle. According to the vita, although Vincent knew only his native dialect of Valencia, Spain, while preaching, he was understood by the large, multilingual crowd in a number of languages:

> Many Greeks, Germans, Sardinians, and Hungarians, and others born in other places, who did not know how to speak anything except their native tongue nor did they understand another, when they came to the places in which Vincent was preaching, they gathered with others in order to hear him, and at last, when his words came to an end, they revealed that they had understood the words of the man of God no less than if they had heard him speaking their own language. In that region of Gaul, which in our time is called Brittany, there are certain people, whom the French call Breton-speaking Bretons, whose tongue is known only to themselves, and although many of them know how to speak the language of the French, nevertheless many speak only their own language, and do not understand any other. These, however, clearly understood the man of God as he

15. "Ad praedicationem ergo procedite singulis diebus, vt eorum violentia confutata quiescat, noscens Christianam fidem vltimis terrae finibus diuulgatam. Obediunt imperio, praedicant singuli per singulos dies, fit grata praedicatio, plures conuertunt ad fidem, alios roborant: perfectis omnibus patriam conantur redire." *AASS*, Mar. I, 44–45. The *Life* of Padern records: "Ad urbem Hierusalem tandem accedentes, nobilissime post Apostolos praedicabant, contra Judaeos & haeresim ibidem ortam: nam unusquisque in lingua sua eos loquentes intelligebant." *AASS*, Apr., II, 380.

16. Doble, *Lives of the Welsh* Saints, 176. Doble notes that this motif was called attention to earlier by François Duine in *La Métropole de Bretagne* (Paris: Champion, 1916), 59.

17. "Cadocus tandem Hierusalem veniens, loca sancta visitauit; cui et dominus gentium idioma, per quas transibat, contulit, variisque linguis loqui coepit." *Nova Legenda Anglie*, 1:168; see also *AASS*, Jan., II, 604. The "Vita Cadoci" was written in the late eleventh century; see J. S. P. Tatlock, "Caradoc of Llancarfan," *Speculum* 13 (1938): 139–52.

spoke his mother tongue, so that each child and woman too reaped the greatest profit from his salutary teaching.[18]

Ferrer's hagiographer clearly focuses on the audience of translation receivers in this passage. The vita goes to great length to assert that no one could understand one another, for each only spoke his/her own tongue. Indeed, the languages mentioned (Hungarian, Greek, German, and Sardinian) seem carefully chosen for their linguistic diversity. Of course, just how or to whom each person revealed that he or she had understood Vincent's words is not clear; in the face of Vincent's miraculous translation, the mundane translational issues experienced by the audience afterward are of little importance to the hagiographer.

According to the account, Ferrer was also understood in the difficult language of the Bretons, and the Breton women and children in particular benefited from hearing him in their own tongue. The hagiographer emphasizes the linguistic isolation of both Vincent Ferrer (who spoke a Spanish dialect), as well as the isolation of the numerous peoples (the Hungarians, Sardinians, "and others born in other places," etc.), who could not understand each other. The narrative places great weight on the needs of women and children who are particularly isolated by their Celtic tongue. Ferrer is similarly feminized by his initial linguistic challenge, as he can only speak his particular dialect; the xenoglossic remedy allows him to fulfill his duties as cleric and spiritual leader, as he aids the vulnerable in their devotions.

In addition to receiving xenoglossia for the sake of preaching to the masses, friars could also receive the gift of tongues to facilitate preaching to other religious. The renowned Franciscan preacher St. Anthony of Padua (d. 1231), who allegedly attracted crowds as large as thirty thousand, is said to have received a gift of tongues that enabled him to preach to an audience of ecclesi-

---

18. Translation mine. "Multi quoque Graeci, Teutonici, Sardi, Hungari, & alii in aliis locis nati, qui non nisi materna lingua loqui sciebant, nec aliam intelligebant, devenientes ad loca in quibus praedicebat Vincentius, cum aliis ad audiendum concurrerunt & tandem facto verborum ejus fine fassi sunt se singula viri Dei verba percepisse, non minus quam si eorum lingua eum loquentem audissent. In illa Galliae regione, quae nostro tempore Britannia dicitur, sunt quidam populi, quos Galli vocant Britones Britonizantes, quorum lingua solis ipsis cognita est, & quamvis plurimi eorum lingua Gallorum loqui sciant, multi tamen non nisi sua lingua loquuntur, & nullam aliam intelligunt: qui tamen virum Dei, suo materno idiomate loquentem, distincte intelligebant, ita ut singuli quoque pueri & feminae maximum fructum ex salutifera ejus doctrina perceperint." AASS, Apr., I, 495. For an exploration of Vincent's canonization process, see Laura A. Smoller, "Miracle, Memory, and Meaning in the Canonization of Vincent Ferrer, 1453–1454," Speculum 73 (1998): 429–54.

astical elite.[19] The fourteenth-century *Actus Beati Francisci et Sociorum Eius* and its Italian translation and adaptation, *I Fioretti* or *The Little Flowers of St. Francis*, describe in some detail the episode, which is usually attributed to the year 1227:[20]

> At one time that wonderful vessel of the Holy Spirit, St. Anthony of Padua, one of the chosen followers and companions of St. Francis, whom St. Francis used to call his bishop, was preaching before the Pope and Cardinals in a consistory where there were men from different countries—Greeks and Latins, French and Germans, Slavs and English—and men of many other different languages and idioms. And being inflamed by the Holy Spirit and inspired with apostolic eloquence, he preached and explained the word of God so effectively, devoutly, subtly, clearly, and understandably that all who were assembled at that consistory, although they spoke different languages, clearly and distinctly heard and understood every one of his words as if he had spoken in each of their languages. Therefore they were all astounded and filled with devotion, for it seemed to them that the former miracle of the Apostles at the time of Pentecost had been renewed, when by the power of the Holy Spirit they spoke in different languages.
>
> And in amazement they said to one another: "Is he not a Spaniard? How then are we all hearing him in the language of the country where we were born—we Greeks and Latins, French and Germans, Slavs and English, Lombards and foreigners?"[21]

19. Raphael M. Huber, *St. Anthony of Padua, Doctor of the Church Universal: A Critical Study of the Historical Sources of the Life, Sanctity, Learning, and Miracles of the Saint of Padua and Lisbon* (Milwaukee, WI: Bruce Publishing, 1948), 54.

20. "To the year, 1227, is usually ascribed the sermon in Rome before Pope Gregory IX, the cardinals *in Curia*, and an innumerable multitude of men of all nations, all of whom miraculously heard him, as once did the multitudes of Apostles addressed on the first Pentecost Sunday, preaching in their own tongues." Huber, *St. Anthony of Padua*, 13.

21. "Little Flowers of St. Francis," 1390–91. The following Latin passage can be found in both Paul Sabatier's edition of the *Actus Beati Francisci et Sociorum Ejus* and his Latin edition of the *Fioretti*: "1. Vas admirabile sancti Spiritus sanctus Antonius de Padua, unus de electis discipulis beati Francisci, quem sanctus Franciscus suum episcopum appellabat, quum praedicaret in consilio coram papa et cardinalibus, ubi erant Graeci et Latini, Francigenae et Teutonici, Sclavi et Anglici et multi alii diversarum linguarum, 2. Spiritu sancto afflatus, lingua apostolica inflammatus, eructans mellifluum verbum, omnes illos tam diversarum linguarum in dicto consilio congretatos, luculentissime et clare ipsum audientes et distincte intelligentes, reddidit tanta admiratione et devotione suspensos, 3. ut videretur renovatum illud antiquum apostolorum mirabile admirantium et dicentium: 'Nonne iste Hispanus est? Et quomodo nos omnes audimus per eam linguam nostram in qua nati sumus, Graeci et Latini, Francigenae et Teutonici, Sclavi et

In this case, Anthony was not preaching to crowds he needed to convert, for the *Actus* describes his gift as occuring in the presence of other religious.[22] In a direct echo of Acts 2:8 ("And how is it that we hear, each of us in our own native language?"), this passage focuses on the amazement of those Christian elite who witness Anthony's translation. The account is particularly concerned with demonstrating that the most promiment ecclesiastical figures in western Christianity recognize the similarity of Anthony's gift to that of the apostles.

Even the famed preacher St. Francis of Assisi (d. 1226) is credited with a gift of vernacular xenoglossia in the thirteenth-century *Legenda aurea* of Jacobus de Voragine, although the claim does not appear in other versions of his vita. According to Jacobus's legend, Francis was named such in part due to his experience of xenoglossia: "Francis was born in Assisi, he was first named John but later was called Francis. It appears that there were several reasons for this change of names. The first was to call attention to a miracle, because he is known to have received miraculously from God the power to speak in the French language. Hence we read in his legend that whenever he was filled with the ardor of the Holy Spirit, he burst out with ardent words in French."[23] In the legend, Jacobus does not explore exactly how Francis used his miraculous French; did he burst out in French in public or in the privacy of his own cell? *The Second Life of St. Francis,* by Thomas of Celano, describes the holy man singing in French when he was particularly inspired, but Thomas does not suggest that the French was a miraculous gift.[24]

Anglici, Lombardi et Barbari?' 4. Papa etiam stupens ad tam profunda de scripturis divinis a sancto Antonio prolata, dixit, 'Vere iste arca testamenti et divinarum Scripturarum armarium est,'" in *Actus Beati Francisci et Sociorum Ejus,* ed. Paul Sabiatier, *Collection d'études et de documents* 4 (Paris: Librairie Fischbacher, 1902), and *Floretum S. Francisci Assisiensis, Liber aureus qui italice dicitur I Fioretti di San Francesco,* ed. Paul Sabatier (Paris: Librairie Fischbacher, 1902) 159–60.

22. A passage included in the *Acta Sanctorum* makes it clear that there were also a number of pilgrims from different lands attending the council: "quem idem sanctus Pater, propter vitam & praedicationis famam, suum Episcopum appellabat; cum Romae in Concilio, de mandato summi Pontificis, peregrinis innumerabilibus, qui illuc propter Indulgentias & Concilium convenerant, praedicaret (erant enim ibi Graeci, Latini, Francigenae, Theutonici, Sclavi, & Anglici, & aliarum linguarum diversarum) sic Spiritus sanctus linguam, ut quondam sanctorum Apostolorum, mirificavit; quod omnes, qui audiebant, non sine omnium admiratione ipsum clare intelligebant: & unusquisque audiebat linguam suam, in qua natus erat. Et tunc tam ardua & melliflua eructavit, quod omnes reddiderit stupore & admiratione suspensos: propter quod Papa ipsum, Arcam testamenti vocavit." *AASS,* June, II, 724.

23. Jacobus de Voragine, *The Golden Legend,* 2:222. "Franciscus prius dictus est Iohannes, sed postmodum mutato nomine Franciscus uocatus est. Cuius mutationis multiplex causa fuisse uidetur. Primo ratione miraculi connotandi; linguam enim gallicam miraculose a deo recepisse cognoscitur, unde dicitur in legenda sua quia semper cum ardore sancti spiritus repleretur ardentia uerba foris eructans gallice loquebatur." Jacobus de Voragine, *Legenda aurea,* 2:1016.

24. "When the sweetest melody of spirit would bubble up in him, he would give exterior expression to it in French, and the breath of the divine whisper which his ear perceived in secret

Indeed, Jacobus's claim is problematic because other lives of Francis indicate that his appellation can be attributed to nonmiraculous reasons. Several vitae mention that Francis's father traveled to France on business and that he was away in France at the time of his birth. *The Legend of the Three Companions*, for example, states that his father changed the baby's name to Francis when he returned from his trip.[25] The claim of miraculous language in Jacobus's legend can perhaps be explained by recognizing Jacobus's emphasis on miraculous language throughout the *Legenda aurea*, which highlights miracles of the tongue more so than other collections.[26] It could be suggested that,

---

would burst forth in French in a song of joy." Thomas of Celano, *The Second Life of St. Francis*, trans. Placid Hermann, in *St. Francis of Assisi: Writings and Early Biographies; English Omnibus of the Sources for the Life of St. Francis*, ed. Marion A. Habig, 3rd ed. (Chicago: Franciscan Herald Press, 1973), 467. "Dulcissima melodia spiritus intra ipsum ebulliens, exterius gallicum dabat sonum, et vena divini susurrii, quam auris eius suscipiebat furtive, gallicum erumpebat in iubilium," in *Analecta Franciscana sive Chronica aliaque varia documenta ad historiam Fratrum Minorum spectantia*, ed. Patribus Collegii S. Bonaventurae, *Legendae S. Francisci Assisiensis: saeculis XIII et XIV conscriptae* (Quaracchi, Florence: Ad Claras Aquas, 1926–1941), 10:205.

25. For example, St. Bonaventure's *Minor Life of St. Francis* states, "He was called John by his mother, but his father changed his name to Francis. He retained the name his father gave him without forfeiting the privilege indicated by the one his mother chose." Trans. Benen Fahy, in *St. Francis of Assisi: Writings and Early Biographies*. Habig, 793; "primumque '*Iohannes* vocatus a matre,' dehinc Franciscus a patre, nominationis quidem paternae vocabulum tenuit, sed et rem materni nominis non reliquit" *Analecta Franciscana*, 654. *The Legend of the Three Companions* states that Francis's mother "gave birth to her blessed son in the absence of his father who had gone to France on business." Trans. Nesta de Robeck, in *St. Francis of Assisi: Writings and Early Biographies*, ed. Habig], 890; the legend continues, "When Peter returned from France, he insisted that his son should be called Francis after the country he had recently left" (891). The *Analecta Franciscana* notes one reference to the gift of miraculous speech in a verse legend of Francis: "Fertur ob hoc tandem Francisci nomen adeptus, / Quod sibi Francorum sit caelitus indita lingua; / Qua fervens in laude Dei consuerverat uti" (494). The editor adds that although this is not mentioned in Thomas or Bonaventure, it is a natural evolution of the legend (494n5). The *Acta Sanctorum*, commenting on Jacobus de Voragine's attribution of tongues to Francis, states: "*Haec omni Jacobus de Voragine, quae plane frigida aut frivola esse, facile perspiciet, quisquis vetustas Vitas & haec ipsa ratiocinia consideraverit. Quod miraculo didicerit* Franciscus *linguam Gallicam, ex nulla vetustiori Vita colligi potest, neque ipse admittit Waddingus, verius existimans,* Franciscum *a patre dictum fuisse ex Gallicano affectu, prompteque apprehensa lingua Francica, quam expedite loquendo, quasi* Francus *evasisse poterat videri. Hunc in finem probat, id temporis vocem* Franciscus *idem significasse, quod* Francicus & Francus; *idque verum est. Ex Vitis quoque novimus,* Franciscum *lingua Gallica libenter usum fuisse, sed addunt Tres Socii mox laudandi;* Licet ea recte loqui nesciret. *Denique ne credam, inde nomen* Francisci *ei datum esse, obstant iidem Socii, ex quorum relatione omnino dicendus videtur nomen illud accepisse a patre in infantia sua, ac proinde antequam linguam Gallicam didicerat. Incertum porro est, an id pater ita voluerit, quod ille natus esset sibi versanti in Francia; an, quod idem nomen jam haberet in cognatione sua, sive alia de causa mihi ignota.*" Oct., II, 559, n75.

26. "The Life of St. Christopher," as recounted in the *Legenda aurea*, presents an intriguing example of vernacular xenoglossia used for strengthening the resolve of vulnerable Christian martyrs undergoing torture. After Christopher bears Christ across the river, the legend recounts: "After that, Christopher went to Samos, a city in Lycia. He did not understand the language spoken there, and prayed the Lord to make him able to understand it. As he prayed, the judges thought he was insane and left him alone; but when the favor he had prayed for was granted, he

because Jacobus was a Dominican, he was particularly aware of legends of missionary saints who miraculously spoke foreign languages. Although Donna C. Trembinski has suggested that Jacobus "refrains from stressing Francis's christomimetic qualities," in his attribution of xenoglossia to Francis, however, Jacobus is stressing his apostolic connections.[27] Because Jacobus doesn't imagine *how* Francis uses the gift, the "message" of his account is not necessarily *what* was said xenoglossically but rather that Francis was inspired in the way that the apostles were, so much so that the memory of the Pentecostal gift was both predicted and preserved in his very name.

Anecdotes of xenoglossia for the sake of wide-scale preaching did not end with the Middle Ages. By the early modern period, the scope of the claims had greatly increased. Perhaps the best-known xenoglossic saints today are not medieval but rather early modern. Attributions of the gift of tongues were included in the canonization processes of SS. Louis Bertrand (d. 1581) and Francis Xavier (d. 1552), missionaries to South and Central America and the Far East, respectively. The Dominican Louis Bertrand was reported to have converted tens of thousands of American inhabitants through the help of the miracle of xenoglossia,[28] and the Jesuit Francis Xavier's seventeenth-century canonization process records that he was given the gift of tongues to facilitate his massive-scale conversion efforts in Asia, although Francis himself discussed his translational difficulties in his letters.[29]

---

covered his face and went to the place where Christians were being tortured and executed, to speak to them and give them courage in the Lord" Jacobus de Voragine, *The Golden Legend*, 2:12. "Post hoc autem Samon, in ciuitatem Licie, uenit; ubi dum eorum linguam non intelligeret orauit dominum ut illius lingue sibi concederet intellectum. Dum autem in prece consisteret, iudices eum insanum putantes reliquerunt. Assecuto Christophorus quod petebat uultum operiens ad locum certaminis uenit et christianos et qui torquebantur in domino confortabat." Jacobus de Voragine, *Legenda aurea*, 2:666–67.

27. Donna Trembinski, "*Non Alter Christus*: Early Dominican Lives of Saint Francis," *Franciscan Studies* 63 (2005): 69–105, at p. 85.

28. While preaching to a number of different peoples in diverse places, St. Louis Bertrand was understood in his native Spanish language: "& inde ad diversos Indorum populos missus evangelizavit, incolentibus scilicent Tubaram, Cipacoam, Paluatum, Mompoix, Serram sanctae Marthae, Tuncarum, Tenerifem, & aliis, ibique plura, & mirabilia perpetravit. Orationibus a Deo obtinuit, ut lingua sua Hispana, in qua natus erat, evangelizando absque interprete intelligeretur ab Indis" *AASS*, Oct., V, 483. See also *AASS*, Oct., V, 322 and 382. Louis Bertrand was canonized in 1671.

29. Francis Xavier's canonization bull states that when he was a missionary his Portuguese was miraculously understood by Chinese and Japanese audiences. Stanley M. Burgess, "Medieval Examples of Charismatic Piety in the Roman Catholic Church," in *Perspectives on the New Pentecostalism*, ed. Russell P. Spittler (Grand Rapids, MI: Baker Book House, 1976) 21. A discussion of the development of xenoglossia in Francis's legends can be found Andrew Dickson White, *A History of the Warfare of Science with Theology in Christendom* (New York: D. Appleton, 1898), 2:19–23. See also *Analecta Bollandiana* 16 (1897): 52–63; 48 (1930): 441–45, and *Monumenta Xaveriana ex autographis vel ex antiquioribus exemplis collecta* (Matriti: Typus Augustini Avrial, 1899–

Of course, with many of these vitae, it is difficult to assert with any certainty exactly when a particular legend of xenoglossia developed. Such is the case with St. Bernardino of Siena (d. 1444), the famed Franciscan preacher, who allegedly preached to audiences as large as fifty thousand throughout Italy. In 1439, the Council of Florence convened with the goal of reuniting the Greek and Roman churches; the meeting was "preached partly in Greek for the benefit of the Orthodox representatives."[30] Bernardino, who could not speak Greek, attended that council, and was later said to have miraculously spoken in Greek to the Greek members. John Moorman suggests that it is Wadding who makes this event "more miraculous" in the seventeenth century;[31] it appears, however, that Bernardino's xenoglossia was also recorded by the hagiographer Laurentius Surius in the late sixteenth century.[32] To be able to pinpoint the exact date when the claim of xenoglossia was first made is difficult. Certainly, the attribution in Bernadino's life could be an example of a sixteenth-century expectation of tongues; or, it could reflect a legend that had originally developed in the fifteenth century and was only copied down later. The attribution of xenoglossia does serve to emphasize Bernardino's connection with the xenoglossic Vincent Ferrer. Legend states that once while Vincent was preaching to a large crowd (in 1401–1402 or 1406–1407) in which Bernardino was in attendance, Vincent predicted that a member of his audience would become a greater preacher than himself.[33] Once again, we note

---

1912), 710. Francis was canonized in 1622; Burgess asserts that the xenoglossic claim was made by Francis's first biographer, Horatius Tursellini, *De vita Francisci Xaverii* (Rome) in 1594. See Burgess, "Medieval Examples," 21n15.

30. Moorman, *History of the Franciscan Order*, 465.

31. According to Moorman, "Wadding (*An. Min.* xi, p. 59) makes the thing more miraculous by saying that Bernardino preached entirely in Greek, a language of which he had no knowledge" (465n6). The *Annales Minorum seu Trium Ordinem a. S. Francisco Institutorum*, compiled by Lucas Wadding, states: "Interfuit huic Concilio sanctus Bernardinus Senensis, & magno quidem fructu, tum suae vitae exemplo, tum privatis colloquiis & publicis praedicationibus Graecos, ad unionem alliciendo. Laudabili studio volebat ille veram salutis & veritatis viam docere, sed magno animi dolore cruciabatur, quod Graecorum non calleret idioma. Secum autem cogitans admiranda Dei opera, qualiter suis Apostolis contulerit ut possent omnium gentium linguis loqui, obnixe rogabat ut largiretur Graecis intelligentiam eorum quae dicturus esset ad illos. Mox ferventi spiritu, multa in Deum fiducia fretus, ascendit suggestum, Graeceque concionatus est, de Catholica fide Graecos summo studio erudiens: ita ut mirarentur omens dicerentque eum, non minus probe nosse Graece, quam si in Graecia natus esset; sed Deus movebat linguam ejus & loquebatur per eum. Cum enim a suggestu descendisset, & omnes laudarent ejus Graece dicendi facultatem & copiam, ille Deo soli honorem omnem tribuens, Graecae linguae expers, sicuti antea fuerat, remansit," in Lucas Wadding Hiberno, ed., *Annales Minorum sue Trium Ordinum a. S. Francisco Institutorum*, 11 (1734), 59.

32. See *AASS*, May, V, 311, for a similar passage found in Surius.

33. Franco Mormando, "Signs of the Apocalypse in Late Medieval Italy: The Popular Preaching of Bernardino of Siena," ed. Paul Maurice Clogan, *Medievalia et Humanistica* 24

that medieval xenoglossia did not occur in "isolated cases"; rather, these accounts of Vincent and Bernadino demonstrate the strong connections between holy people and emphasize how important it was believed to be that diverse audiences had unfettered access to their speech.

Xenoglossia on a Smaller Scale: The Semiprivate Miracle

The public preaching model experienced by men on such a massive scale was not the only model of xenoglossia in the Middle Ages. Holy men could also receive a variation on the public preaching model for the sake of smaller-scale preaching, counseling, and confession, revealing other ways that the Christian community could be strengthened through translation and shared language. The semiprivate version of this miracle, that is, xenoglossia granted for the sake of communication between as few as two participants, shows the great adaptability of the hagiographic trope. The examples of semiprivate xenoglossic experiences are numerous. As with large-scale preaching, the accounts focus on different aspects of the miracle, including the purpose and mechanics of the miracle, as well as the benefits to the audience. The accounts also exhibit differing investments in exploring the social hierarchies of language made apparent by the gift.

Two examples of xenoglossia attributed to St. Dominic (d. 1221), the founder of the Order of Preachers, call attention to the purpose of the miraculous translation, that is, why the holy man prays for a xenoglossic ability, as well as to the audience (the translation receivers and users) who immediately benefit from his translation. An early legend of Dominic reports that the saint was given the gift of xenoglossia when he met with another religious with whom he wanted to converse but was unable because neither knew the other's language:

> Once, on a journey, the servant of God happened to meet a certain religious whose saintly manner he could see, but whose speech and language were utterly foreign to him. Saddened by the fact that he could not refresh himself by conversing about divine things with this holy person, he prayed and obtained from the Lord the favor that each one would speak in the language of the other. By thus convers-

ing, they were able to understand each other for the three days they traveled together.[34]

The purpose for xenoglossia is clear in this account: Dominic wishes to converse with a holy person who will offer him spiritual enlightenment, and his traveling companion will also benefit from the exchange. As both holy men are granted the gift, both men become translation receivers and users. In this narrative, the specific language miraculously spoken by Dominic is not even mentioned, for this is the least important aspect of the miracle; instead, the narrative emphasizes why Dominic prays for the xenoglossic ability as well as the duration of the gift (three days), which indicates how lengthy the men's spiritual conversations are. Whereas other prominent medieval preachers receive xenoglossia to facilitate their missionary work, Dominic's account of miraculous translation focuses on his more intimate, personal desires for spiritual refreshment and conversation and includes the saint among the audiences that benefit.

In a similar xenoglossic narrative, Dominic and his companion Friar Bertrand are also reported to have received the miraculous ability to speak German when they encountered a group of pious pilgrims in France. Hearing the pilgrims reciting psalms and prayers, Dominic and Bertrand joined the group. Not wanting to consume the pilgrim's supplies without offering some spiritual sustenance in exchange, the saint prayed to the Lord for the gift of German, which was immediately granted to both Dominic and Bertrand:

> Then one day Blessed Dominic said to his companion, "Brother Bertrand, I feel terrible eating the food provided by these pilgrims and giving them no spiritual food in return. If it is agreeable to you, let us kneel down and ask the Lord to make us understand and speak their language, so that we may be able to speak to them about the Lord Jesus Christ." Then, to the amazement of the pilgrims, they began to speak intelligibly to them in German and, for the next four

34. From Constantine of Orvieto, *Legenda Sancti Dominici*, ed. D. H. C. Scheeben, Monumenta Ordinis Fratrum Praedicatorum Historica 16 (Rome, 1935), 203–352, quoted in *Saint Dominic: Biographical Documents*, ed. and trans. Francis C. Lehner (Washington, D.C.: Thomist, 1964), 53. The *Acta Sanctorum* describes this miracle in these words: "Contigit enim aliquando, Viro Dei iter agente, associari sibi religiosum quemdam conversationis quidem sanctitate domesticum, sed loquela & lingua penitus alienum. Dolens itaque, quod de divinis verbis una cum illo mutua se collocutione refovere non posset, tandem a Domino orationum suarum instantia, ut unus lingua loqueretur alterius, verbisque sic alterutrum variatis sese per triduum, quo videlicet simul ituri erant, intelligerent, impetravit." *AASS*, Aug., I, 405. See also *AASS*, Aug., I, 570.

days, they went with them speaking about the Lord Jesus until they reached Orleans.[35]

This particular narrative emphasizes Dominic's motives for praying for a gift of xenoglossia; rather than imagining Bertrand and himself benefiting from the Germans' conversation (as he did with the holy man in the first miracle account), Dominic reasons that the pilgrims will learn and be nourished by his own words. The text indicates that the gift is only experienced by Dominic and his companion; it also is quite specific about the language (German), the occasion (a pilgrimage), and the duration of the miracle (four days). Dominic's newly acquired language becomes a kind of currency or barter with which he can repay his generous hosts for their food, as he and his companion become masterful German interpreters and speak of spiritual matters for several days until they reach their destination. The gift of xenoglossia therefore enables Dominic and Bertrand to serve as spiritual guides for the German pilgrims as they prepare themselves for the devotional sites they will witness and experience in Chartres, the destination of the pilgrims.

Xenoglossia could also be imagined to facilitate confession and spiritual guidance among and between religious men. A later medieval vita of St. Pachomius (d. c. 346), the Egyptian desert father who is credited with the founding of cenobitic monasticism, features the story of how the saint prayed for and received a permanent gift of all the languages in the world to be able to listen to confessions and to counsel those monks who depended on his guidance. His gift of linguistic boundary-crossing is a lifetime gift, granted for the continuing growth and prosperity of both the faith and the newly developing monastic community. A version of the vita recorded in an eleventh-century manuscript describes how the holy man visited a cell of monks and wished to converse with them, but he could not speak their languages.[36] In particular, he wished to speak with an articulate Roman monk, who asked to confess to

---

35. Lehner, *Saint Dominic*, 52, from Gerardus de Frachet, *Vitae Fratrum Ordinis Praedicatorum*, ed. Benedictus Reichert, Monumenta Ordinis Fratrum Praedicatorum Historica 1 (Louvain: Typis E. Charpentier & J. Schoonjans, 1896). The *Acta Sanctorum* records the following: "Quarta die ingemiscens beatus Dominicus socio suo dixit: Frater Bertrande, vere laesam habeo conscientiam, quod istorum peregrinorum carnalia metimus, cum eis spiritualia non seminamus. Si placet, flexis gentibus oremus Dominum, ut linguae eorum nobis det intelligentiam pariter & loquelam, ut eis dominum Jesum annuntiare possimus. Qui cum orassent, stupentibus illis, intelligibiliter idioma Theutonicum sunt locuti, per aliosque dies quatuor ambulantes & loquentes cum eis de domino Jesu, tandem Aurelianis venerunt." *AASS*, Aug., I, 589.

36. It is not known when this story was incorporated in the vita of Pachomius; earlier versions of his vita state that he received the language of angels. For the dating of the Greek manuscript, see *Sancti Pachomii Vitae Graecae*, ed. François Halkin, Subsidia Hagiographica 19 (Brussels: Société des Bollandistes, 1932), 11–18.

Pachomius alone, without an interpreter. With hands stretched out to heaven, Pachomius prayed to God for three hours, beseeching him, "O All powerful Lord God, if I am not able to be a help to these brothers, whom you deign to send to me from diverse parts of the world, because I am utterly ignorant of their language, I pray what use will it be to them?" After three hours, a single written page suddenly fell from heaven. When Pachomius had read it, he became master of the languages of all nations and was able to offer confession to this monk and many other monks speaking Latin and Greek.[37]

Although the miracle is initially experienced intimately between two (Pachomius and the monk), it is described as having a more wide-reaching effect, as the holy man can afterward speak to and hear the confessions of a number of other monks in Greek and Latin and, indeed, in any other language necessary. Thus, the translation receivers and users become all those monks who have gathered around Pachomius for guidance and benefit from his language learning. Having prayed for the miraculous ability, Pachomius becomes a skilled translator after studying the page or leaf of writing; the heaven-sent document represents a compression of traditional, literate clerical education, which the holy man must master for the sake of oral interpretation. The account emphasizes that Pachomius prays for the ability, signaling his willingness to guide this newly formed community. The Egyptian-speaking holy man realizes that he must learn the most prominent languages (Latin and Greek) of the developing Christian community to guide his fellow religious successfully, rather than asking that his own language be miraculously understood by others.

That xenoglossia could encourage conversation and spiritual guidance between male religious was part of the popular medieval imagination. Similar to the legend of St. Pachomius, the *Life* of St. Basil the Great (d. 379) imagines that xenoglossia can repair or equalize linguistic hierarchies. A legend that developed in the early Middle Ages, and which was frequently retold in the later Middle Ages, records that the hermit Ephrem (a prominent theologian and Syriac writer, d. 373) sought out Basil (a Greek Doctor of the Church) after receiving a vision. The *Legenda aurea* relates:

37. Translation mine. "Extensis deinde in caelum manibus, hoc modo Deum deprecatus est: Domine Deus omnipotens, si Fratribus auxilio esse non possim, quos a diversis mundi partibus ad me dignaris mittere, propterea quod linguam eorum penitus ignorem, quid oro utilitatis eis proventurum est? Si ergo salvos per me effici eos cupis qui sub me degunt, istud mihi, Domine, largire, ut ad recte gubernandos eorum animos, lingua quoque illorum uti valeamus. Cui rei exorandae postquam tres omnino horas impendisset, multisque Deum hac super re esset deprecatus, repente e caelo charta ad eum conscripta fuit delata; quam ut perlegit, omnium mox nationum linguas perdidicit." *AASS*, May, III, 341.

When he [Ephrem] saw the bishop clothed in shining white vestments, moving solemnly in procession with his clergy, he said to himself: "I know now that I have gone to all this trouble for nothing! This man, who enjoys such honor, certainly cannot be the great saint I expected to see!" . . . Basil knew in spirit what was going through Ephrem's mind and had the hermit brought before him; and when he came into the bishop's presence, he saw a tongue of flame coming out of his mouth as he spoke. "Truly Basil is great," Ephrem exclaimed, "truly Basil is a column of fire, truly the Holy Spirit speaks through his mouth!" And to the bishop Ephrem said: "I beg of you, my lord, to obtain for me the ability to speak Greek." "You have asked for something very difficult," Basil replied. Nevertheless he prayed for the hermit, who at once began to speak in Greek.[38]

By imagining the Syriac-speaking Ephrem's urgent wish to speak with Basil the Great, the vita expresses a desire to show these two great church writers as seeking out a way to communicate with each other directly. The narrative also exposes the linguistic hierarchy of the Greek and Syriac languages in the hagiographers' minds at the time of the text's composition, as Ephrem is shown asking for the more prominent language so that he can communicate with the Church Doctor. David G. K. Taylor, however, challenges this conclusion, suggesting:

the gift of Greek in particular could also be interpreted not as a condescending gift to a provincial Syrian, or as an attempt by a Syrian biographer to bestow posthumous cultural respectability upon his subject, but as an attempt to include Ephraim within the fold of the Greek-speaking theologians, rather than leave him as a notorious

---

38. Jacobus de Voragine, *Golden Legend*, I:108. For this episode in the (Pseudo) Amphilochius' *Life* of St. Basil, see *AASS*, June, III, 431. "Veniens igitur in ciuitatem in die epiphaniae ut tantum uirum uidere posset, cum uidisset eum stola candida indutum cum clericis uenerabiliter procedentem ait intra se: 'Vt uideo, in uacuum laboraui. Iste enim, cum in tali sit honore positus, nequaquam talis potest esse quemadmodum uidi. Nos enim qui portauimus pondus diei et estus, nihil tale consecuti sumus; et hic cum in tali honore et constipatione positus sit, columpna ignis est? Miror ista.' Basilius igitur in spiritu hoc uidens fecit eum ad se introduci. Qui cum introductus esset, uidit linguam igneam per os eius loquentem et ait Effrem: 'Vere magnus Basilius, uere columpna ignis Basilius, uere spiritus sanctus loquitur per os eius.' Dixitque illi Effrem: 'Obsecro domine ut mihi impetres quod grece loquar.' Cui Basilius: 'Rem difficilem postulasti.' Pro eo tamen orauit et continuo grece loqui coepit." Jacobus de Voragine, *Legenda aurea*, 1:180.

and disquieting example of a divine who was able to produce out-standing theology unhindered by possessing only "tourist Greek."[39]

Taylor also points out that in Syriac versions of the Acts of St. Ephrem, it is Basil who receives a gift of Syriac.[40]

A gift of Syriac and Greek xenoglossia is also featured in the vita of St. Andrew the Fool for Christ (also known as Andreas Stultus or Andreas Salus). This vita plays with the idea of public/private xenoglossia and focuses on its effect on the audience, as Andrew's xenoglossia makes possible "private" conversation in a more public setting. Andrew's vita describes how he, a Scythian slave of a rich man in Constantinople, became a holy fool and attracted a disciple, the wealthy young man Epiphanios.[41] The vita records two separate instances of Andrew being gifted with tongues, for the purpose of both private counseling and more public preaching.

Andrew's first experience of xenoglossia occurred when he was invited to dinner and spent the night at the home of Epiphanios's father. The holy man was first approached by a tearful servant who wished to follow his way of life. Andrew changed the slave's speech into Syriac so that, although in the presence of his master and other slaves, the two could speak together privately.[42] The miracle of xenoglossia thus allows Andrew to counsel a servant who is indeed quite vulnerable, for he wishes to desert his master and follow Andrew.

---

39. David G. K. Taylor, "St. Ephraim's Influence on the Greeks," *Hugoye: Journal of Syriac Studies* 1.2 (1998), http://syrcom.cua.edu/Hugoye/Vol1No2/index.html (accessed August 15, 2008), paragraph 4.

40. See T. J. Lamy, ed., *Sancti Ephraem Syri Hymni et Sermones*, II (Malines 1882), 5–90, discussed in Taylor, "St. Ephraim's Influence on the Greeks," at note nine.

41. According to François Halkin, editor of *Manuscrits Grecs de Paris: Inventaire Hagiographique*, Subsidia Hagiographica 44 (Brussels: Société des Bollandistes, 1968), this manuscript, containing the vita originally composed by Nikephoros in Greek (which was later translated by the Bollandists), was written in 1286 (206). Lennart Rydén, editor and translator of *The Life of St Andrew the Fool*, 2 vols. (Uppsala: Uppsala University, distributed by Stockholm: Almqvist & Wiksell, 1995), explains the somewhat complex narratological situation. The author of the vita identifies himself as "Nikephoros" and claims to have known Andrew personally. He sets the story in the early Byzantine period, placing Andrew's life in the reign of Emperor Leo (d. 474; 1:143); other vitae of the saint place his death in the tenth century. Although there is some argument over the original date of composition, Rydén asserts that the vita is from the tenth century (1:56; 1:143).

42. "The righteous man understood in his spirit what the boy wanted to obtain, and as he wished to speak with him in private, through the power of the Holy Spirit changed the boy's language to that of the Syrians and sat down and talked with him in fluent Syriac." Nikephoros, *Life of St Andrew the Fool*, 2:87. For the Greek original, see Nikephoros, *Life of St Andrew the Fool*, 2:86, and *AASS*, May, VI, 33. The Latin translation in the *Acta Sanctorum* reads, "Sanctus autem, quid alter supplicibus obtinere precibus niteretur cognoscens; cupiensque seorsim cum solo colloqui, mutavit sancti Spiritus virtute vernaculam servi linguam in Syriacam; locutusque Syriace cum illo est, quaecumque vellet." *AASS*, May, VI, 33.

His changing the servant's tongue to Syriac turns the typical master-servant power relationship on its head, as he enables a servant to speak openly in front of his master's son, without fear of reprisal; Andrew temporarily turns the servant into a holy fool but must relent at the insistence of Epiphanios, who fears his father's wrath.

Andrew's second experience of xenoglossia occurred later that night. When the other servants, "driven by ardent love," gathered around the holy man, Andrew saw the sins that each had committed and began to speak in parables to them. The servants' reaction was extraordinarily strong, for each thought Andrew was speaking directly to him: "They on their side gave ear to the holy man's words, some turning red as fire for shame, others becoming dizzy and trembling, while still others were ashamed and went away, for the righteous man's plain speech bluntly exposed the sins of each, revealing why and how and where they had committed them. And the most wonderful of all: each one understood what he said in his own language. They all assumed, 'This man is speaking about me!'"[43] Andrew's experience of tongues is a strange mixture of private and public, of secrecy and openness. The saint's words are, through the grace of God, changed into a kind of universal language that all can understand; when Andrew speaks to the servants as a group, each imagines that his sins are exposed to the holy man and perhaps to the rest of the audience. For Andrew, therefore, the xenoglossic ability to be both translator and translated enables him to preach publicly and counsel privately, simultaneously. Andrew actually speaks in two levels of translation here: as his words are translated into the servants' own tongues, he also speaks in parables to encourage their "translation" of his allegorical words to fit their own individual situations. His role is therefore as reprover and teacher, as he facilitates the inner conversion of the heart in the Christian servants who listen to him.

In sum, in medieval saints' lives, only men experience xenoglossia for the sake of public preaching, and the claims are an important part of their reputations as religious leaders and teachers. Variations of this apostolic preaching miracle for men take the form of xenoglossia received for more private spiri-

43. Nikephoros, *The Life of St Andrew the Fool*, 2:89, 91. For the Greek original, see Nikephoros, *The Life of St Andrew the Fool*, 2:88, 90, and *AASS*, May, VI, 33: "Considentibus itaque illis & Epiphanium corona cingentibus, vidit Andreas perspicaci mentis oculo, quid quisque operatus esset, quos errores delictave commisisset: cumque omnibus recte consultum vellet, exordio dicendi facto, parabolam quamdam in medium protulit. Illi vero ejus verba sensumq; assequentes, pudore suffusi sunt, non secus quam si flamma ignis abstitisset a facie eorum; alii rigebant horrore, a sensibus fere abibant alii ac trepidabant, nonnulli prae verecundia se subducebant: simplex enim & incompta viri sancti oratio universa eorum peccata praecise redarguebat, pandebatque quo modo & fine commissa essent. Qua in re illud imprimis mirandum venit, quod cuilibet suum in sua lingua manifestaret peccatum, pensitantibus dicentibusque apud se: Isthunc mea homo ille causa sermonen instituit." *AASS*, May, VI, 34.

tual conversation, counseling, and confession or to guide a spiritual community. The gift is asked and prayed for by the men, who become masters of that language, sometimes for an evening (in the case of Andrew), several days (Dominic), or a lifetime (Pachomius).[44]

Part 2: Women's Vernacular Xenoglossia

Not surprisingly, medieval holy people were imagined to experience xenoglossia in ways that reflected understandings of "appropriate" social and religious behavior for men and women. Whereas xenoglossia for men is often granted for the sake of the public conversion of others, for women, it is accidental, limited, and, in many cases, the "fame" we might expect for the miraculous experience is downplayed. The female version of the miracle is almost always semiprivate, and it often emphasizes vulnerability and a certain lack of control or limited control over the language. Whereas men's gifts tend to last for longer periods and often give full command of a language, women's gifts are typically shorter in duration and much more circumscribed in nature.

There are very few examples of vernacular xenoglossia in the vitae of medieval women. Connections with Pentecost and the gift of omnilingualism are emphasized in two accounts, but the descriptions are frustratingly brief. The first occurs in an aside in the early thirteenth-century *Life* of Lutgard of Aywières by the Dominican theologian Thomas of Cantimpré. Thomas mentions a woman whom he has witnessed speaking in tongues on the Day of Pentecost. He refuses to give her name (or, indeed, any other information about her), and it appears to have only occurred that particular day: "I myself once saw a woman who had knowledge of all languages from terce to vespers on Pentecost, but I do not wish to give her name because she is still alive."[45] The second instance of women's xenoglossia being directly connected to Pen-

---

44. According to Burgess in "Medieval Examples," St. Stephen also received a gift of Greek, Turkish, and Armenian (20), as cited in Giuseppe Silos, *Historiarum Clericorum Regularium a Congregatione Condita* (Rome: Panormi, 1650–1666), 2:13. I have been unable to consult Silos's book for this project.

45. Thomas de Cantimpré, *The Life of Lutgard of Aywières*, trans. Margot H. King and Barbara Newman, 211–96 in *Thomas of Cantimpré: The Collected Saints' Lives; Abbot John of Cantimpré, Christina the Astonishing, Margaret of Ypres, and Lutgard of Aywières*, ed. Barbara Newman, trans. Margot H. King and Barbara Newman, Medieval Women: Texts and Contexts 19 (Turnhout: Brepols, 2008). "Vidi unam quae in die Pentecostes ab hora tertia usque ad vesperam omnium linguarum notitiam habuit: sed hanc adhuc prodere nolo, quia adhuc in vita degit." *AASS*, June, III, 252.

tecost is a short reference in the *Life* of St. Colette of Corbie (d. 1447), the founder of the Colettine Reformed Clares. According to the vita written shortly after her death by Pierre de Vaux, Colette shared many similarities with the apostles: "The apostles were speaking in various tongues and understood all languages. In the same way she herself understood all languages, namely Latin and German and the rest."[46] Piere then quickly goes on to list other aspects Colette shared with the apostles, including an ability to survive poison.

In contrast with the wealth of examples of men who convert non-Christians to Christianity through xenoglossia, I have found only one narrative of a xenoglossic woman who converts non-Christians, and it is an early modern legend, not medieval. Significantly, the account does not describe exactly *how* the woman converts them, whether through preaching, pious conversation, or example. The vita of a sixteenth-century Franciscan from Toledo, Sor Juana de la Cruz (Blessed Joan of the Cross), describes how, when the bishop gave two Muslim slaves to Juana's convent, "mores which he had brought from the conquest of Oran," the slaves could not be induced to convert to Christianity. Juana, however, was granted the gift of "Algauaria," their native language, and converted them. The holy woman was also heard speaking "in diuers languages, of which she neuer had any former knowledge, especially in Latin, Arabick, and others."[47] Juana's miracle is experienced and performed semiprivately on a much smaller scale than the conversions experienced by prominent male preachers like Patiens or the Welsh saints Teilo, Padarn, and David. There are no such examples of medieval women being granted xenoglossia for the sake of the conversion of non-Christians, although they do use their gift for the inner "conversion" of wayward Christian men and women.

Vernacular xenoglossia could be granted to women who found themselves in especially vulnerable situations. Colette of Corbie, who was reported to be omnilingual, also experienced a short-lived gift of tongues in what was possibly a life-threatening situation. Her vita describes how Colette was granted

46. The Latin translation of Colette's original French life reads, "Apostoli varijs linguis loquebantur & omnia idiomata percipiebant. Pariformiter ipsa cuncta percipiebat idiomata, videlicet Latinum & Alamanicum & reliqua." *AASS*, Mar., I, 576. Colette's French vita states, "Les apôtres toutes langues parlaient et entendaient. Pareillement, tous langages du monde, et latin, et allemand, et autres, par la grâce de Dieu, elle entendait," quoted in Nancy Bradley Warren, "Monastic Politics: St Colette of Corbie, Franciscan Reform, and the House of Burgundy," in *New Medieval Literatures* 5, ed. Rita Copeland, David Lawton, and Wendy Scase (Oxford: Oxford University Press, 2002), 203–28, at p. 220. See also Marie Richards, "Community and Poverty in the Reformed Order of St. Clare in the Fifteenth Century," *Journal of Religious History* 19 (1995): 10–25, for a discussion of the vitae.

47. Antonio Daca, *The Historie . . . of the Blessed Virgin, Sister Joane, 1625*, ed. D. M. Rogers, English Recusant Literature, 1558–1640 (volume) 335 (Yorkshire: Scholar Press, 1977), 149–50.

the gift of a foreign vernacular language when armed men fell upon the saint and a party of fellow nuns while they were journeying in an unidentified strange region. Colette spoke with them in such a way that "their evil designs are transformed into 'amour et charite,'"[48] a defensive act that enables the saint and her religious companions to protect their own goods and honor from violent masculine attack. This "feminine" version of the conversion gift converts the desires of men from lust of body and goods to charity, from *cupiditas* to *caritas*; the holy woman therefore performs her own kind of a conversion miracle that features not the wide-scale baptisms performed by xenoglossic male preachers but rather the conversion of a few men's inner hearts to "charite."

In three cases, medieval women are given xenoglossia when approached by another in need. However, the women's experiences are briefer in duration and appear to offer less command of language than men's experiences of xenoglossia do. The *Life* of the Augustinian nun St. Clare of Montefalco (d. 1308) describes how the holy woman was given the gift of French to converse with a pious female pilgrim who visited her nunnery for a short time.[49] In the descriptions of the miracle that appear in her vita and canonization process, we also see that Clare's xenoglossia is included as an indication of her prophetic abilities; xenoglossia, therefore, becomes just as much of a message of Clare's divine grace in this sense as a medium of that grace.

The *Life* of Clare records a number of the holy woman's divine gifts, including heightened spiritual understanding of Scripture, prophetic visions,

48. Warren, "Monastic Politics," 220. The *Acta Sanctorum* records: "Fuit cum ego aliaeque complures ab ea duceremur per regionem peregrinam, cuius nulla nostrum nouerat idioma: hic per locum formidinis plenum syluosumque transeuntibus obuiam se dat subitus militum an latronū globus, qui latuerat in insidijs; & currum stipans (cuius commoditas vt quaereretur, Matris filiarumque imbecillitas coegerat) magna cum violentia & incondita vociferatione in nos impetum facit. Recitauerat de more Litanias Coleta: igitur velut Apostolicū linguarum sortita donum, sua inuasores lingua alloquitur, & inuitos quoque blandissimis verbis reuocat ad mansuetudinem, vsque adeo vt comites se in viam reliquam defensoresque offerrent, qui spoliaturi accurrerant: tanta erat morum in diuersa mutatio!" *AASS*, Mar., I, 607, as originally narrated in French by Sister Petrina de Balma.

49. Although St. Clare has been claimed by both the Franciscans and Augustinians, according to Enrico Menestò in "The Apostolic Canonization Proceedings of Clare of Montefalco, 1318–1319," she "observed the Rule of St. Augustine from 1290 to her death" (104), in *Women and Religion in Medieval and Renaissance Italy*, ed. Daniel Bornstein and Roberto Rusconi, trans. Margery J. Scheider (Chicago: University of Chicago Press, 1996): 104–29. As André Vauchez explains, "Clare of Montefalco and her companions formed a community of recluses living according to the rule of St Augustine. But their entourage (confessors etc.) were all Friars Minor" (262n.b) in *Sainthood in the Later Middle Ages*, trans. Jean Birrell (Cambridge: Cambridge University Press, 1997). For a translation of her vita, see Berengario di Donadio, *Life of Saint Clare of Montefalco*, ed. John E. Rotelle, trans. Matthew J. O'Connell, Augustinian Series 9 (Villanova, PA: Augustinian Press, 1999).

and on one occasion, the gift of French. The vita was written by Berengario di Donadio (Béranger de Saint-Affrique or Berengario di San Africano), who, as vicar general of the Spoletan diocese, had been called in to investigate the claim that her fellow nuns had seen the marks of the passion on Clare's heart after her death.[50] Berengario's *Life* states that "Clare often foretold the arrival of holy persons and the reason for their coming." On one particular day, Clare prophesied the visit of a foreign pilgrim and began preparing for her arrival. When the French pilgrim arrived, she was greatly surprised by Clare's greeting:

> When Clare called her, she approached the grill, and Clare said to her: "I saw you yesterday better than I do now, and I knew that you would be coming today.". . . It seem [*sic*] amazing that Clare had foreseen the lady and knew her in advance; another wonderful thing was that Clare understood her speech. The nuns who were with Clare at the grill could not understand what Marguerite was saying. Clare, on the contrary, understood, grasped her meaning completely, and answered in an entirely appropriate way. But why was it wonderful or surprising? He who had enabled Clare to see the woman before she came also saw to it that the speech was understood.[51]

In addition to emphasizing the linguistic miracle, this narrative calls attention to the holy woman's prophetic ability to foretell the arrival of the pilgrim.

Clare's gift of xenoglossia, in combination with the gift of prophecy, was deemed important enough to be included in her canonization process. The event appears as number 91 of the *articuli interrogatori* in the process of 1318–1319; the event is described in a manner similar to that of the vita, which can no doubt be explained by the common practice of drawing the canonization process articles directly from the vita.[52] Three witnesses give testimony regard-

---

50. Berengario, *Life of Saint Clare*, 1. In addition to the vita, a number of depositions from her canonization processes remain, making her perhaps "the most fully documented saint of the Middle Ages" (2).

51. Berengario, *Life of Saint Clare*, 49–50.

52. Number 91 of the articles of canonization states: "Item quod sancta Clara . . . dixit sororibus suis dicti monasterii hec vel similia verba: 'Cras habebitis hic unam peregrinam de longinquis partibus et est mulier sancta et devota.' Et in crastinum, de mane, fecit sancta Clara parari comestionem pro peregrina ventura. Et postea, circa tertiam, venit ad gratem ad recipiendam peregrinam predictam. Ed ecce quod mulier quedam, que vocatur Margarita provincialis et dicitur esse de civitate Carcasonensi, intravit oratorium dicti monasterii, et sancta Clara aperuit fenestram, et cognoscens quod illa erat illa peregrina que fuerat ei per revelationem ostensa, vocavit eam ad se, et postea vocavit sorores aliquas dicti loci dicens eis: 'Venite, venite, quia peregrina nostra venit.' Et sancta Clara recepit ipsam peregrinam caritative, et ambe simul fue-

ing this article.[53] Certainly, these records are extremely valuable because they offer first-hand accounts of how xenoglossia could be experienced or interpreted, as well as its effect on the audience observing the phenomenon. Of course, the questions asked of witnesses shape and form the articulation and content of the answer, so even these eyewitness accounts undergo a process of mediation. That the Latin of the *Processus* is being translated from the witness's vernacular Italian also complicates this linguistic puzzle.

The testimony of Sister Joanna, a contemporary of Clare's, emphasizes her own (and others') witnessing of the miracle. Joanna also describes how the miracle was enacted, specifically that the miracle was one both of orality (speaking French) and of aurality (hearing and understanding French):

> And with the sisters of the aforementioned monastery present and with the witness herself present and listening, Clare herself and the aforementioned pilgrim spoke much together about the Lord and about spiritual things, with the aforesaid Marguerite speaking in her own tongue and the aforesaid S. Clare understanding her and responding to her. And, as the witness herself heard from the aforesaid sister Clare, Clare herself was understanding the language of the aforesaid Marguerite in all the things that she was saying, and treated the pilgrim lovingly.[54]

Witness 38, Sister Marina, also provides an eyewitness account of the event and comments on the length of the conversation. Marina also asserts that Clare herself claimed the miraculous event: "The same witness heard that they spoke together with spiritual words so long that a man could have said

---

runt diu locute de Deo et fuerunt in colloquio spirituali, et sancta Clara bene intelligebat Margaritam et bene ei respondebat, quamvis Margarita non esset de illa lingua" (13–14) in *Il Processo di Canonizzazione di Chiara da Montefalco*, ed. Enrico Menestò, Quaderni del Centro per il Collegamento degli Studi Medievali e Umanistici nell'Università di Perugia 14 (Perugia: Regione dell'Umbria, and Firenze: La Nuova Italia, 1984).

53. A number of witness accounts have been lost from the original canonization process, including the account of Marguerite of Provence, the pilgrim with whom Clare shared the linguistic miracle. See Berengario, *Life of Saint Clare*, 50n1.

54. Translation mine. [Soror Iohanna magistri Aegidii de Montefalco]: 'Et ibidem, presentibus sororibus dicti monasterii et ipsa teste presente et audiente, ipsa Clara et dicta peregrina locute sunt multum ad invicem de Deo et de spiritualibus, predicta Margarita in lingua sua loquente et dicta s. Clara eam intelligente et ad singula respondente. Et, ut ipsa testis audivit a dicta sorore Clara, ipsa s. Clara intelligebat linguam dicte Margarite in omnibus que dicebat, et tractavit eandem peregrinam caritative." *Il Processo*, 48. The account continues, "Dixit etiam dicta testis . . . quod postea dicta Clara dixit sibi testi quod ipsa Clara intelligebat clare et distinct linguam dicte Margarite et omnia que dixerat ea" (49).

100 Pater Nosters in the whole time that they spoke, and this witness was in no way, as she says, able to understand the aforesaid pilgrim. She said, however, that she heard from Clare herself that she (Clare) understood her (Marguerite) in her own language."[55] Just whose language is referred to in that last line is not entirely clear, although it does appear from the other accounts that Clare was hearing and understanding Marguerite in the Frenchwoman's own language. A third witness, Sister Thomassa, supports this by stating that Clare "was both hearing (*audiebat*) and understanding (*intelligebat*) Marguerite."[56]

Although this appears to be a private miracle, experienced by two religious women engaged in intimate, spiritual conversation (if only for the length of one hundred Pater Nosters), it is also a rather public miracle, occurring in front of a number of witnesses who observed the event and whose witnessing means that their testimonies can be included in the canonization process. Even though the other nuns do not appear to have understood the actual conversation, it is enough for them to know (and to have confirmed by Clare herself) that a linguistic miracle has occurred. The private, sacred translational performance therefore takes on a wider audience and becomes transformative, not just for the two women involved but also for all those observing.[57] That the miracle is then included in her vita and canonization process means that an even wider audience could learn of the miraculous event and would come to think of Clare as blessed. In its presentation in both the vita and the canonization process, her gift of French is intimately related (or even subordinate) to her prophetic ability; this further points to the gift of miraculous translation as a message in itself, for the words themselves are not as important as what is indicated by them, that is, that Clare has the divinely given ability to foresee the future.

The clarity of Clare's xenoglossic experience can be contrasted with the obscurity of an account in the *Relevaciones* (*Revelations*) of the visionary St. Bridget of Sweden (d. 1373), the founder of the Bridgettine Order. Book 6 of Bridget's *Revelations* features a confusing account of what is quite possibly

55. Translation mine. "Audivit etiam ipsa testis quod locute fuerunt ad invicem verba spiritualia quod homo potuisset dicere C Pater noster per totum spatium temporis (quo) locute fuerunt, et ipsa testis nullo modo, ut dicit, poterat intelligere dictam peregrinam. Dixit tamen quod audivit a dicta sancta Clara quod ipsa intelligebat eam in linguam suam." *Il Processo*, 139.

56. "et ipsa sancta Clara audiebat et intelligebat linguam suam valde bene et referebat verba sua sororibus abstantibus." *Il Processo*, 215.

57. According to Mary A. Suydam, "Beguine Textuality: Sacred Performances," in *Performance and Transformation*, ed. Suydam and Ziegler, 169–210, "The performative dimension of holy women's sacred actions were critical components of their success in being recognized as truly holy, and had to be continually repeated in order to guarantee such success" (176). Although this event is directly experienced by two, it is actually witnessed and therefore experienced by many.

an example of vernacular xenoglossia or perhaps even xenoglossia denied. Sometime in the years between 1350 and 1373, when Bridget was residing in Rome, a Finnish pilgrim approached the Swedish-speaking holy woman with a pressing translation problem: "A man who did not know how to speak the Swedish language came to Rome from the Diocese of Aboe. Since no one in Rome understood him and he could not find a confessor, he consulted Bridget about what he should do. Then Bridget heard in her spirit (Jesus Christ, the Son of God, spoke): 'That man who seeks you out laments that he does not have anyone to listen to his confession. Tell him that his will to confess is sufficient.'"[58] It is not clearly stated how Bridget understands the Finnish pilgrim and then conveys Christ's command to him. On the one hand, this appears to be an example of xenoglossia denied because it suggests that Bridget is most definitely not given a gift of xenoglossia, which would enable her to act as an interpreter for the pilgrim during his confession to the priest. On the other hand, a miraculous gift of xenoglossia would seem to be the only way possible to communicate with him, since she did not speak Finnish and he presumably did not speak Swedish or even understand it. Christ therefore appears to be responding to the Finn's need for translation by rendering that need unnecessary through Bridget's xenoglossic words.[59]

If we assume Bridget has received a gift of vernacular xenoglossia, then, similar to a number of late medieval holy men and women, Bridget experiences the miraculous ability to remedy an interpretive impasse and to aid a linguistically isolated pilgrim made vulnerable by his lack of foreign language skills, namely, his lack of the more politically advantageous Scandinavian language of Swedish or even Italian, the dominant vernacular in Rome. But since this vision is not so much concerned with Bridget's Pentecostal gift as it is with Christ's statements regarding the value of inner will, it does not describe the mechanisms of how his message is conveyed. Because Bridget's visionary text, the *Revelations*, focuses on the holy woman's prophetic reception and interpretation, the metaphoric "translation," if you will, of the divine message

58. *Revelations*, 6:115. Translation mine. "Quidam de dyocesi Aboensi venit Roman ignorans ydeoma Sueuicum. Quem cum nullus in Roma intelligeret nec confessorem habere poterat, consuluit dominam, quid ageret. Tunc domina in spiritu audiuit (Ihesus Christus, filius Dei loquitur): 'Homo ille, qui te consuluit, plorat, quod non habet auditorem confessionis sue. Dic ei, quod sufficit voluntas,'" *Revelaciones, Book 6*, ed. Birger Bergh, Samlingar utgivna av Svenska Fornskriftsällskapet, Ser. 2, Lakinska skrifter 7:7 (Uppsala: Almqvist & Wiksells International, 1991), 274.

59. In *St Birgitta of Sweden*, Studies in Medieval Mysticism 1 (Woodbridge, UK: Boydell, 1999), Bridget Morris questions how Bridget understands the pilgrim: "What language she communicated with him in is unclear, as it is extremely unlikely that she could understand Finnish" (113n61).

into earthly language, translation between human languages therefore is of concern when it is involved in the articulation of that message. Bridget's own words are not of any importance here, for she is a prophetic mouthpiece for the Lord, the vehicle through which the more obscure Finnish can travel.

If we compare two xenoglossic episodes from very different time periods and settings, that of Bridget of Sweden and Pachomius (the omnilingual Egyptian holy father), we can appreciate how gender may affect issues of linguistic agency. Both gifts are granted to facilitate confession; one narrative imagines the hermit Pachomius possessing all the languages of the world, whereas the other is not even clear regarding how the holy woman communicates Christ's message that the Finn's confession need not be translated. Rather than focusing on Bridget's active command of the language, the account emphasizes the visionary's role as prophetic mouthpiece of the Lord. Both Pachomius's and Bridget's accounts describe situations of men's linguistic isolation. The former features the isolation of the desert father who only speaks Egyptian and cannot understand the languages of the younger monks. He admires their linguistic ability and recognizes his own limitations in not being able to speak the two most prominent Christian languages. Receiving the gift therefore allows him not only to become a full participant in the Latin- and Greek-speaking monastic community for the rest of his life but a leader of it as well. In Bridget's example, the linguistic isolation is experienced by a vulnerable Finnish-speaking pilgrim, who can find no one to confess him in Rome; Bridget's aid does not so much remedy the isolation as ensure the pilgrim that the isolation is bearable, even desirable, since his inner will can be easily understood by Christ. Compared with Pachomius's experience, Bridget's is fleeting and more focused on her role as the mouthpiece of God rather than on the language in her mouth. And if hers is not a Pentecostal gift but rather a denial of xenoglossia, then her gendered experience is emphasized still further.

Certainly, the idea of an omnilingual confessor must have been quite attractive to medieval audiences, many of whom might have experienced their own difficulties finding a confessor who spoke their native tongue while traveling abroad. A keen devotee of Bridget, the fifteenth-century English visionary Margery Kempe is also rendered linguistically isolated and therefore vulnerable without an English-speaking confessor when she is on pilgrimage in Rome. Although I will discuss her example in detail in Chapter 3, I shall mention here that her *Book* claims that Margery is granted an intriguing version of vernacular xenoglossia and repeatedly calls attention to the strange mechanics of the miracle. Not suddenly, but rather after thirteen days of prayer, Margery receives the ability to understand German and a German priest to understand her English, so that she may confess to him. She also uses this mutual xenoglossic gift to receive spiritual counseling, as well as to prove her prophetic and visionary abilities to the German priest and to other clerics who do not believe her.

Women's Lack of Xenoglossia

Bridget of Sweden's ambiguous experience of xenoglossia suggests that, for some, translational difficulties increase devotion and therefore xenoglossia is not the desired answer. The *Lives* of St. Lutgard of Aywières (d. 1246) and Blessed Ida of Nivelles (d. 1231) demonstrate quite clearly how women's spiritual authority and lack of linguistic agency are intimately connected. For these two thirteenth-century Cistercian holy women from the Southern-Netherlandish region, translation difficulties, either miraculously aided or not, form an important part of their devotional experiences. The women's passive response to their difficulties encourages their spiritual and contemplative growth, which ultimately lends them spiritual authority as opposed to administrative authority.

Whereas xenoglossic men often receive reward, promotion, and recognition for their linguistic gifts, one thirteenth-century woman, however, actually prays to Mary for a gift of *disglossia* to protect her from having to fulfill a more public administrative role in her nunnery. St. Lutgard was a Benedictine nun at St. Catherine of Sint-Truiden until her mid-twenties, when she transferred to the Cistercian order in Aywières. The Flemish-speaking Lutgard had been hesitating to join the convent in Aywières because "the French nuns there spoke a different language," preferring initially to enter a Cistercian monastery in Herkenrode, where Flemish was spoken.[60] At the insistence of the Lord, her spiritual advisor, and others, Lutgard entered the French-speaking convent, but the issue of language soon came to the forefront, when a number of newly founded French-speaking houses wished her to be their abbess:

> Thus the fame of the blessed Lutgard's virtues expanded everywhere. During this period new monasteries were beginning to be built in

60. For discussion of miraculous language in Lutgard's *Life*, see Alexandra Barratt's excellent essay, "Language and the Body in Thomas of Cantimpré's *Life* of Lutgard of Aywières," *Cistercian Studies Quarterly* 30 (1995): 339–47. Scholars translate the Latin term *Teutonica* as either "Flemish" or "Dutch"; I have chosen to follow the choice of the translator but am aware that the decision of the translator can be politically motivated.

the French-speaking districts, and several of them longed to have Lutgard as abbess had she learned even a little French. When the gracious Lutgard learned of this, she was horrified and, turning to the glorious Virgin Mary, tearfully entreated her to avert this from her. The blessed Mother appeared to her and said, "Do not worry at all about this because I will set the shield of my protection before you." . . . Lutgard was barely twenty-four years old when she entered Aywières and yet, in the forty years she lived among French-speaking companions, she could barely learn more French than she needed to ask for bread correctly when she was hungry.[61]

The "shield of protection" cast by Mary, therefore, is a shield against linguistic acquisition, protection from an oral French competency that would enable her to hold an office of pastoral care and authority over others. The miracle of disglossia allows Lutgard to remain a nontranslator living in quiet, private Flemish contemplation, quite unlike the xenoglossic holy men SS. Norbert, Patiens, and others, who were granted miraculous translation abilities so that they could succeed in prominent public preaching positions and guide their communities.

What control is Lutgard imagined to have over language and translation? On the one hand, unable to speak French, she is linguistically vulnerable and certainly quite isolated in the French-speaking community. On the other hand, that she prays for the inability means that she has as much control over her inability as xenoglossic men have over their ability. Her desire is *not* to learn the dominant language, and Mary, who is often imagined as a teacher of language for women, in this case agrees to make Lutgard incapable of learning. Thus, Lutgard's vita offers us an interesting variation on the (usually masculine) practice of praying for xenoglossia to guide an ever-growing flock. The hermit Pachomius embraced the need for linguistic translation, prayed to God, and was granted the ability to miraculously learn and speak all lan-

---

61. Thomas de Cantimpré, *Life of Lutgard*, 239. "Igitur cum virtus piae Lutgardis ubique crebresceret, coeperunt nova monasteria in Gallicis partibus construi & ad electionem illius, dum modo parum de Gallico didicisset, multipliciter anhelare. Quod ut pia Lutgardis cognovit, multum exhorruit; & conversa ad gloriosam virginem Mariam, eam ut hoc averteret cum lacrymis exoravit: cui beata Mater apparens ait: Nullo modo paveas in hoc verbo: quia scutum meae protectionis opponam. Et vide, Lector, quali modo aversum hoc fuerit, & videbis quam mera veritas respondentis. Vix viginti quatuor annorum tempus attigerat, cum Aquiriam intravit; & tamen talis in quadraginta annis, quibus postea inter socias Gallicas vixit, tantum vix sermonis Gallici addiscere potuit, ut panem recto modo Gallice peteret, cum esurivit. Quod ubi palam omnibus factum est, dilecta hynnula Christi in somno contemplationis pausare permissa est; nec suscitavit eam aliquis, neque evigilare ad curam pastoralem fecit, donec ipsa vellet; nec unquam accidit, ut hoc vellet." *AASS*, June, III, 243.

guages; Lutgard, however, refused to learn and embraced nontranslatability to avoid any position of control over other nuns that would have taken her away from her private devotions.

Lutgard's French disglossia was miraculously reversed on two occasions, enabling her to serve in important semiprivate advisory positions. One day when none of her fellow Cistercian sisters were able to help a despairing Frenchwoman who arrived at the nunnery, they introduced her to the pious Lutgard, who they assumed could at least pray for the unfortunate visitor. The two women conversed together quietly in a corner, and soon the whole abbey was wondering what they could possibly have to say to each other, since neither one spoke the other's language. Thomas of Cantimpré's vita describes the scene in great detail:

> Now a certain woman came to her in utter despair, lacking all hope of pardon. When she entered the parlour, the nuns pleaded with her to be consoled and set her hope in God. . . . Their efforts were in vain, for she tried to flee, but they held her back and begged her to wait for the gracious Lutgard. Although Lutgard was Flemish and could not give her any words of consolation (for the woman spoke only French), nevertheless she could pray to the Lord for her. As soon as Lutgard was brought in, she withdrew into a far corner with the woman, for she sensed in her spirit that she was in deep distress. Everyone began to laugh and wonder how they could communicate, since neither knew the other's language. But after they had been sitting there together for a long time, the woman got up, recalled to the fullest confidence and hope. She returned to the parlour and said to the nuns, "Why did you say that this most holy lady was Flemish? Indeed, I have found by experience that she is quite French!" . . . It is no wonder that the two women could communicate for awhile without knowing each other's language, for Lutgard was filled with the same Spirit that filled the assembled disciples with a variety of tongues.[62]

62. Thomas de Cantimpré, *Life of Lutgard*, 267–68. "Veniens ergo quaedam mulier, ab omni spe veniae penitus desperata, locutorium introivit. Rogabant autem Moniales ut consolationem reciperet, & spem in Deum poneret, qui non vult mortem peccatoris, sed ut convertatur & vivat. Illa autem casso labore fugere nitebatur: retenta tamen ea rogabant, ut expectaret piam Lutgardem; quae etsi ei ad consolationem loqui non posset, tamquam Teutonica, pro et tamen Dominum exoraret: erat autem mulier penitus Gallica. Nec mora pia Lutgardis adducta, ad remotum locum cum muliere secessit: sensit enim in spiritu supra modum feminam tribulatam. Mirari omnes ac ridere coeperunt, quomodo ignotae sibi invicem linguae in colloquio convenirent.

According to her vita, the holy woman was also miraculously gifted on another occasion, so that she could converse with a visiting bishop, who "was as completely ignorant of the Flemish language as she was of French," and they were "conversing and understanding each other."[63] Thus, in Lutgard's example, private devotional counseling or conversation is understood to be a worthy reason for xenoglossia; the Virgin Mary, however, supports Lutgard's decision that obtaining the position of abbess is definitely not a worthy cause and allows the pious woman to focus on her personal spiritual development rather than the day-to-day functioning of her religious order.

We see similar concerns regarding women's linguistic agency and spiritual development in other vitae of the same period. I would now like to consider a case of a woman who is pointedly not given a gift of xenoglossia, Ida of Nivelles. Similar to that of Lutgard, Ida's example is valuable because it demonstrates how a woman's spiritual growth is nurtured by her linguistic isolation and vulnerability, rather than by her mastery over the region's dominant vernacular. Ida's linguistic isolation encourages a particularly pious feminine experience as she learns to rely on God for her communication. Like Lutgard, translation difficulties bring Ida closer to Christ, and it is for this reason that her lack of control over the Flemish or Dutch language is repeatedly called attention to.

The *Life* of Ida of Nivelles demonstrates a linguistic struggle when a pious woman moves into a new region after she decides to enter a religious order. Ida's life, written by the Cistercian Goswin of Bossut, describes how the young woman, a French speaker, had to learn to speak Dutch when she entered a Cistercian nunnery at Kerkom, which was situated just to the north of the medieval French/Dutch linguistic divide in the Low Countries. Ida did eventually learn Dutch in an entirely unmiraculous way; her vita is thus interested not in attributing miraculous linguistic powers to her but rather in chronicling both her linguistic difficulties and the spiritual benefits that arise as a result of her lengthy linguistic isolation.

According to the two extant manuscripts of her vita, Ida fled her home when she was nine to avoid an impending marriage. Taking her Psalter with her, she sought refuge with a collective of beguines dedicated to poverty and

---

Postquam ergo ibidem diutius consedissent, surrexit mulier, ad plenissimam spei fiduciam revocata; & reversa in locutorium Monialibus dixit: Cur dixistis istam sanctissimam. [*sic*] Dominam esse Teutonicam, quam prorsus Gallicam sum experta?" *AASS*, June, III, 252.

63. Thomas de Cantimpré, *Life of Lutgard*, 268. "Refert Pater Bernardus, quod vidit eam, & virum venerabilem ac Deo dignum Magistrum de Guiardum Cameracensem Episcopum, qui penitus, linguam Teutonicam, sicut & ipsa Gallicam, ignorabat, mutuo colloquentes, & invicem intelligentes." *AASS*, June, III, 252.

remained with them for seven years.[64] At the age of sixteen, she was admitted to the Cistercian nunnery at Kerkom, a move her vita claims she made because she wanted "to unburden herself of concerns of possessing absolutely nothing of her own (RB 33.3) and also to receive the holy Eucharist frequently from the priest at mass, as do the monks and nuns of the Order."[65] The nunnery was then soon moved to Jauchelette and was known as La Ramée, where Ida remained until her death.[66]

Ida's vita describes her initial difficulties in understanding when she first entered the Dutch-speaking nunnery, her isolation that resulted, and the humility she learned from this experience. First, we are told that, when Ida joined the Cistercian order, she was required to learn what her hagiographer calls "Teutonic," or a medieval form of Flemish, an early form of Dutch.[67] The *Life* describes the difficulties she faced: "While in this monastery, Sister Ida used to hear the sisters speaking words quite foreign and unfamiliar to her, since almost all of them spoke Dutch, and she did not understand their tongue. Yet despite her ignorance of it, there was one religious gentleman who used to preach the word of God in that tongue, and whenever she listened to him, the Holy Spirit breathed into her soul and tears flowed from her eyes, tears too copious for her to hold back, her heart being in the grip of so agreeable a savour."[68] Linguistically isolated from most of her sisters, Ida is spiritu-

---

64. Goswin of Bossut, *Send Me God: The Lives of Ida the Compassionate of Nivelles, Nun of La Ramée, Arnulf, Lay Brother of Villers, and Abundus, Monk of Villers*, ed. and trans. Martinus Cawley (Turnhout: Brepols, 2003; University Park: Pennsylvania State Univeristy Press, 2006), 31. As described by Cawley, the Latin *Life* of Ida of Nivelles is extant in two manuscripts and was printed by Chrisostomo Henriquez in *Quinque prudentes virgines* (Antwerp, 1630), 199–297. All Latin quotations from Ida's *Life* are from Martinus Cawley's *Lives of Ida of Nivelles, Lutgard, and Alice the Leper* (Lafayette, OR: Guadalupe Translations, 1987), which contains Cawley's Latin edition and his earlier English translation of her *Life*. For the importance of Ida fleeing from her house with her Psalter, see Walter Simons, " 'Staining the Speech of Things Divine': The Uses of Literacy in Medieval Beguine Communities," in *The Voice of Silence: Women's Literacy in a Men's Church*, ed. Thérèse de Hemptinne and María Eugenia Góngora. Medieval Church Studies, 9 (Turnhout: Brepols, 2004), 85–110, at pp. 88–89.

65. Goswin of Bossut, *The Life of Ida of Nivelles*, 34. "Duabus itaque de causis sicut ipsa perhibebat, transtulit se ad ordinem. Ut scilicet onmnibus expedita curis, nihil omnino proprium haberet, & ut etiam frequenter a sacerdote in Missa sanctam acciperet Eucharistiam, sicut moniablius in ordine consuetudo est." Cawley, *Lives of Ida*, 10.

66. Simons, "Staining the Speech," 89.

67. Barbara Newman states, "Whatever the state of her Latin skills, we know she was bilingual in the vernacular. French was her native tongue, but early in her religious life she mastered the language Goswin calls 'Teutonic,' the form of Dutch native to Beatrice [of Nazareth]." Preface to Goswin of Bossut, *Send Me God*, xxxviii.

68. Goswin of Bossut, *Life of Ida of Nivelles*, 34. "In hoc ergo monasterio cum esset Venerabilis Ida, audiebat sorores barbara quaedam & ignota sibi verba loquentes, nec intelligebat linguam eam eo quod omnes fere lingue Theutonica loquerentur. Et quamvis linguam Theutonicam nesciret, tamen cum interdum audiebat virum religiosum lingua Theutonica praedicante verbum

ally touched by one Dutch preacher. On the one hand, this description suggests she experiences something akin to a miracle of vernacular xenoglossia, for she appears moved by the Holy Spirit to understand his discourse; on the other hand, this experience could also be interpreted as a gift of divinely infused spiritual understanding of his words.

The vita continues to emphasize Ida's inability to understand Dutch. Rather than limiting her spiritual growth, however, the inability encourages her to search inward more deeply and to develop her own meditative strength: "Not understanding what her sisters were saying, Ida frequently conversed with herself and God alone, remarkably combining meditative prayer and prayerful meditation. In doing this, she would bring to mind various visible, bodily creatures for consideration, and in admiring them she would contemplate *their Creator* (Wisd. 13.5), an exercise in climbing to higher things, one little step at a time."[69] Thus, linguistic isolation encourages and forces Ida to advance spiritually, as her conversation is restricted to a dialogue between herself and God. Because of the order's emphasis on silence (except in the *loquarium*) and inner meditation, Ida's linguistic inability encourages her growth as a contemplative Cistercian.

It is in the midst of this discussion over her difficulties with Dutch and her resulting inward contemplation that we are told about Ida's (in)ability to read Scripture, as well as the comfort she took in Scripture despite (or perhaps because of) the fact that she could not read the text: "As for sacred Scripture, she loved it as a mirror for her soul. Of course, *the law of the Lord was in the heart*, not in the hardbound tome (Ps. 36.31), but some volumes there were in which she could spot terms like *God* or *Christ*, or *Emmanuel*, and other terms too, fragrant with spiritual sweetness. These volumes she would press to her chest and hug so tightly in her bosom that the books' rugged embossing left her bruised."[70] Even though Ida could not read Scripture, she was able to

---

Dei flante Spiritu Sancto interius in anima ejus, fluebant ab oculis suis lachrymae, nec poterat se continere quoniam magna cordis suavitate tenebatur." Cawley, *Lives of Ida*, 10.

69. Goswin of Bossut, *The Life of Ida of Nivelles*, 34. "Et quoniam, ut dictum est, non intelligebat ea quae a sororibus dicebantur, frequenter Deo soli & sibi loquebatur, & miro modo orationem habens meditativam ac meditationem orativam, in consideratione mentis suae creaturas visibiles & corporales considerabat. In quarum quodammodo admiratione perfusa contemplabatur earum Creatorem ut hoc studio posset paulatim ad altiora, quasi quibusdam graduum profectibus ascendere." Cawley, *Lives of Ida*, 10.

70. Goswin of Bossut, *Life of Ida of Nivelles*, 35. "Scriptorum sacram tanquam quoddam speculum animae valde diligebat, libros tamen in quibus inveniebat has dictiones, scl. Deus, vel Christus vel Jesus vel Emanuel vel aliud quid quod spiritualem redoleret dulcedinem, eosdem pectori suo applicabat & tam fortiter in ulnis suis amplectabatur quod ex duritia asserum eorundem librorum non modice laedebatur." Cawley, *Lives of Ida*, 11.

recognize certain holy words; these words left their imprint in her heart as well as their imprint on her skin. Her inability to speak "Teutonic," therefore, made her appreciate the utter comfort offered by the holy names in Latin Scripture, even more than she had appreciated previously.

Immediately after this scene, Goswin returns to the subject of Ida's vernacular difficulties and successes, calling attention to how she attempted to cheer even those with whom she could not communicate orally:

> There was one of her sisters whom she would sometimes see unusually downcast, and, though unable to speak to her in Dutch, she would sit beside her and lend her at least the serenity of an outward good cheer to clear away the clouding of her face. Her visitors too, men and women, whether or not religiously inclined, used to get great consolation from her exemplary conduct and from the abundant grace they were confident she possessed. And in any case, she gradually mastered the Dutch language and became able to speak suitably to her sisters and to people of that tongue.[71]

The vita emphasizes that Ida is able to communicate silently through her pious conduct (her outward performance of her increasing inner peace), including her physical actions, facial features, tears, pious expressions, and physical embrace of Scripture. Ida's grace is readable from her countenance, a grace that is emphasized by her inability to communicate linguistically. Her inability becomes a way for the holy woman to deepen and to grow spiritually, as well as for others to appreciate her piety, and for the vita's audiences to experience and witness her exemplary behavior through her actions, not just her words.

This focus on Ida's vernacular difficulties and the deepening of spiritual growth that resulted no doubt is influenced by contemporary Southern-Netherlandish vitae such as Lutgard's, which focus on women's miraculous linguistic isolation as spiritually desirable and ultimately supported by God. Xenoglossia, as well as its opposite, linguistic isolation, can foster and support

---

71. Goswin of Bossut, *The Life of Ida of Nivelles*, 35. "Si quando videbat aliquam sororum suarum solito tristiorem, quamvis ei loqui Theutonice nesciret, tamen residebat juxta eam & obnubilationem faciei ejus exterior saltem serenabat hilaritate. Religiosi siquidem & non religiosi tam viri quam mulieres venientes ad videndum ipsam, ex honestis ejus moribus & ex abundantia gratiae quam in ea esse credebant consolationem magnam reportabant. Ipsa auditem paulatim didicit linguam Theotonicam, ut tam sororibus quam ejusdem linguae gentibus, congrue loqueretur." Cawley, *Lives of Ida*, 11. For Cawley's discussion of the translation of this passage, see Goswin of Bossut, *Life of Ida of Nivelles*, 35n18.

the deepest of pious experiences in women. Perhaps accounts like Ida's convinced other hagiographers that vernacular xenoglossia need not hold such a prominent position in medieval women's religious experience as it did in the lives of medieval men.

Conclusion

In this chapter, I have explored the remarkable adaptability of vernacular xenoglossia in medieval vitae, which include experiences ranging from wide-scale preaching to more private one-on-one spiritual conversations. I have argued that medieval men and women are described as receiving and practicing their miraculous gifts of translation in markedly different ways. Whereas xenoglossic men can be both public preachers and counselors, women are usually granted vernacular xenoglossia when approached by another in need, for a brief period of time. These differing experiences of xenoglossia raise significant questions concerning linguistic agency. What access to and control over language are men and women imagined as having in these accounts? That men often pray for the ability that is then granted to them suggests that they desire to be proficient in that language; they are then described as masters of that language for lengthy periods of time. We could, for example, imagine St. Dominic speaking on a variety of religious and spiritual topics, as well as discussing food, shelter, and perhaps even the weather (if necessary), with those German pilgrims over the course of several days. For women, however, their control over language is often much less defined. St. Clare, for example, was said to have spoken for the length of one hundred Pater Nosters with Marguerite in French. But could they have sustained a conversation for several days on a variety of spiritual topics?

In several cases, the more mundane scope of women's gifts might suggest a recording of actual lived experience. Whereas many legends about the apostles or earlier saints developed long after the subjects lived (or, in some cases, were alleged to have lived), actual witnesses testified in a canonization process that they saw Clare speaking with Marguerite. Of course, witnesses' testimonies are shaped by the questions asked of them and the circumstances of the process, but Clare's sisters do appear to believe that they observed Clare communicating with another woman for a brief time, in a language the witnesses did not understand themselves. We can perhaps explain this by imagining that Clare and Marguerite, who both spoke romance languages, could understand some of what each other said and could also communicate through gestures and expressions. Or perhaps one of the two possessed a more passive or receptive understanding of the other language, an ability to comprehend but not to express. In Lutgard's case, although she was said to never have learned French, Thomas mentions that the holy woman did learn enough to be able to beg for bread. Perhaps her conversation in French with the visiting bishop involved her listening more than speaking, or she had acquired enough simple phrases to engage in a brief dialogue. In all of these cases, what appears to be a very limited or narrow scope of xenoglossia may actually reflect the desire on the communities' or hagiographers' parts to describe more ordinary occurences as miraculous.

There is a danger, of course, in drawing conclusions about gendered experiences based on so few examples of vernacularly xenoglossic holy women. Although the gift of vernacular tongues is relatively common in men's lives, I have only found several attributions of vernacular xenoglossia in the lives of medieval women. Two other instances of possible xenoglossia have been suggested by scholars, but it is not at all clear in the texts that we are meant to understand the events as xenoglossic.[72] Perhaps holy women, their communities, and their hagiographers could not imagine situations in which miraculous vernacular translation would be necessary other than one-on-one spiritual guidance, preferring instead to imagine how linguistic isolation could foster women's spiritual growth.

As I argue in the next chapter, holy women's vernacular miracles must be

---

72. Margot H. King has suggested a possible instance of xenoglossia in Thomas of Cantimpré's *Life of Margaret of Ypres*, although I do not read it as such. Thomas describes how Margaret (d. 1237) was approached by a sinful man who wished to improve his life. He sought out Margaret, and although he did not understand her words, he immediately experienced remorse: "Scarcely was anyone so perverse and stubborn that the sight of her countenance and disciplined bearing would not influence him for the better. Wherefore a certain thing happened as I shall tell. There was in the remoter parts of Flanders a man who, having heard the rumor of her sanctity, decided to see her. This man had been lax and remiss in his actions all the days of his life. Without delay, when he saw her countenance and heard her words—which he did not understand—he was attracted by the wonderful grace in her. Visibly struck by remorse in his heart, he received an improvement of life quite unexpectantly," in The *Life of Margaret of Ypres*, trans. Margot H. King and Barbara Newman, in *Thomas of Cantimpré: Collected Saints' Lives*, 163–206, at pp. 173–74. For the Latin, see G. Meersseman, "Vita Margarete de Ypris," appendix in *Les Frères Prêcheurs at Mouvement Dévot en Flandre au XIII Siècles*, Archivum Fratrum Praedicatorum 18 (Rome: Institutum Historicum Fratrum Praedicatorum, 1948), 106–30, at p. 112. According to King, "This could either mean that he did not understand the dialect Margaret was speaking, or that she was speaking too obscurely, or 'in tongues'" (174n45). I do not read this as a case of xenoglossia, since there is no indication that the man actually understood Margaret's words; rather, he appears to have been affected by her obvious grace. For a possible claim of vernacular xenoglossia in the letters of St. Catherine of Siena, see Chapter 2.

seen in combination with their gifts of Latinity and imbued spiritual knowledge, gifts that are far more common than vernacular xenoglossia in their vitae. Miraculous gifts of being able to read, to understand, or to speak Latin potentially allow women to participate in realms normally limited to clerics; how women choose to participate (if at all) is at stake in these miracle accounts, for they address a number of significant concerns about the appropriateness of women engaging with and translating Latin Scripture. The next chapter therefore examines a group of texts and experiences that appear to offer women far more significant, and problematic, roles as translators.

TWO

MIRACULOUS LITERACIES:
MEDIEVAL WOMEN'S MIRACULOUS EXPERIENCES OF LATIN

In Chapter 1, I explored the remarkable adaptability of vernacular xenoglossia in medieval vitae, which include experiences ranging from wide-scale preaching to more private one-on-one spiritual conversations. I demonstrated that few women receive vernacular xenoglossia and argued that when they do, their gifts are usually limited in scope and duration. Whereas men often receive the full command of the language for their use in the company of many, lasting from an evening to an entire lifetime, medieval holy women typically experience miraculous translation for briefer periods (one conversation) in one-on-one situations, when approached by another in need. This suggests that when medieval hagiographers imagined vernacular xenoglossia they described experiences that were highly gendered and reflected their expectations of men's and women's "appropriate" social behavior.

In this chapter, I examine an important variation of xenoglossia in the lives of later medieval women, one that is central to their reputations of blessedness. Although relatively few women were said to have been given gifts of vernacular xenoglossia, a much greater number are reported as having experienced miraculous Latinity. Women's gifts of Latin xenoglossia take a variety of forms and emphasize the importance of God's grace over study and learning. Women are infused with divine knowledge of Latin scriptural and liturgical texts such as the Psalter and Divine Office, and they become admired authorities on these texts. This gift of infused spiritual knowledge and its resultant Latinity is granted for many purposes, including private devotional reading

and translating, participating in liturgical activities, and teaching and translating for other female religious. It is a more problematical gift than vernacular
xenoglossia, however, because reading, translating, and becoming an authority on Latin Scripture in the later Middle Ages are for the most part masculine,
clerical endeavors, activities that women traditionally appealed to masculine
authority to provide.

Women's gifts of miraculous scriptural knowlege have attracted the attention of a number of scholars who explore how the gifts emphasize *sapientia*
over *scientia*, or an internalized, "felt" understanding infused by God, over
intellectually derived knowledge gained from traditional education.[1] Two
studies appearing in 2004 have been particularly illuminating. Anneke Mulder-Bakker has emphasized how gifts of sapientia for many medieval and
early modern women and men actually indicate other nontraditional routes
of learning, including "seeing and hearing,"[2] and Katrien Heene has suggested
that accounts of women's gifts of sapientia in thirteenth-century religious
texts are careful to emphasize that the women do not challenge masculine,
clerical privilege, even though they claim a divine gift of wisdom.[3] While

---

1. For the distinction between *sapientia* ("affective knowledge") and *scientia* ("intellective
knowledge"), see Nicholas Watson, *Richard Rolle and the Invention of Authority*, Cambridge Studies in Medieval Literature 13 (Cambridge: Cambridge University Press, 1991), 23–24; A. J. Minnis,
Medieval Theory of Authorship: Scholastic Literary Attitudes in the Later Middle Ages (Philadelphia:
University of Pennsylvania Press, 1988), especially chapter 4; and Anne Clark Bartlett, "Miraculous Literacy and Textual Communities in Hildegard of Bingen's *Scivias*," *Mystics Quarterly* 18
(1992), 43–55, at p. 44.

2. Anneke B. Mulder-Bakker, ed., introduction to *Seeing and Knowing: Women and Learning in Medieval Europe, 1200–1550*, trans. Myra Scholz, Medieval Women: Texts and Contexts 11
(Turnhout: Brepols, 2004), 1–19, at p. 11. Mulder-Bakker observes that medieval male and female
litterati and *illiterati* have "two distinct routes" for acquiring knowledge open to them: "the
world of written knowledge on the one hand, and the oral world of mainstream medieval culture
on the other" (4). Thirteenth-century women such as Beatrice of Nazareth, who composed a
collection of vernacular sermons heavily infused with theology, and Juliana of Mont-Cornillon,
who spearheaded the establishment of the Feast of Corpus Christi, are excellent examples of
women whose knowledge acquired through "seeing and knowing" rather than traditional study
rivals the knowledge of learned clerics (1–4).

3. In her 2004 essay, "*De litterali et morali earum instruccione*: Women's Literacy in Thirteenth-Century Latin Agogic Texts," in *The Voice of Silence: Women's Literacy in a Men's Church*,
ed. Thérèse de Hemptinne and María Eugenia Góngora, Medieval Church Studies 9 (Turnhout:
Brepols, 2004), 145–66, Katrien Heene describes two kinds of learning that appear in men's and
women's hagiographic literature: knowledge that is gained from the actual study of texts and that
achieved through a divinely infused gift. As Heene explains, a number of thirteenth-century men
and women are said to be educated by the Holy Spirit and infused with understanding of God's
Word so that they become spiritual authorities. Holy men and women experience gifts of divinely
infused knowledge in gendered ways: for men, "it was used to compensate their lack of formal
schooling"; for women, "it was not only important to stress that they possessed the necessary
knowledge to acquire spiritual authority and to become a saint, but also to make clear that this
knowledge—whatever its origin—did not incite them to claim clerical prerogatives" (161–62).

scholars have investigated claims of sapientia in localized areas and individual lives, my aim in this chapter is to offer a wider exploration of this trope in later medieval women's vitae, which range from the earliest examples (late twelfth century) through the end of the Middle Ages. I shall explore how women's gifts of Latinity speak to the issues of agency and performance that were raised in the first chapter. The goal of later chapters will be to discover how the late medieval authors Margery Kempe and Geoffrey Chaucer adapt this feminine model in their own writings.

Although women's miraculous Latinity could be the subject of a book on its own, my interest in these fascinating accounts focuses on the intersection between sapientia and language. What kind of access to the Latin language is afforded by a gift of sapientia? I argue that in imagining women's gifts of sapientia, hagiographers describe gifts that offer access to Latin scriptural, liturgical, and devotional texts in a way that is different from and superior to the traditional route of masculine education. At the same time as they admire the gifts, however, the hagiographers are hesitant to show women as masters of Latinity who exhibit a full range of clerical abilities, including reading, writing, speaking, and understanding. In fact, no woman with a gift of infused spiritual understanding gains a linguistic ability that fully approximates clerical proficiency. The vitae therefore appear to be split by two desires: at the same time that the hagiographers admire the knowledge afforded by sapientia, they are also invested in demonstrating that the gift does not provide the range of literate abilities that clerical study can.

I shall argue that similar to vernacular xenoglossia, women's gifts of Latinate ability and infused scriptural understanding appear limited in scope. An ability to translate Latin Scripture into the vernacular becomes proof of the miraculous gift of infused scriptural understanding, but that translation is limited in significant ways. Women do become translators for themselves and others, but many of the miracles appear quite unmiraculous or even mundane in their description and seem to suggest that the women have been granted miraculously what they might reasonably have been expected to learn on their own. This hesitancy to imagine women as masterful Latin translators can be explained by two different impulses: first, many of the miracle accounts seem to reflect actual lived experiences of women gaining access to Latin texts in nontraditional ways. The hagiographers, communities surrounding the holy women, and perhaps even the women themselves are heavily invested in presenting their nontraditional learning as miraculous. Second, I argue that in several cases, hagiographers appear concerned that women's miraculous Latinity could potentially challenge their own clerical authority, and therefore they imagine the women with gifts that are limited in both scope and practice.

Toward the end of the Middle Ages, however, a variation on this gift emerges that actually affords women more control over their own Latinity. The vitae of several prominent holy women describe how Mary commands them to learn Latin and even tutors them. It is this miraculous tutelage that allows St. Bridget of Sweden, founder of the Bridgettine Order, to become proficient in speaking, understanding, and reading Latin, in order that she may oversee the translation of her *Revelations* from Swedish into Latin. Women's xenoglossia, therefore, is imagined as authorizing actual textual practices, a motif that the English writers Margery Kempe and Geoffrey Chaucer develop in their own writings.

Part 1: Medieval Women's Miraculous Latinity

For women, the gift of the Latin language without an accompanying gift of infused spiritual understanding is quite rare. One such miracle account concerning St. Thomas Becket describes how a very pious *inclusa* (a recluse or anchoress) repeated to some monks a sentence she received in Latin "from a very beautiful woman," that is, the Virgin Mary, without understanding what the words meant. The monks mourning the death of the Archbishop then realized that the message was meant for them.[4] In contrast, a woman could also be imagined with a much deeper gift of the Latin language. As mentioned in Chapter 1, the fifteenth-century vita of St. Colette of Corbie reports that, like the apostles, she could understand all languages, "namely Latin and German and all the rest." What exactly is meant, however, by this gift of Latinity is not developed. Could Colette understand spoken Latin and written Latin? Did her ability extend to an understanding of political, scientific, and theological Latin, for example, or only scriptural or liturgical Latin? Nancy Bradley Warren has argued that this linguistic claim asserts Colette's authority over the male religious whom she is reforming; it is significant, however, that the

---

4. "Quaedam etiam inclusa sanctissima, quae nec Latinum noverat sermonem nec Gallicum, monachis Cantuariae in brevi post mortem archiepiscopi mandavit se a muliere pulcherrima accepisse, sed non intellexisse, hoc Latinum, 'Noli flere pro archipraesule tuo, quia caput ejus in sinu Filii mei requiescit,'" in James Craigie Robertson, ed., *Materials for the History of Thomas Becket, Archbishop of Canterbury* (London: Longman & Co., 1876), 2:290.

vita imagines her as passively undertanding Latin rather than producing it, for the apostles are attributed more active tongues.[5]

For many medieval male religious, however, purely linguistic gifts of Latin or even Greek offer a clerical mastery of language. The life of St. Pachomius, for example, as we also recall from Chapter 1, describes how, by reading a heavenly sent page, the holy man learned all the languages of the world, including Latin, so that he could hear confessions and take spiritual care of the monks who were forming the first monastic community around him. The description of his reading the page and learning the languages of the world mimics a clerical education, and we are told that Pachomius retained his linguistic ability for life. Similarly, the Spiritual Franciscan Angelo Clareno (d. 1337) learned the entire Greek language in one night so that he could translate difficult theological texts into Latin.[6] Xenoglossic holy men, therefore, can become fully proficient in a clerical language; holy women, however, are never imagined as mastering a clerical language fully so that they can participate in all aspects of Latin literacy, including reading and writing.

The vita of St. Catherine of Siena (d. 1380) describes a kind of sudden Latin ability that perhaps comes closest to a clerical mastery; however, the specific access to Latinity offered by the gift is quite ambiguous and points to the problematic nature of medieval women's gifts of literacy. Catherine's vita was composed several years after her death by her spiritual advisor, the Dominican Master General Raymond of Capua, to promote her canonization. Whereas extant epistolary evidence suggests that Catherine claimed a gift of vernacular xenoglossia for herself, Raymond asserts that she received a Latinate gift, no doubt thinking it was more convincing evidence of her blessedness.[7] Raymond describes how, to be able to say the Latin Psalms and perform

5. "Apostoli variis linguis loquebantur et omnia idiomata percipiebant. Pariformiter ipsa cuncta percipiebat idiomata, videlicet Latinum et Alamanicum et reliqua." *AASS*, Mar., I, 576. For Colette's authority over friars, see especially Nancy Bradley Warren, "Monastic Politics: St Colette of Corbie, Franciscan Reform, and the House of Burgundy," in *New Medieval Literatures* 5, ed. Rita Copeland, David Lawton, and Wendy Scase (Oxford: Oxford University Press, 2002), 216–67.

6. "Abiit *autem* cum illis Angelus Clarenus; *etiam ipse reversus ex Armenia, ibidemque in Achaia* divinitus edoctus *est* Graecum idioma, in nocte nativitatis Domini sub anno MCCC; *eoque sic instructus*, plures aliorum lucubrationes Latinitate donavit." *AASS*, June, II, 1094).

7. Just three years before her death, Catherine of Siena sent a letter to Raymond of Capua, in which she appears to claim that God had given her, an illiterate woman, the ability to write in Italian through the aid of John the Baptist and Thomas Aquinas: "This letter and another I sent you I've written with my own hand. . . . He [God] provided for my refreshment by giving me the ability to write—a consolation I've never known because of my ignorance—so that when I come down from the heights I might have a little something to vent my heart, let it burst. . . . Shortly after you left me, I began to learn in my sleep, with the glorious evangelist John and Thomas Aquinas" (2:505) in Catherine of Siena, *The Letters of Catherine of Siena*, trans. Suzanne

the prayers of the Divine Office and canonical hours, the holy woman decided to learn how to read. After many unsuccessful weeks of trying to learn the alphabet from a fellow nun, Catherine prayed to the Lord for help and was suddenly granted the miraculous ability to read both Scripture and prayers.[8] Raymond describes the strange nature of her Latinity:

> Then a marvel happened—clear proof of God's power—for during this prayer she was so divinely instructed that when she got up she knew how to read any kind of writing quite easily and fluently, like the best reader in the world. When I realized this I was flabbergasted, especially when I discovered that though she could read so fast she could not read separate syllables; in fact, she could hardly spell the words. I believe that the Lord meant this to be a sign of the miracle that had taken place. From then on Catherine began to hunt for books of the Divine Office and to read the Psalms and anthems and the other things fixed for the Canonical Hours. She was especially struck by the verse with which each Hour begins and remembered it to the end of her life, "O God, come to my assistance; O Lord, make haste to help me." She often used to repeat this in the vernacular.[9]

Noffke, Medieval and Renaissance Texts and Studies, 2 vols. (Tempe: Arizona Center for Medieval and Renaissance Studies, 2001). The Italian original reads, "Questa lettera, e un'altra ch'io vi mandai, ho scritte di mia mano . . . [Dio] m'aveva dato, e proveduto con darmi l'attitudine dello scrivere; acciocchè discendendo dall'altezza, avessi un poco con chi sfogare 'l cuore, perchè non scoppiasse." Letter 272, from Le Lettere di S. Caterina da Siena, ed. Niccolò Tommasco, 4 vols., rev. Piero Misciattelli, 6 vols. (Florence: C/E Giunti-G. Barbera, 1940), 4:158–72, at p. 172, quoted in Karen Scott, "Mystical Death, Bodily Death: Catherine of Siena and Raymond of Capua on the Mystic's Encounter with God," in Gendered Voices: Medieval Saints and Their Interpreters, ed. Catherine M. Mooney (Philadelphia: University of Philadelphia Press, 1999), 136–67 and 238–44, at p. 241n25. There has been some debate over whether Catherine actually wrote this letter, or if it was included later to promote her canonization; see Scott, "Mystical Death, Bodily Death," 150–51. On whether this represents a miraculous ability, see also Catherine of Siena, Letters of Catherine of Siena, 2:505–6n51.

8. Raymond describes Catherine's efforts to learn the alphabet in the conventional way with the aid of a fellow nun. After many weeks of not being able to learn she prayed to the Lord: "If you want me to learn to read so that I can say the Psalms and sing your praises in the Canonical Hours, deign to teach me what I am not clever enough to learn by myself. If not, thy will be done: I shall be quite content to remain in my ignorance and shall be able to spend more time in meditating on you in other ways." Raymond of Capua, The Life of St Catherine of Siena, trans. George Lamb (New York: P. J. Kenedy & Sons, 1960), 95. "Domine, si placitum est tibi, ut sciam legere, ut psalmodiam & tuas laudes valeam decantare per Horas canonicas, tu me docere digneris, quod per memetipsam apprehendere nequeo: sin alias, fiat voluntas tua: quia in simplicitate mea libenter permaneo, & tempus a te mihi concessum, in aliis meditationibus tuis magis libenter expendo." AASS, Apr., III, 881.

9. Raymond of Capua, Life of St Catherine of Siena, 97. The Acta Sanctorum reads: "Mira res, & divinae virtutis manifestum indicium! Antequam de oratione surgeret, ita divinitus est edocta, quod postquam ab ipsa surrexit, omnem scivit litteram legere, tam velociter & expedite,

What is remarkable in this account is how Raymond imagines Catherine's Latinate ability as so different from his own clerical mastery. First, he emphasizes that she cannot even learn her letters. Second, he tests the gift and demonstrates that Catherine is both fully literate and illiterate at the same time. On the one hand, the holy woman becomes an accomplished, fluent Latin reader (a *doctissumus*) who devours books with a speed marveled at by the learned hagiographer. On the other hand, her Latinity is not a traditional, grammatical literacy, for she cannot spell or even discern individual syllables. Raymond's description makes it unclear what kind of access to Latinity Catherine receives. Can she read and understand the Latin of any kind of text? Or is this a gift of divinely facilitated understanding of certain scriptural or liturgical texts, accompanied by the ability to speak the Latin words, without any actual mastery of the Latin language per se? This account suggests that the holy woman has been given a gift of sapientia, or spiritual wisdom divinely infused by God, which manifests itself as an ability to "read" the Latin of the Divine Office, Psalms, and anthems.

As we see in Catherine's example, gifts of sapientia offer a vehicle for Latin xenoglossia quite different from a gift of simply producing or understanding another language. Miracles of sapientia occur in both men's and women's lives and are extremely popular ways of demonstrating people to be divinely inspired. The gift is reported to have been experienced by a range of recipients, from illiterate nuns and lay brothers and sisters to the most learned of male clerics and theologians.[10] For example, the thirteenth-century *Life* of the

---

sicut quicumque doctissimus. Quod ego ipse dum fui expertus, stupebam: potissime propter hoc, quod inveni, quia cum velocissime legeret, si jubebatur syllabicare, in nullo sciebat aliquid dicere: imo vix litteras cognoscebat: quod aestimo pro signo miraculi ordinatum a Domino tunc fuisse. Hoc facto, coepit libros quaerere divinum Officium continentes, & in ipsis legere psalmos, hymnos, & reliqua quae pro canonicis Horis sunt deputata. Inter alia vero verba quae tunc dicebat, signanter notavit & tenuit usque ad mortem verbum psalmi, per quod quaelibet hora inciptiur, scilicet: Deus in adjutorium meum intende, Domine ad adjuvandum me festina: quod in vulgari reductum, frequentius repetebat." AASS, Apr., III, 881.

10. In *de doctrina Christiana*, Augustine cautions, "But now as to those who talk vauntingly of Divine Grace, and boast that they understand and can explain Scripture without the aid of such directions as those I now propose to lay down. . . . I would such persons could calm themselves so far as to remember that, however justly they may rejoice in God's great gift, yet it was from human teachers they themselves learnt to read. Now, they would hardly think it right that they should for that reason be held in contempt by the Egyptian monk Antony, a just and holy man, who, not being able to read himself, is said to have committed the Scriptures to memory through hearing them read by others, and by dint of wise meditation to have arrived at a thorough understanding of them; or by that barbarian slave Christianus, of whom I have lately heard from very respectable and trustworthy witnesses, who, without any teaching from man, attained a full knowledge of the art of reading simply through prayer that it might be revealed to him; after three days' supplication obtaining his request that he might read through a book presented to him on the spot by the astonished bystanders," in Augustine of Hippo, *Nicene and*

Cistercian lay brother Arnulf of Villers (d. 1228) claims that the illiterate holy man was schooled by grace to the extent that learned men would seek him out with complicated scriptural questions, which he could answer beautifully; thus he could deeply understand Scripture without being able actually to read it.[11] Another thirteenth-century Cistercian, Beatrice of Nazareth (d. 1268), who learned to read her Psalter at age five, was also illuminated by the Holy Spirit while she was reading difficult passages so that she could understand their deep inner meaning: "Thus is often happened that, if ever her reading concerned some mysterious matter in the divine pages of Scripture which she could not at all understand with her limited powers—lest her spirit weary itself in vain for a long time—, the grace of the Holy Spirit was suddenly present enlightening her intellect."[12] The gift of deep understanding could therefore be given to someone like Beatrice, who already possessed some literate ability, or to someone like Arnulf, who was said to be entirely uneducated.

Gifts of sapientia could also aid men in achieving clerical mastery. For example, the Life of Yvette (Jutta) of Huy (d. 1228) records how her wayward son reformed his sinful ways and then wished to enter a Cistercian monastery. Since he lacked the necessary education, however, the Holy Spirit increased the speed and depth of his learning, an education that would have required a proviciency in speaking, reading, writing, and understanding Latin.[13]

Post-Nicene Fathers, First Series, vol. 2, Augustin: City of God, Christian Doctrine, ed. Philip Schaff (New York: Christian Literature Company, 1887; reprinted in Peabody, MA: Hendrickson, 1995), 519–20.

11. "Such a simple man, but educated by grace in the school of supreme divinity, where he learned what many of the wise of this world, for all their wisdom, never have discovered!" Goswin of Bossut, Send Me God: The Lives of Ida the Compassionate of Nivelles, Nun of La Ramee, Arnulf, Lay Brother of Villers, and Abundus, Monk of Villers, ed. and trans. Martinus Cawley, Medieval Women: Texts and Contexts 6 (Turnhout: Brepols, 2003; University Park, PA: Pennsylvania State University Press, 2006), 165–66.

12. The Life of Beatrice of Nazareth, 1200–1268, ed. and trans. Roger de Ganck, Cistercian Fathers Series 50 (Kalamazoo, MI: Cistercian Publications, 1991), 111. "Vnde frequenter accidit, vt de profundis misteriorum diuine pagine, siquando lectio suis se conspectibus ingessisset quam, proprij viribus ingenioli, nullatens intelligere valuisset; ne diutus incassum fatigaretur illius spiritus, repente gratia spiritus sancti, illuminans intellectum illius." Life of Beatrice of Nazareth, 110. The hagiographer also writes, "Divine grace had opened the beloved's faculties to understand the Scriptures, and therefore she was zealous to form all her actions and affections, within and without, according to the counsel of the Scriptures" (109). "Aperuerat quippe diuina gratia sensum dilecte sue vt intelligeret scripturas; et propterea omnes, tam actionum suarum quam affectionum motus, intrinsecos videlicet et extrinsecos, iuxta consilium scripturarum informare studuit" (108).

13. "And therefore as the days went by she attempted to persuade her son that he should wish to transfer himself to a certain convent of the Cistercian order. He replied that nothing stood in his way except that he must first learn sacred letters. . . . He was remitted to things which suited an adolescent when a man fully grown and in a shorter time than one might believe he was seen to progress until soon he transcended even those who had frequented the schools since infancy in the spirit of wisdom and understanding. No wonder. For how can there be delay

Whereas gifts of sapientia are often given to men to assist their *scientia*, as in the case of Yvette of Huy's son, more often than not, in women's lives, sapientia is said to come to the wholly illiterate, who are blank slates waiting to be written on by God. For example, the Cistercian Ida of Louvain (d. 1300), who entered a convent later in life after living as a beguine for many years, was described as formally illiterate. Although "she had never been taught letters in her entire life," she is imagined to have an interior bookshelf that she could read inwardly, suggesting that sapientia provides an alternative to traditional literacy.[14]

The vitae emphasize the women's illiteracy, but what does this really mean? The term *literatus* often referred to an ability to read and understand Latin texts, not vernacular ones.[15] As Brian Stock defines, medieval literacy "indicated a familiarity, if not always a deep understanding, of Latin grammar and syntax," the ability to "read and write a language for which in theory at least there was a set of articulated rules."[16] An ability to read or write in a vernacu-

---

in learning when the Holy Spirit is the teaching master . . . ? And when he had been completely instructed, following his mother's will, he entered the Cistercian monastery of Trois-Fontaines and made such progress that he was soon adept in all the grades of the priesthood." Hugh of Floreffe, *The Life of Yvette of Huy,* trans. Jo Ann McNamara (Toronto: Peregrina, 1999), 81–82. "Euolutis igitur diebus aliquot, cum persuadere tentaret filio, vt ad aliquod coenobium se transferre vellet Cisterciensis ordinis, respondit ille, nulla se id facturum ratione, nisi primo sacras litteras didicisset. . . . Remittitur ad prima rursum elementa adolescens iam pene vir adultus, & in breuissimo spatio temporis plus quam credi possit profecisse visus est; ita vt etiam eos qui ab infantia scholas frequentauerant in breui spiritu sapientiae & intellectus transcenderet ampliori. Nec mirum. Nulla quippe in discendo mora est, vbi in docendo Spiritus sanctus magister est. . . . At vbi competenter instructus est, secundum consilium matris transtulit se ad Ecclesiam Triumfontium Cisterciensis ordinis, & in tantum profecit quod post non multum temporis sacerdotij gradum feliciter adeptus est." *AASS,* Jan., I, 875.

14. The vita notes, "Again, just as Mary, in childbirth, had brought the incarnate Word forth into the world for the salvation of all, so, too, with a reversal of roles and for the nourishment simply of her own soul, Ida was consigning that same Word to an inner library of many shelved [*sic*], to be brought forth and fed upon as in a holy reading." *Ida of Louvain: Mediaeval Cistercian Nun,* trans. Martinus Cawley (Lafayette, OR: Guadalupe Translations, 1990), 18. See also *Ida the Eager of Louvain: Mediaeval Cistercian Nun,* trans. Martinus Cawley (Lafayette, OR: Guadalupe Translations, 2000), 22. "Maria denique Verbum divinitus incarnatum, ad salutem omnium, in mundo pariendo produxit: & ad salutarem animae suae pastum, hoc ipsum Ida Venerabilis vice versa, per Lectionis esum, in alvi sui receptacula delegavit." *AASS,* Apr., II, 164. For commentary on the difficult Latin phrasing, see Cawley, *Ida the Eager of Louvain,* 18.

15. For the definition of medieval literacy as the ability to read and write in Latin, see, for example, Anthony Goodman, *Margery Kempe and Her World* (London: Longman, 2002), 7, and Jocelyn Wogan-Browne, Nicholas Watson, Andrew Taylor, and Ruth Evans, eds., *The Idea of the Vernacular: An Anthology of Middle English Literary Theory, 1280–1520* (University Park: Pennsylvania State University Press, 1999), which characterizes the distinction between *illiteratus* and *litteratus* as "shifting definitions along the fault line dividing Latin from vernacular" (xv).

16. Brian Stock, *The Implications of Literacy: Written Language and Models of Interpretation in the Eleventh and Twelfth Centuries* (Princeton: Princeton University Press, 1983), 6; see also

lar language was not necessarily thought of as "literacy." The terms *illiteratus/
a* and *non literatus/a* are similarly difficult to define and equally unstable. On
the most basic level, *illiteratus* referred to a person who could not read and
understand Latin texts. The term could indicate a complete lack of knowledge
of Latin letters; however, *illiteratus* could also indicate someone who had not
been tutored formally, but who nevertheless could understand or even read
something in Latin. For example, the *Life* of Blessed Veronica of Binasco (d.
1497) reports that she was illiterate, except for knowing the Hours of the
Virgin.[17] For the author of her vita, Veronica's grasp of the Latin Hours did
not negate claims of her illiteracy; perhaps Veronica, like many women, had
learned the text informally, as she heard it being read or chanted repeatedly.

In other cases, textual evidence seems to contradict claims of complete
illiteracy. For example, Anne Clark points out that the twelfth-century German visionary St. Elisabeth of Schönau was claimed by her brother and hagiographer to be completely illiterate (a point he elaborates on at some length),
and therefore, it was entirely miraculous when she uttered "appropriate"
Latin phrases when she came out of a spiritual trance; at another point in her
visionary text, however, Elisabeth is described as reading from a Latin prayer
book.[18] Asserting complete illiteracy, therefore, is very obviously a trope in
women's lives and is none the more evident than in the life of the visionary
St. Umiltà of Faenza (d. 1310), a married woman who became a Benedictine
nun, anchoress, and then abbess of the Vallombrosan Order. Although her
vita reports that she had been given a female tutor to teach her to read Latin
and that she did learn, Umiltà's visionary text (which she dictated to female

---

Herbert Grundmann, "Litteratus-illiteratus. Der Wandel einer Bildungsnorm vom Altertum zum
Mittelalter," *Archiv für Kulturgeschichte* 40 (1958): 1–65.

17. "Repetendum hoc loco est Veronicam religionis habitum subeuntem litteras ignorauisse,
horis supremae Virginis exceptis, quas lectitare consueuerat." *AASS*, Jan., I, 899.

18. "But then, after a long trance, when her spirit had been gradually restored, she would
suddenly utter in Latin certain very divine words that she had never learned from anyone else
and that she could not have made up herself since she was unlearned and had little or no skill in
speaking Latin. Also, she frequently announced—without any premeditation—testimonies from
canonical scripture and other expressions from the divine office that were appropriate to what
she had seen in spirit." *Elisabeth of Schönau: The Complete Works*, ed. and trans. Anne L. Clark
(New York: Paulist Press, 2000), 41. That Elisabeth possessed some proficiency in Latin is suggested by the following: "When I had hardly finished reading one psalm, I threw far from me
the psalter which had always been a pleasure for me. Again, thinking it over and wondering to
myself at what had happened to me, I picked it up again [and] read." Anne L. Clark, *Elisabeth of
Schönau: A Twelfth-Century Visionary* (Philadelphia: University of Pennsylvania Press, 1992), 30.
See also Elisabeth Gössman, "Das Menschenbild der Hildegard von Bingen und Elisabeth von
Schönau vor dem Hintergrund der frühscholastischen Anthropologie," 24–47, in *Frauenmystik
im Mittelalter*, ed. Peter Dinzelbacher and Dieter R. Bauer (Ostfildern: Schwabenverlag, 1985).

scribes) claims that she was completely illiterate and had never learned any Latin whatsoever.[19] What these examples demonstrate is that claims of illiteracy are so important that they are asserted in contradiction to physical evidence that suggests otherwise; they also suggest that the term *illiterata* is so slippery that a medieval audience might not have perceived a contradiction.

Assertions of illiteracy were of such importance in the vitae of holy women that the female subjects, their communities, and hagiographers often downplayed the women's literate abilities. The Benedictine St. Hildegard of Bingen (d. 1179) is perhaps the earliest example of what Barbara Newman has identified as the trope of the "illiterate and therefore divinely inspired."[20] Hildegard claims to have never learned Latin formally (although she did learn the Psalter from the anchores Jutta of Sponheim)[21] but rather to have been infused with the knowledge of Scripture by the Holy Spirit. Her vita, composed by Gottfried of St. Disibod and Dieter of Echternach between 1177 and 1181, includes a passage from Hildegard's first book, *Scivias*, to support this claim of her initial ignorance of Latin grammar, as well as her continued formal illiteracy after she experienced the gift: "When I was forty-two years and seven months old, a blazing fiery light came from the open heaven and poured over my whole head and heart and breast like a flame. . . . Immediately I knew how to explain the books of the Psalter, gospel and other catholic volumes of the Old and New Testament. However, I did not know how to interpret the words of their text, nor the division of syllables, nor the knowledge of cases and tenses."[22] Here Hildegard claims that she understands the deeper meaning of

19. For a discussion of the contradictory evidence of literacy in Umiltà's vita and sermons, see Catherine M. Mooney, "Authority and Inspiration in the *Vitae* and Sermons of Humility of Faenza," *Medieval Monastic Preaching*, ed. Carolyn Muessig, Studies in Intellectual History 90 (Leiden: Brill, 1998), 123–43.

20. See Barbara Newman, *Sister of Wisdom: St. Hildegard's Theology of the Feminine* (Berkeley and Los Angeles: University of California Press, 1987), 1–41, esp. pp. 34–41. "Yet although the seer was self-conscious about her 'unpolished' style, she seems to have cherished it as a mark that her inspiration must be divine because she herself scarcely knew how to write" (23).

21. Ibid., 5. In her letter to Guibert of Gembloux, Hildegard writes, "But what I do not see, I do not know, for I am not educated, but I have simply been taught how to read. And what I write is what I see and hear in the vision. I compose no other words than those I hear, and I set them forth in unpolished Latin just as I hear them in the vision, for I am not taught in this vision to write as philosophers do." Newman, *Sister of Wisdom*, 7.

22. Gottfried of Disibodenberg and Theodoric of Echternach, *The Life of the Saintly Hildegard*, trans. and ed. Hugh Feiss (Toronto: Peregrina Publishing, 1996; reprinted 1999), 26–27. "Cum quadraginta duorum annorum, septemque mensium essem, maximae coruscationis igneum lumen aperto coelo veniens, totum cerebrum meum transfudit, & totum cor, totumque pectus meum, velut flamma, non tamen ardens, sed calens, ita inflammavit . . . Et repente intellectum expositionis librorum, videlicet Psalterii, Euangelii, & aliorum Catholicorum, tam veteris quam novi Testamenti voluminum sapiebam, non autem interpretationem verborum textus

the scriptural texts but not the Latin words and grammar in and of themselves.[23] Of course, whereas we know that the historical Hildegard was an accomplished, hermeneutically literate reader, writer, listener, and speaker of Latin, Hildegard in the vita is presented initially as an unskilled Latin grammarian, unable to complete even the simplest grammatical exercise. If she did eventually gain a proficiency in Latin, this is not made clear in the vita, for such a linguistic command would have detracted from the miraculous aspects of her visions.[24] Her visions in Latin, therefore, are imagined to come *through* her and not to be affected in any way *by* her, a particularly important claim for all female visionaries who articulate visions fully or partly in Latin.

Similarly, the fourteenth-century *Life* of St. Clare of Montefalco (d. 1308) goes to great lengths to demonstrate that the holy woman's miraculous Latin learning could not have been possible through traditional means. Formally illiterate yet gifted with understanding "way beyond the scope of the human intellect," Clare became a teacher of the Divine Office for her fellow nuns:

> Beginning with herself, she said it [the Divine Office] devoutly, and she taught the other nuns to read and recite it. It is said that she possessed this knowledge as infused by God rather than having acquired it through a practice in reading, because even though it is recorded that as a child she had learned seven psalms and a morning lesson, but nothing more, that certainly did not enable her to know the office by her natural powers; moreover, even if she had known it, so long a time had passed that she must have forgotten it, espe-

---

eorum, nec divisionem syllabarum, nec cognitionem casuum aut temporum habebam." *AASS*, Sept., V, 680.

23. Hildgard's infused knowledge of texts goes well beyond Scripture. The second book of her biography incorporates Hildegard's own words from *Scivias* into the text: "In the same vision I understood the writings of the prophets, evangelists, and other saints and of certain philosophers without the benefit of any human teaching. I explained some of them although I had scarcely any knowledge of letters. An uneducated woman had taught me." Gottfried and Theodoric, *Life of the Saintly Hildegard*, 46. "In eadem visione scripta Prophetarum, Euangeliorum, & aliorum sanctorum quorumdam philosophorum, sine ulla humana doctrina intellexi, ac quaedam ex ille exposui, cum vix notitiam literarum haberem, sicut indocta mulier me docuerat." *AASS*, Sept., V, 684.

24. Distinguishing between accomplished and unaccomplished readers and listeners is, according to David Rollo, distinguishing between the "hermeneutically proficient" and the "grammatically competent" (xv) in *Glamorous Sorcery: Magic and Literacy in the High Middle Ages*, Medieval Cultures 25 (Minneapolis: University of Minnesota Press, 2000). Barbara Newman has argued that by asserting her own ignorance of formal grammar, Hildegard "stakes her claim to prophetic authority" (21) in "Hildegard and Her Hagiographers: The Remaking of Female Sainthood," in *Gendered Voices*, ed. Catherine M. Mooney, 16–34 and 195–202.

cially since up to this point there had never been office books in the monastery. That Clare's knowledge was inspired by God could easily be appreciated by various experts, since on other occasions, despite not having read books or learned the disciplines, she gave exhaustive answers to readers and to theologian-preachers regarding doubtful points and profound questions. From this time forward, she recited the office in the proper order, rarely looking at the book, even when she had not learned it, and she taught the nuns.[25]

Clare's hagiographer, Berengario, anxiously emphasizes that the holy woman does not possess traditional literacy. He points out her very limited education (she was only tutored in the seven psalms and a morning lesson), which was not enough for her to know the office; moreover, he argues that it had been so long ago that she could not possibly remember any of it, and last, there were no books in the monastery from which she could have refreshed her memory. Even the detail of Clare not looking at the book while she spoke is meant to suggest the divine origin of her knowedge, although perhaps it only indicates that she had memorized the text aurally.

The insistence on illiteracy in these accounts often leads hagiographers to emphasize how some women initially wanted to learn Latin but were unable, with the result that they had to ask God for a gift, or that the women themselves rejected their tutors in favor of relying on God, thereby rejecting traditional methods of literacy and privileging sapientia. Indeed, the claim of illiteracy is so important that several lives describe gifts of miraculous Latinity being granted after the holy women are proven entirely unable to learn to read in more traditional ways. The cowherd Vernonica of Binasco, for exam-

25. Berengario di Donadio, *Life of Saint Clare of Montefalco*, ed. John E. Rotelle, trans. Matthew J. O'Connell, Augustinian Series 9 (Villanova, PA: Augustinian Press, 1999), 71–72. "Et a se ipsa incipiens officium deuote dicebat, alias dominas legere et officium dicere edocebat. Quam scientiam dicitur habuisse a Deo infusam potius quam per exercitium lectionis, quia quamuis tempore pueritie vij. psalmos et unam lectionem matutini et non plus didicisse dicatur, non ob hoc tamen ex humano ingenio officium scire potuit, et si sciuisset propter diuturnitatem temporis obliuioni tradere debuisset. Maxime quoniam libri in quibus officium legeret usque ad hoc tempus in ipso monasterio non fuerunt. Et inspirata diuinitus Clare scientia a quocumque perito facile poterat deprehendi quoniam cum Clara alias nec libros legisset nec scientias didicisset lectoribus et predicatoribus in theologia de quibuscunque dubijs et profundis questionibus sufficientissime respondebat et diuinum officium raro librum respiciens a dicto tempore in antea quamuis non didicerat, ordinate dicebat et dominas edocebat" (213–14) in Berengario di San Africano, "Vita di S. Chiara da' Montefalco," ed. M. Faloci Pulignani, 193–266, in *Archivo Storico per le Marche e per l'Umbria*, ed. M. Faloci Pulignani, G. Mazzatinti, and M. Santoni, vol. 2, no. 6 (Foligno: Presso la Direzione, 1885).

ple, tried to teach herself to read in the evenings after working all day in the fields, but she was unable to learn the alphabet. As we saw with the example of Catherine of Siena, the holy woman prayed for the gift when she was unable to learn even her letters after weeks of studying under a female teacher.[26] Because their mundane efforts at acquiring literacy fail, these women are often described as being taught by holy figures, including Christ, Mary, and the saints. For others, miraculous literacy comes when women reject traditional tutelage and turn themselves over to God. Umiltà of Faenza's successor as abbess, the Blessed Margaret of Faenza (d. 1330), rejected the female tutor assigned to her, insisting that God would teach her whatever she needed to know.[27] What is lauded, therefore, in these accounts is the holy women's complete ignorance of Latin, the lack of which calls into relief the miraculous aspects of the gift they are given.

Medieval women's Latinate gifts are used for a variety of devotional and spiritual performances. Women read and translate for themselves; they participate in liturgical activities with fellow religious and even teach those texts to other nuns. In this way, the gift imagines women as authoritative Latin translators of particular texts, sanctioned by God and the Holy Spirit. But the resulting Latin literacy is not at all clear in many cases. It is not a clerical kind of literacy that will allow the recipients to read a wide range of Latinate texts and function in a range of Latinate situations; rather, it gives the women the ability to understand particular scriptural texts and the Latin of those texts alone, like the Psalter or Hours of the Virgin, which is all the women are imagined as wanting and needing to know. Thus, the gift of miraculous literacy seems to afford these women enhanced versions of the same kind of literate access and practice that actual religious women were either observed to

---

26. "Narrabat etenim mihi de semetipsa, quod cum pro divinis laudibus & Horis canonicis depromendis, decrevisset addiscere litteras; scripto sibi alphabeto, per quamdam suam sociam docebatur: sed cum per plures hebdomadas laborasset, & nullatenus illud posset addiscere; cogitavit gratiam adire coelestem, pro perditione temporis evitanda." *AASS*, Apr., III, 881.

27. "When the most holy Umiltà, the aforesaid abbess, gave a female teacher to Blessed Margaret, so that she might teach Margaret letters, the unrivaled nun [Umiltà] said to her: 'Learn, continue to learn to read, for you will become abbess.' Very shortly after, Margaret let the teacher go, for she firmly believed that the all-powerful God would open his meaning fully in her mind so that she could understand Scripture" (translation mine). "Cum sanctissima Humilitas, abbatissa praefata, B. Margaritae magistram dederit, ut eam litteras doceret, monachaque unica ei diceret: Disce, addisce legere; abbatissa enim fies: mox magistram reliquit, credens firmiter, quod omnipotens Deus aperiret sensum ipsius, ad intelligendum Scripturam penitus hinc ad mentem: cui cum ego Joannes praedictus legerem semel ei, petens eam, si vellet, me vulgariter legere: respondit: Minime, quia bene intelligo." *AASS*, Aug., V, 851. The vitae often make it clear that the holy woman is assigned a female teacher of Latin (as in the examples of Umiltà of Faenza, Margaret of Faenza, and Catherine of Siena).

have or perhaps in some circumstances even expected to have. For women who give voice to all or part of their visions in Latin, their vitae emphasize the subjects' continued ignorance of the language to assert that they do not correct or amend the Latin text in any way, often in the face of concrete evidence of their literate abilities.

Part 2: Miraculously Mundane Gifts of Latinity

As I have argued, the emphasis on miraculous literacy, as "other" than traditonally acquired literacy, leads hagiographers to focus on the formal illiteracy of their female subjects. The actual Latin linguistic ability generated by a gift of infused knowledge is difficult to determine. Indeed, often these miraculous gifts of sapientia look suprisingly mundane, for they offer women access to Latin scriptural and liturgical texts that they might have reasonably been expected to acquire on their own. Women's gifts of Latinity therefore seem limited in scope and duration when compared with men's more frequent gifts of mastery.

I would like to suggest two reasons for this mundane quality of medieval women's xenoglossia. First, women's gifts of Latinity appear quite mundane because the accounts may be interpreting and presenting instances of nontraditional literacy as miraculous. Because the medieval definition of literacy often emphasizes formal knowledge, claims of illiteracy in the women's vitae overlook or ignore, either purposefully or unconsciously, nontraditional ways of acquiring Latin, which include rote repetition or rehearsal ("repeating the names of items or objects to be memorized"), listening or reading with selective attention for certain key words or phrases (as Ida of Nivelles did with holy names of Scripture), inferencing (guessing meanings and completing "missing parts"), memorizing others' translations, and so on.[28] Second, I argue that, in many accounts, women's gifts of Latin also appear quite mundane because hagiographers do not want to imagine women as masters of Latinity because the women would challenge their own clerical authority;

---

28. Rosamund Mitchell and Florence Myles, "Cognitive Approaches to Second Language Learning," in *Second Language Learning Theories*, ed. Rosamund Mitchell and Florence Myles (London: Arnold, 1998), 72–99, at p. 91. Second-language acquisition theory is particularly helpful in identifying how adults learn second languages in formal education settings as well as informally. See also J. Michael O'Malley and Anna Uhl Chamot, *Learning Strategies in Second Language Acquisition* (Cambridge: Cambridge University Press, 1990).

women are therefore imagined as limiting their performance so as not to infringe on clerical privilege.

In arguing this, I believe many of these medieval miracles accounts to reflect both the lived experiences of historical figures, as well as the imagination and desire of hagiographers and communities, mediated through several layers of interpretation (holy person, community, hagiographers, audiences) for a large number of related purposes, including, but not limited to, asserting the blessedness of the person, strengthening the faith in general, and creating, preserving, or commemorating community identity. Those witnessing, narrating, and writing down the miracles have been preconditioned to read and to shape the miraculous in a certain manner that fits preconceived notions of holiness, as well as to craft the presentation of experiences in the most rhetorically powerful and persuasive form possible.

In a number of instances, these accounts seem to be interpreting nontraditional literacy as miraculous. Many of these experiences of medieval holy women seem quite mundane and could easily have a nonmiraculous explanation. Examples of women miraculously learning their Psalter, for example, might suggest that they simply learned these scriptural texts either aurally, through rote recitation, or informal tutoring and translation. Veronica of Binasco, for example, is said to have been able to read and to understand her Psalter miraculously after many years in a convent; certainly, she might have memorized the text on her own after all that time.[29] Margaret of Faenza was miraculously able to translate a scriptural passage for herself after she rejected her tutor and depended on God to supply her with sapientia. Her hagiographer relates, "When I, John, once was reading to her and asked her if she wished me to read to her in the vernacular, she responded, 'No, since I understand well.'"[30] The passage seems to suggest that John was in the habit of reading to Margaret and translating for her, and it should not be surprising that she learned to translate this particular passage for herself.

An account in the *Life* of Ida of Louvain offers an example of a miracle of Latinity that could easily have a mundane explanation. Her vita reports that the illiterate Ida was gifted with deep scriptural understanding, as well as with the ability on several occasions to understand and translate the Latin Gospel, both for her fellow Cistercian nuns and for her confessor:

29. "Huius ancillae suae humilitatem respiciens summus Opifex, totum psalterium illam edocuit, tantoque munere diuinarum litterarum sapientiam infudit, vt psalmos quosque Dauid & legeret & intelligeret." *AASS*, Jan. I, 899.

30. For the Latin, see footnote 27.

We would also like to mention that Ida had never in her life learned Latin or had any schooling, not even enough to enable her to decipher the letters of a Latin text and pronounce the sounds, and yet many a time when she heard things chanted or read aloud by the nuns, she received inspiration from the Holy Spirit and understood their meaning. This was especially the case in Lent, when Gospel texts were recited; even though they were read to her in a language she did not know, she would readily recite them back, in the vernacular, with the correct sequence and context, to anyone who wished to hear and as often as she deemed it opportune.[31]

At another time, when Ida heard the Antiphon, "I have the power to lay down my life," sung by the choir, she heard an angelic choir repeating the same in a higher and "more elegant mode." Ida understood fully what was sung, with the grace of the Holy Spirit, and in a discerning (or discreet) manner recited it in her own tongue afterward, to her confessor.[32] The miracle therefore offers Ida the opportunity to join in liturgical activities with other nuns and to translate both for herself, her fellow nuns, and her spiritual advisor, to whom she submitted her translation for approval.

This anecdote is notable because of the wholly unmiraculous quality of the event. According to the hagiographer, Ida is illiterate, having been a beguine earlier in life and entering the convent at a more advanced age. Although it is presented as a miracle, the account seems to describe little more than Ida's ability to paraphrase accurately (in "correct sequence and context") a liturgical text she already knew well. Similarly, fourteenth-century *Schwesternbucher,* or *Sisterbooks* of Dominican German nuns, record that on occasion certain sisters received a sudden, divinely infused understanding of the Latin liturgi-

31. *Ida of Louvain: Medieval Cistercian Nun,* Cawley, 83. "Sed & hoc mirabile credimus in Dei Virgine reputandum, & inter cetera divinitus sibi collata mirabilia recitandum; quod cum in omni vita sua litteras aut elementa scholaria minime didicisset, neque haec absque quolibet eorum intellectu legere, proferre vel exprimere potuisset; saepissime tamen ea quae cantabantur aut legebantur a monialibus, inspirante gratia Spiritus sancti, intellexit; in Quadragesimina praecipue, cum sancta recitarentur Evangelia; quae licet inexperto sibi legerentur eloquio, vulgari tamen lingua, quoties opportunum id esse credidit, eorum seriem, ordinem, & tenorem in auribus haec audire volentium apertissime retractavit." *AASS,* Apr., II, 188.

32. *Ida of Louvain: Mediaeval Cistercian Nun,* Cawley, 83. "Unde Quadragesimali quodam tempore, cum illa in choro psallentium altisona voce decantatam auscultasset, Antiphonam Potestatem habeo ponendi animam meam; a choris Angelicis hanc eamdem audire promeruit, altiori multum & elegantiori modo repetitam; quam eo quoque tempore plenissime, revelante sibi gratia sancti Spiritus, intellexit; & illi suo Confessori, sub vulgaris linguae postmodum idiomate, discretissime recitavit." *AASS,* Apr., II, 188.

cal texts they were singing.[33] Miracles such as these could certainly reflect lived experiences of women's nontraditional literacy, as well as the intense desire of women to understand more deeply the texts they were reciting.

A more mundane explanation for what is described as miraculous Latinity may shed light on the complicated situation found in the *Life* of St. Umiltà of Faenza. The vita reports that, unlike other nuns who had grown up in the convent, Umiltà was illiterate when she decided to enter the Benedictine house.[34] Miraculously, one day she began to read and speak in Latin for the benefit of her fellow nuns, who wished her to read for their "relaxation" or perhaps to make fun of the unlearned woman:

> One particular day, when she was still illiterate, some sisters called on her and bade her read at the second meal, as is the custom among nuns. I think they commanded her to do this for their own relaxation [or, as a joke].[35] She bowed her head and took up the book so that she might obey. Having picked it up, she carried it to the appropriate place, opened it and began at this verse: "Despise not the works of God, since they are all true and just." What is more, she spoke such lofty words, keeping her eyes always raised to heaven, that she excited the entire convent, who came running to see this spectacle, marvelling in wonderment. And when the sign was given for her to con-

33. Gertrud Jaron Lewis, *By Women, for Women, About Women: The Sister-Books of Fourteenth-Century Germany*, Studies and Texts 125 (Toronto: Pontifical Institute of Mediaeval Studies, 1996). Lewis offers several fascinating examples of women divinely gifted with scriptural understanding and Latinate ability. For example, novice Kathrin Brúmsin admitted to St. John in a dream vision that she could not read Latin; St. John led her to a book "and suddenly she was able to read twenty-four verses of a sequence." Upon waking, Kathrin could recite the verses from memory (278). For nuns' rote learning of Latin texts, see Eileen Edna Power, *Medieval English Nunneries, c. 1275–1535* (Cambridge: Cambridge University Press, 1922), 244–45, cited in Paul Lee, *Nunneries, Learning, and Spirituality in Late Medieval English Society: The Dominican Priory of Dartford* (Woodbridge, UK: York Medieval Press, 2000), 136–38.

34. According to Mooney, Umiltà's Latin vita was composed sometime between the years 1311 and 1322; a second vita, in Italian, was written in 1345. "Authority and Inspiration," 124–25.

35. It is quite possible that the nuns wished to amuse themselves at the expense of an uneducated woman who entered the convent later in life. Mooney suggests that they ask her to read in order to perhaps have "a bit of fun" ("Authority and Inspiration," 130); "solatiose" could also be translated as "as a joke" or "for their own entertainment." If the latter is true, then the gift is given as a kind of reprimand to the uncharitable nuns and as a way to protect Umiltà from their ridicule. In addition to causing her to be recognized as a holy figure, the gift allows her to participate fully at that moment in the practice of the religious community and to silence their cruelty. In this way, it is similar to the account of vernacular xenoglossia in the vita of St. Lutgard, who was granted a gift of French that certainly silenced the laughter of the nuns who wondered what she had to say to the despairing French-speaking woman who visited at the convent at Aywières.

clude her reading, by saying "you, however," as was appropriate, taught by the Holy Spirit, she concluded in the best possible way. Inside that volume no one was ever able to find the passages that she had read, neither before nor after. From that time on, the convent took care to teach her letters—which she did learn—by getting a woman teacher for her.[36]

As Catherine M. Mooney has argued in her valuable essay, "Authority and Inspiration in the *Vitae* and Sermons of Humility of Faenza," Umiltà's actual gift is quite confusing, as is the language it occurs in. It is not really a gift of reading, since her eyes are lifted off the page, and no one could find the passage afterward; however, the biographer refers to the passage as one that was "read," and the nuns continue to look in the book, therefore suggesting that it was thought to be a gift of reading.[37] This event, therefore, can be understood as either a gift of miraculous Latinity (Umiltà as divinely inspired and reading the Latin text or even sermonizing in Latin) or a gift of divinely infused understanding of the Latin passage that she was supposed to read but could not. But this could also represent a moment in which the illiterate holy woman, unable or barely able to read the actual text in front of her, under much stress began sermonizing in Italian, drawing from her own prior understanding and knowledge of the subject matter. The convent responded to her "miraculous" sermonizing by ensuring that she learn to read in a traditional manner. Assigning her a female tutor can be seen as the convent's way of inviting her into the monastic textual community, so that she could perform with them in all the necessary liturgical duties and readings. Or perhaps she was given a tutor because of the potential the nuns saw in Umiltà as a future

36. "Life of St. Umiltà, Abbess of the Vallombrosan Order in Florence," 121–50, in *Consolation of the Blessed*, ed. and trans. Elizabeth Petroff (New York: Alta Gaia Society, 1979), 124. "Die quadam Sorores, cum esset illiterata, eam vocarunt, & ut legeret secundae mensae, ut mos est Monialium, solatiose ut aestimo injunxerunt. Illa vero caput flexit, & ut obediret librum sumpsit: quem ad locum aptum accedens aperuit, ea voce incipiens, Nolite despicere opera Dei, quia omnia vera & justa sunt: super quo tam ardua, in coelum erectis semper luminibus, dixit, quod totum Conventum currentem ad spectaculum ac admirationem mirabilem excitavit: & dum sibi signum terminationis factum fuit, dicendo, Tu autem, uti decuit, Spiritu sancto edocta optime terminavit. Quae autem legit, nullus umquam in praefacto codice prius vel post penitus adinvenit; & ex tunc Conventus, data sibi doctrice, ipsam litteras, quas & didicit, discere procuravit." *AASS*, May, V, 206. As Mooney points out, the Italian vita states that she "non fusse in leggere molto ammaestrata" [She had little education in reading"], and does not state that a woman had been assigned to teach her. Mooney, "Authority and Inspiration," 131.

37. Mooney states, "Cleary, the fact of her relative or total lack of Latin literacy, miraculously overcome in the above incident, is central to the passage's meaning." Mooney, "Authority and Inspiration," 131.

abbess, who would need to be formally educated. When Umiltà later desired to give herself over entirely to prayer and to leave this particular convent, she was miraculously whisked over the convent's high walls; at the top of the wall, she left behind her Psalter, the text from which she was no doubt learning to read.[38] In addition to serving as proof of the miracle, the forgotten book suggests that she had little need for the actual physical Psalter because of her divinely infused understanding. It is in effect her own rejection of traditional literacy, for in her later sermons she claimed that she never studied letters.

A description of Umiltà's miraculous linguistic ability from her vita has been used to argue that medieval women could on occasion be imagined as commanding a clerical mastery of Latinity, but the passage turns out to be a much later addition to the *Life*: "It was a thing marvelous in all respects to see Blessed Umiltà who had never learned letters, not only reading at table [as it is said in her vita], but even discoursing and speaking in the Latin language, as if she had studied much in it, dictating very beautiful sermons and lovely tractates on spiritual things, in which there appeared profound doctrine, expressed in the aptest words, even when speaking of the more sublime mysteries of sacred theology."[39] In this passage, Umiltà appears to possess and practice a full, miraculous control of both written and oral Latin; she therefore appears to be a late medieval female version of a learned cleric. The problem, however, is that this passage was added by a Vallombrosan monk who edited the vita in the seventeenth century. The holy woman's access to Latinity, as described in the medieval version of the vita, is much less clear and much more limited. This addition expands the topos and exaggerates her level of mastery.

In many medieval accounts, it is not at all clear who is overlooking or ignoring the possibility of women's nontraditional literacy. Is it the saintly woman herself who downplays her learning to claim divine inspiration? Is it the immediate community surrounding the woman that claims the miracle on her behalf, or the wider communities that narrate and retell versions of the vita and miracles as the fame of the woman grows? Or is it the hagiogra-

---

38. *Life of St. Umiltà*, 125. In the examples of Umiltà of Faenza, Margaret of Faenza, and Clare of Montefalco, each require some Latinate skills to be made abbess. Lutgard is the extreme, for she protects herself from being abbess by denying herself the ability to learn any French.

39. Translation in Petroff, ed., *Consolation of the Blessed*, 9, and cited in Muessig, "Prophecy and Song," 148, as an example of a medieval woman preaching. "Fuit res omnino admirabilis, videre B. Humilitatem, quae numquam litteras didicerat, non solum legentem super mensa, uti dicitur in Vita; sed etiam discurrentem loquentemque Latina lingua, quasi multum in ea studii posuisset; dictando sermones & tractatus pulcherrimos de rebus spiritualibus, in quibus apparet profunda doctrina, aptissimis expressa verbis, etiam circa sublimiora sacrae Theologiae mysteria, cum descriptione dilucida gloriae immensae Beatorum." *AASS*, May, V, 213.

pher, the male cleric who is particularly intrigued with a miracle that offers in an instant what he had to acquire through hard study, and therefore he either overlooks, ignores, or simply does not see the women's nontraditional literacy?

To claim a miracle of Latinity serves several purposes. First, it gives authority to the women as interpreters and translators. Umiltà's miraculous sermonizing in the refrectory gained her much admiration and respect, and even resulted in the nuns assigning her a female tutor. Ida's joyous outbursts allowed her to translate for whomever would listen and gained the admiration of her spiritual counselor and hagiographer. Clare became a teacher of nuns and an authority that theologian-preachers could appeal to, question, and test. Women's nontraditional literacy, therefore, is given much authority, as it is easily attributable to miraculous means.

In addition to representing lived experiences, the limitations of the women's Latin xenoglossia in the accounts (that women are not imagined as possessing a full proficiency in or mastery of the language) may indicate a desire on hagiographers' part to represent women's Latinity as nonchallenging and to demonstrate these women as behaving properly and not overstepping clerical bounds. In some cases, women are actually presented as limiting their own translation practice and performance of miraculous Latinity so as not to infringe on clerical power.

Certainly, it is to be expected that saintly women are described as behaving properly, under clerical supervision. But the emphasis on how and for whom the gift of miraculous literacy is practiced is quite striking in many of these accounts and indicates a deep investment in showing these women as limiting their own performance of Latinity. For example, Ida of Louvain, who translated the gospel texts openly for any of her fellow religious who would listen, was careful to translate her Antiphon for her confessor's testing and approval. Catherine of Siena was given a gift so that she could read and translate the Divine Office, Psalms, and Anthems for her own personal devotional practice. Clare of Montefalco was granted her gift so that she could teach the nuns in her convent; she would answer questions put to her by male authorities, but only humbly and reluctantly. In each of these instances women are shown as using their gift discreetly, under male eyes that are both admiring and watchful.

Two holy women from the Southern Netherlandish region, the lay (or beguine-like) Christina Mirabilis (Christina the Astonishing) and the Benedictine turned Cistercian St. Lutgard of Aywières, both refuse to use their gifts of Latin scriptural understanding to translate for others because they are described as humbly believing that their interpretation would infringe on clerical roles. The pious women are imagined to limit their own practice and performance of miraculous Latinity; paradoxically, therefore, their linguistic agency consists of their ability to exercise control over their own utterances and to limit their own translations.

As we saw in Chapter 1, the vitae of Southern Netherlandish holy women, edited or composed by the Dominican hagiographer Thomas of Cantimpré, are highly invested in describing scenes of vernacular xenoglossia. His *Life* of Lutgard of Aywières features the holy woman's disglossic and xenoglossic experiences of French, and Thomas mentions that he has seen another woman, whom he refuses to name, speak in tongues from morning to night on the Day of Pentecost.[40] Thomas's attention to vernacular and Latinate xenoglossia could either reflect his own personal interest or his awareness as a Dominican of the importance of xenoglossia in the medieval tradition; or his attention may in some way reflect lived experiences with language because of the particularly complex linguistic pressures in this geographical region, as women were frequently required to travel and relocate across the French and Flemish or Dutch linguistic borders. The women not only had to negotiate vernacular pressures and obstacles, but they also experienced the pressure of differing expectations of Latinate ability, as they moved between orders and religious houses.

Thomas of Cantimpré's vitae feature two prominent accounts of miraculous Latinity. The *Life* of Christina the Astonishing describes how the young woman received gifts of miraculous Latinity on several occasions and practiced her gifts in three different ways. First, she performed privately; second, she performed by leading nuns in song; and third, she refused a more public role as teacher and scriptural authority because she did not want to infringe on the jurisdiction of clerics. Because her fellow townspeople believed Christina was crazed, they tied her to trees and attempted to restrain her exuberant behavior.[41] In addition to calling attention to her blessedness, therefore, Thomas forefronts Christina's self-limiting of her performance of her gift and her recognition of her need for clerical supervision to emphasize the divine

---

40. Thomas of Cantimpré, *The Life of Lutgard of Aywières*, trans. Margot H. King and Barbara Newman, 211–96, in *Thomas of Cantimpré, The Collected Saints' Lives; Abbot John of Cantimpré, Christina the Astonishing, Margaret of Ypres, and Lutgard of Aywières*, ed. Barbara Newman, trans. Margot H. King and Barbara Newman, Medieval Women: Texts and Contexts 19 (Turnhout: Brepols, 2008).

41. See Barbara Newman, "Possessed by the Spirit: Devout Women, Demoniacs, and the Apostolic Life in the Thirteenth Century," *Speculum* 73 (1998): 733–70.

origins of her speech and song in the face of possible doubt regarding the origins of her ability.

Thomas emphasizes that Christina was very humble and discreet in her practice of miraculous Latinity and that she did not wish to promote herself as a linguistic authority. He writes that while Christina was staying with a woman recluse on the border of Germany, she experienced a miraculous gift of Latin song: "While she was in that place Christina went to the vigils of matins every night. Then, after everyone had left the church and the doors were locked, she would walk around the church floor and utter a song so sweet that it seemed to be angelic rather than human singing. This song was so marvellous to hear that it surpassed the music of all instruments and the voices of all mortals. . . . This song [that she sang in church] was in Latin and wondrously adorned with harmonious phrases."[42] To insist that the wondrous song was in Latin is a way of proclaiming the divine origins of her knowledge. Just how Thomas knew it was in Latin is not made clear; perhaps he learned it from the recluse or from other female religious at the church. Thomas is careful, however, to assert that Christina performed the miraculous gift quite discreetly, for she waited until everyone had left the church and the doors were locked before she began her own private concert.

Thomas mentions one more miraculous gift of Latin song in Christina's vita; this time, however, she performed her gift in front of other nuns, who joined in with her singing. Thomas describes how Christina "had become familiar" with the nuns of St. Catherine's, a Benedictine convent near Sint-Truiden. On a certain occasion, she experienced an ecstatic fit and whirled around violently, during which time there arose from the area of her breast and throat a "wonderous harmony." After this had happened, Christina called for the nuns to be brought to her so that they could praise Jesus: "Shortly thereafter the nuns of the convent came running from all sides (for they greatly rejoiced in Christina's solace) and she began to sing the *Te Deum laudamus*. All the convent joined in as she finished her song." He then em-

---

42. Thomas de Cantimpré, *The Life of Christina the Astonishing*, trans. Margot H. King and Barbara Newman, 147–48, in Thomas of Cantimpré, *The Collected Saints' Lives*, 127–57. "Igitur in eodem loco, omni nocte Christina Matutinorum frequentans vigilias, recedentibus omnibus de ecclesia, & obseratis januis, per aream pavimenti ecclesiae deambulans, canticum tantae dulcedinis emittebat, ut potius videretur cantus angelicus quam humanus. Cantus ille tam mirabilis erat auditu, ut omnium musicorum instrumenta, omnium mortalium voces excelleret; minor tamen & longe impar dulcedine illius harmoniae jubilo, qui dum mente excederet, inter guttur & pectus ejus [incomparabilis] resonabat. Cantus, inquam, iste Latinus erat, mirisque consonantium clausulis exornatus." *AASS*, July, V, 657.

phasizes that she "fled for shame and embarrassment" when she was told what had happened.[43]

Thomas presents Christina's singing of the *Te Deum* as a miraculous occurence; it is not immediately clear, however, whether the gift is that of heavenly music to accompany the words of the *Te Deum* that she already knew by rote or whether she is granted a gift of the Latin words as well as the song. Certainly, if we assume this is a reflection of lived experience, Christina could have learned the *Te Deum* and its music while staying at the convent. What Thomas emphasizes here, however, are her audience and her behavior, which assert the divine origins of her gift. Christina's immediate audience for the *Te Deum* is a group of nuns with whom she had associated herself. The gift of Latin song therefore allows the unlearned woman to participate (and even initiate and lead) the nuns' devotions. Although she is humble and embarrassed by her unconscious display, her role as spiritual authority for other women is quite accepted and lauded.

In a third and more developed episode focused on miraculous language, Thomas describes the holy woman as reluctant to use her Latinate gift, thereby limiting her audience to spiritual friends and translating infrequently, because she does not want to encroach upon the role of clerics: "Although she had been completely illiterate from birth, yet she understood all Latin and fully knew the meaning of Holy Scripture. When she was asked very obscure questions by certain spiritual friends, she would explain them very openly. But she did this most unwillingly and rarely, for she said that to expound Holy Scriptures belonged to the clergy and not the ministry of such as her."[44]

43. Thomas of Cantimpré, *Life of Christina the Astonishing*, 145–46. "Cumque diutius sic rotata fuisset, acsi vehementia deficeret, membris omnibus quiescebat; sonabatque proinde inter guttur & pectus ejus, quaedam harmonia mirabilis, quam nemo mortalium vel intelligere posset, vel aliquibus artificiis imitari. Solam flexibilitatem musicae & tonos ille ejus cantus habebat; verba vero melodiae, ut ita dicam, si tamen verba dici possunt, incomprehensibiliter concrepabant. Nulla interim de ore ejus vel naso vox vel anhelitus spiritalis exibat, sed inter solum pectus & guttur harmonia vocis angelicae resonabat. . . . Tunc post aliquanta spatia, ad se paulisper reversa, quasi ebria, & vere ebria consurgebat: clamabat vociferans: Adducite mihi conventum, ut summae benignitatis Jesum, in suis mirabilibus collaudemus. Mox undique concurrente conventu; (laetabatur enim multum Christinae solatio) inchoabat, Te Deum laudamus; & prosequentibus omnibus finiebat. Postea vero cum ad plenum reversa esset ad se, cognosceretque, recitantibus aliis, quid egisset; & conventum ad Christi laudem qualiter invitasset, prae pudore & erubescentia fugiebat, vel si vi ab aliqua detineretur, dolore nimio tabescebat; stultamque se ac fatuam indicabat." *AASS*, July, V, 656.

44. Thomas de Cantimpré, *Life of Christina the Astonishing*, 148. "Intelligebat autem ipsa omnem latinitatem, & sensum in Scriptura divina plenissime noverat, licet ipsa a nativitate litteras penitus ignoraret, & earum obscurissimas quaestiones spiritualibus quibusdam amicis, cum interrogaretur, enodatissime reserabat. Invitissime tamen [ac rarissime] facere voluit; dicens Scripturas sanctas exponere, proprium esse clericorum, nec ad se huiusmodi ministerium perti-

How are we meant to interpret the claim that Christina understood "all Latin"? Is Thomas suggesting that the holy woman comprehended all spoken and written Latin, or perhaps more likely, that she understood the Latin of Scripture and religious literature? He is unclear about the kind of literacy she possesses (i.e., pragmatic, devotional, legalistic, or other) because he is more concerned with how Christina chooses to display her knowledge.

Thomas depicts Christina as completely able, but unwilling, to perform publicly a scriptural knowledge, which, although sanctioned to her by the divine, would infringe on the temporal clergy's jurisdiction. He also empha- sizes that the only reason she did reluctantly give voice to her understanding and translate that knowledge for others was when questioned by her spiritual friends, to whom she owed some level of obedience. Although Christina is said to have resurrected three times, lived in trees for months, and engaged in other extreme ascetic practices, she refused to encroach on the authority of the church by taking it upon herself to preach or teach in any form; she was even reluctant to voice her knowledge to friends. Thomas implies that Christina's "ministry," therefore, was one of extreme pious example rather than that of sharing her clerical-like understanding.[45]

Thomas of Cantimpré explores his concerns with just how, when, and where women can display their miraculous Latinity in another vita, that of Lutgard, who, as we recall from the first chapter, prayed for an inability to learn French so that she would not have to become an abbess. Although, unlike Christina, Lutgard was in a convent and not "in the world," her vita also emphasizes a holy woman's self-limiting access to and performance of miraculous Latinity. In addition to rejecting learning the French language, Lutgard actually prayed for an *inability* to understand and translate the Psal- ter, wishing instead to remain illiterate and not overstep the bounds of clerics. To summarize briefly, Lutgard at first prayed for, and received, a divinely infused understanding of the Psalter. The holy woman then prayed to have the gift removed; Thomas writes that Lutgard gave two reasons for her deci- sion, again reflecting the difficulty in defining the gift itself: first, it was re-

---

nere." *AASS*, July, V, 657. There is an extant Middle English translation; see "The Lyf of Seinte Cristin the Mervelous," ed. C. Horstmann, "Prosalegenden: Di Legenden des MS Douce 114," *Anglia* 8 (1885): 102–96.

45. For Christina's pious example, see Robert Sweetman, "Christine of Saint-Trond's Preaching Apostolate: Thomas of Cantimpré's Hagiographical Method Revisited," *Vox Benedic- tina* 9 (1992): 66–97. Sweetman states, "Given Christina's humble status, it comes as no surprise that on those occasions when she acts in ways strongly reminiscent of the preacher, Thomas is at pains to establish the propriety of her activity" (73).

jected in terms of it being a gift of spiritual understanding only, and second, in terms of it being a gift of limited Latinity.[46]

The first explanation for Lutgard's rejection of her gift imagines the gift to be one of infused understanding alone. According to Thomas's account, Lutgard rejected the gift of Psalmic understanding because she was disappointed with her "progress" after receiving the gift. Thomas attempts to explain why she refused the infused understanding, stating, "The reverence of a veiled mystery is the mother of devotion, what is hidden is the more avidly sought, and what is concealed is looked upon with more veneration."[47] Thomas interprets Lutgard's intended "progress," therefore, not as the search for scriptural enlightenment but rather as a search for the intensification of devotion. Because "what is hidden" leads to reverence, he is suggesting that the unlearned have a particular and even superior access to devotion because of their *lack* of understanding.

The second explanation for her rejection of her Psalmic understanding imagines the gift to be one that offers a kind of Latin literacy as well. Thomas reports Lutgard as asserting, "What use is it to me to know the secrets of Scripture—I, an unlettered, uncultivated, and uneducated nun?"[48] In this case, Lutgard's rejection of scriptural knowledge is based on the fact that she describes herself as unlearned and rustic, able only to speak her mother tongue; her formal ignorance of Latin is what allows her to foster her own particular devotion. Thomas imagines Lutgard as arguing against possessing and using

---

46. For the difficulties in determining Lutgard's literacy, see "Language and the Body in Thomas of Cantimpré's *Life* of Lutgard of Aywières," *Cistercian Studies Quarterly* 30 (1995): 339–47, in which Alexandra Barratt explores the vita's many references to language, arguing that Lutgard's literacy is essentially unclear. Barratt suggests this is because of a desire on the holy woman's part to present herself (and to be presented by Thomas, her biographer) as both illiterate and spiritually infused with understanding. Concerning Lutgard's linguistic abilities Barratt offers the following assessment: "She was certainly illiterate in Latin, in the sense that she could not write it, showed no sign of having had any formal instruction, and indeed did not want to 'understand' the psalter in any sense of the word. But we may suspect that after many years in the religious life, with its constant round of liturgical duties, she had picked up some passive knowledge of Latin phrases, possibily as much oral as written" (347).

47. Thomas of Cantimpré, *Life of Lutgard of Aywières*, 226. As the *Acta Sanctorum* records, "Et illa volo, inquit, ut ad majorem devotionem Psalterium, per quod orem, intelligam. Et factum est ita. Nam ut illo in tempore probatum est, Psalterium tanto lucidius intellexit, quando radiantiori lumine fuerat illustrata. Post haec cum nondum se tantum, quantum putaverat, in hac gratia proficere comperisset, (reverentia enim velati mysterii mater est devotionis, & res celata avidius quaeritur, et venerabilius abscondsa conspicitur) dixit Domino, Quid mihi idiotae & rusticae, & Laicae Moniali Scripturae secreta cognoscere? Cui Dominus: Quid vis? Volo, inquit, [cor tuum]." *AASS*, June, III, 239. For discussion of how Lutgard is "idiotae & rusticae, & Laicae Moniali," see Barratt, "Language and the Body," 342–43, and Thomas of Cantimpré, *Life of Lutgard of Aywières*, 226n62.

48. Thomas of Cantimpré, *Life of Lutgard of Aywières*, 226.

this understanding in terms based on her inability as an uneducated nun to have mastery over, that is, to be able to translate, other languages. Because of her formal illiteracy, she did not desire to have the gift that approximates or exceeds clerical, Latinate understanding of any part of Scripture, even that which would enable her to pray more deeply, for that paradoxically would not increase her devotion. Thomas, therefore, lauds Lutgard for rejecting her heightened linguistic and spiritual ability and because she prefers to gain access to Latinity and Scripture through the clergy.[49] In sum, Thomas imagines Lutgard rejecting a deep understanding of the Latin Psalms because it offers a kind of literacy that he thinks of as unnatural and undesirable for a holy woman. No formal literacy is thought to be best for Lutgard because that way she can approach Christ through the body (his heart) rather than through his words.

Thomas's *Lives* of Christina and Lutgard demonstrate an extreme in the range of imaginings that address just what constitutes appropriate Latin and scriptural knowledge and practice for women. For both women, the kind of literacy they possess is unclear and ill defined. Does Christina understand the Latin language in general or only Latin scriptural texts? Does Lutgard understand the actual Latinate words of the Psalms or their innermost meaning, divorced from the words? It appears to be not so much the extent or nature of the gift of Latin that concerns Thomas but rather the women's practice and performance of their gifts. The women's self-limiting of their practices and translation is praised. For Christina, not voicing her extensive knowledge when others approach her is laudable; she may, however, lead a Latin song for nuns or perform her miraculous Latin music discreetly, without an immediate and obvious audience. For Lutgard, her example argues that having *no* access to Latinity and scriptural knowledge may be preferable for an unlearned woman, lay or religious.

What lies behind the insistence on modest behavior and performance of miraculous Latinity in many of the medieval accounts may also be an awareness that bold Latin performance can also indicate devilish possession. Accounts of the laity speaking Latin through the devil embody the fear of women translating boldly, not under supervision, challenging clerical power and perogative. *The Dialogue on Miracles*, a thirteenth-century collection of religious exempla by the Cistercian Caesarius of Heisterbach, includes an account of a

---

49. At other times, Lutgard is gifted with understanding the Psalter: "It often happened that while she was ruminating the Psalter, the Holy Spirit revealed to her the power and meaning of the verses." Thomas of Cantimpré, *Life of Lutgard of Aywières*, 261. "Frequenter accidit, ut dum Psalmodiam ruminaret, ei Spiritus sanctus virtutem & intelligentiam versuum revelaret." *AASS*, June, IV, 250.

possessed laywoman who spoke Latin confidently when confronted by clerics.[50] Similarly, a later medieval life of St. Amalberga, an eighth-century Carolingian holy woman, describes how an illiterate cloth-fuller suddenly became literate in Latin when he was possessed by the devil. According to the account, the fuller, who had "never learned one letter," was possessed by the devil for fifteen days and was speaking Latin so well that clerks took notice. They led him into the chapel of the blessed Amalberga, who cured his affliction; and "never afterward did he know how to speak Latin."[51]

Women's devilishly inspired Latinity is anything but mundane. The *Life* of St. Norbert, founder of the Premonstratensians, describes the battle between the holy man and the devil for the body and soul of a girl from Nivelles whom the fiend had infested. Boasting that Norbert cannot hurt him, the devil flaunts his power by causing the possessed girl to recite the Song of Songs and to expound on it in Latin and then to translate and develop the exposition into her own vernacular tongue. John Capgrave's fifteenth-century version is particularly descriptive:

> The deuel gan speke and no þing rore;
> But seide oute in Latyn al þat ilk book,
> Whech we Cantica Canticorum calle.
> Euery man gan sterten, waytyn and look,
> For þus þei seide at þat tyme alle,
> Thei herd neuyr no wondir so sodeynly falle.
> For first þe maydin in Latyn al þis book spak,

50. "She was taken into the church of S. Michael the Archangel, and was questioned on various subjects, and when the binding of Lucifer in hell was mentioned, the devil replied by her mouth: 'O fools, do you imagine that my master is bound in hell with any chains of iron? Very different is the reality. Three words of the mass have been laid in silence upon him, and with these he is bound.' Some of the brethren asked: 'What are these three words?' but she was unwilling, or rather afraid, to speak them, only saying: 'Bring me the book, and I will show you.' The missal was brought and handed to her closed; she opened it and found the canon without any difficulty and putting her finger upon the place: *Through Him, and with Him and in Him*, in which a memorial is made of the Supreme Trinity, she said: 'Behold these are the three words with which my master is bound.' Several of the monks present heard this, and knowing that the woman could not read, they were much edified, for they understood the force of the words," in Caesarius of Heisterbach, *The Dialogue on Miracles*, trans. Henry von Essen Scott and C. C. Swinton Bland, 2 vols. (London: G. Routledge & Sons, 1929), 1:333.

51. "Anno eodem, quidam fullo, purus laicus, qui numquam didicerat solam litteram, obsessus per quindenam, ita congrue latinebatur, quod vix aliqui clericorum sibi respondere valuerunt; ductus erat in capella beatae Amelbergae; qui meritis eius ab omni clade diabolica sanabatur: & numquam postea scivit latinum loqui." *AASS*, July, III, 111. There is much confusion over St. Amalberga because there are actually two saints by this name celebrated on the same feast day. See *Analecta Bollandiana* 31 (1912): 401–9, "Les Biographes de Ste. Amelberge," by A. Poncelet.

And aftir þat a exposicioun, witȝouten ony lak,
Rehersed sche þerto; and ȝet aftir this
In hir owne langage, in Teutony tunge,
Opened sche þese wordes witȝouten mys.
This grete merveyle þorw þe town is runge,
That swech a mayde of age so ȝonge
Wheche had not lerned but hire sauter only
Schuld haue swech cunnyng of grete study.

(1071–1085)[52]

Aided by the fiend, the girl participates in a literate practice that imagines
her boldly expounding on Scripture's meaning in Latin and translating or
"opening" in it the vernacular.[53] The semiliterate girl is effectively transformed into a learned scholar/preacher, who performs her translation under
the astonished eyes of clerics surrounding Norbert. Her "opening" of the
Song of Songs, however, with its blatant sexual content, seems not to be a text
particularly appropriate for a girl on the brink of womanhood; it is Scripture,
but the most sexually charged passages of Scripture, and certainly her exposi-

---

52. John Capgrave, *The Life of St. Norbert*, ed. Cyril Lawrence Smetana (Toronto: Pontifical
Institute of Mediaeval Studies, 1977), 58–59. The *Acta Sanctorum* records the episode as follows:
"Nam ibidem aderat quidam pater cujusdam puellae, quae jam per annum a daemonio fuerat
vexata, & vinculis & carcere tenebatur; qui graviter flens & suspirans, dolore filiae affectus, coepit
rogare eum, ut saltem videre eam & tangere dignaretur. Magnum opus! sed non dispar fides in
opere. Adducite eam, inquit, ad me. Adducitur puella jam duodennis, & populi plurima fre-
quentia convenit. Tunc igitur Dei Sacerdos, tempus & locum & materiam videns, ut glorificaretur
Deus, majorem fiduciam concepit. Itaque Stola & Alba indutus, exorcismum agere aggressus est;
coepitque diversa legere Euangelia super caput illius puellae. Ad quae daemon respondit: Hujus-
modi liras frequenter audivi, neque pro te, neque pro his omnibus hodie recedam de habitaculo
isto. Nam pro quibus recedam? Columnae Ecclesiae ruerunt. Cum autem Sacerdos multiplicaret
exorcismum, respondit daemon: Nil agis, quia necdum per coruscum Sanguinem Martyrum me
adjurasti. Tunc igitur, ut vere superbus est daemon, scientiam suam volens ostentare, Cantica
canticorum, a principio usque ad finem, per os puellae edidit: & iterans verbum ex verbo, in
Romanam linguam usque in finem interpretatus est; & reiterans verbum ex verbo, in Teutonico
totum expressit; cum illa puella, dum adhuc sana esset, nihil nisi Psalterium didicisset." *AASS*,
June, I, 834.

53. A number of saints' lives use the term *exponere*, defined as to "set before, make manifest,
set forth, expound, explain," to describe the laying open and translating of Scripture in both
Latin and the vernacular; see Leo F. Stelten's *Dictionary of Ecclesiastical Latin* (Peabody, MA:
Hendrickson, 1994). Translation theorists have discovered that translations have a "higher degree
of explicitness" than nontranslated texts; this process of "making explicit in the target language
language information that is implicit in the source text" is termed *explication*. Kinga Kloudy,
Routledge Encyclopedia of Translation Studies, ed. Mona Baker, assisted by Kirsten Malmkjaer
(London: Routledge, 1998), 80–85, at p. 80, quoted and discussed in Pál Heltai, "Explication,
Redundancy, Ellipses and Translation," in *New Trends in Translation Studies, In Honour of Kinga
Klaudy*, ed. Krisztina Károly and Ágota Foris (Budapest: Akadémiai Kiadó, 2005), 45–74, at p. 46.

tion, which is "without any lack," suggests that it addresses in exhaustive and vivid detail the bodily images that abound within.

The suspicion of laywomen's deep scriptural knowledge and miraculous Latinity is particularly striking in this example. As Barbara Newman has noted, stories such as these echo legends of miraculous inspiration.[54] This legend embodies a fear that sudden mastery of Latin can be devilish in origin, not divine, and serves as a warning against lay or semireligious women participating in activities normally reserved for clerics, such as preaching and scriptural translation and interpretation. If a young woman inspired by the devil can translate as well as or even better than a learned cleric, the question becomes, how do the biographies of holy women, who receive and practice gifts of Latinity and scriptural understanding, show that the women are inspired by God and not the devil? Namely, the vitae emphasize how the holy women all perform their translations in appropriate, limited ways that do not overstep their roles. Thus, while vitae imagine women performing important roles as translators and interpreters in their communities, the limits of the women's practices are emphasized. Even when miraculous gifts are imagined in the vitae, the women are never imagined to possess or perform a fully developed, clerical literacy; the danger of demonstrating such a literacy, as we see in the example of the girl from Nivelles, is clear. A woman who can pronounce, gloss, and translate Scripture boldly like a cleric, in public, in front of clerics, must be possessed by the devil. Only the devil would give women such a fully developed gift of Latinity, one that the hagiographers imagine they clearly did not need.

As we have seen thus far in this chapter, the boldest, most challenging miraculous Latin translation is made by a young woman possessed by the devil, who after her exorcism is rendered completely illiterate. Only this young woman approximates a cleric in her command and performance of her Latinity; other women are seen as practicing their more limited gifts discreetly and humbly, for the benefit of themselves and their fellow religious. In the final

---

54. Barbara Newman, "Devout Women and Demoniacs in the World of Thomas of Cantimpré," in *New Trends in Feminine Spirituality: The Holy Women of Liège and Their Impact*, ed. Juliette Dor, Leslie Johnson, and Jocelyn Wogan-Browne (Turnhout: Brepols, 1999), 35–60. "In their diabolically 'inspired' charismatic role, such demoniacs bear a startling if superficial resemblance to prophetic female saints, who gained their religious authority by speaking *in persona Dei*. Just like clairvoyant and mystical saints, demoniacs of this kind might possess miraculous literacy and knowledge of Scripture" (47). See also Newman, "Possessed by the Spirit: Devout Women, Demoniacs, and the Apostolic Life in the Thirteenth Century," *Speculum* 73 (1998): 733–70, at pp. 733, 749. Similarly, Nancy Caciola, *Discerning Spirits: Divine and Demonic Possession in the Middle Ages* (Ithaca: Cornell Univeristy Press, 2003) notes that demoniacs could on occasion exhibit xenoglossia (54).

section of this chapter, however, I will turn to a later medieval variation of the gift of Latinate xenoglossia: divine tutoring or the divine call to learn Latin, which does offer women a way to explain and legitimize their actual literate practices. In many ways, miraculous tutelage is the most mundane or least miraculous of the xenoglossic miracles, for it simply describes the learning process as miraculously guided or inspired; in terms of actual linguistic agency, however, it is the most useful.

Part 3: Miraculous Tutelage

The gift of the accelerated learning of Latin, under the tutelage of Mary, Christ, and the saints, is a variation of the gift of Latin xenoglossia that appears to offer its female recipients much more control and mastery over the Latin language than instantaneous gifts of sapientia. The difference between the two kinds of Latinate experience (an instantaneous gift or miraculously aided learning) in women's vitae is that, in the former, the mastery is limited to the particular text in which an understanding is granted and presumably could never extend to another text without another divine gift; in the latter, the mastery is one of the Latin language and could theoretically be performed on a variety of Latinate texts. Claims of miraculous tutelage are no doubt offered in part as a way to defend and to explain what was perceived as unusual literacy in women and to give sanction to the women's educative efforts.

Men's and women's saints' lives claim quite frequently that their subjects learned to read or write "in the school of the divine spirit." Many vitae attribute intense or rapid learning of Latin Scripture to the hands of God, Christ, and Mary.[55] The Life of Blessed Isabelle (Elisabeth; d. 1270), sister of the French King Louis IX, states that she was an "exceptional student in the school of our Lord Jesus Christ, who said to his disciples, 'Come, learn from me'"; Isabelle then dedicated herself to understanding sacred Scripture.[56] The

---

55. For the image of Mary as teacher, see Mulder-Bakker, "*Maria doctrix*: Anchoritic Women, the Mother of God, and the Transmission of Knowledge," in Mulder-Bakker, ed., *Seeing and Knowing*, 181–99.

56. "Discipula enim fuit singularis in schola Domini nostri Jesu Christi, qui discipulis suis dixit: Venite, 'discite a me, quai mitis sum & humilis corde.' . . . Venerabilis haec atque excellens Domina in juventute sua libentissime manebat in cubiculo, studebatque intelligere sacram Scripturam. . . . Postquam litteris abunde imbuta erat, ex serico quaedam componere discebat, stolasque componebat, aliaque sanctae Ecclesiae ornamenta." *AASS*, Aug., VI, 798–99. For a discussion of Isabelle's Old French *Life* by Agnes of Harcourt, see Sean L. Field's *Isabelle of France: Capetian Sanctity and Franciscan Identity in the Thirteenth Century* (Notre Dame: University of Notre

vita of the German beguine Christine of Stumbeln (Christine of Stommeln; d. 1312) also attributes to holy figures a woman's modestly miraculous ability to read Scripture. Christine learned to read when she was eleven years old; her vita records that, after just seven weeks of studying, she was able to read the entire Psalter. This was, it is said, because "she had the bridegroom Christ and the Angels as teachers."[57] The *Life* of St. Leonorius (d. sixth century), however, describes a much more rapid acquisition of literacy. He is said to have learned to read in three days: on the first day, he mastered his letters; on the second, how letters joined in spelling; and then on the third, the symbols of writing. Having learned to read and write in only half a week, Leonorius could quickly turn his attention to learned study of sacred Scripture.[58] This three-day ability is certainly more striking than Christine's gift of being able to read the Psalter in seven weeks. While it may be misleading to draw assumptions based on just one or two examples, it seems significant that a man can be imagined to learn to write Latin in three days; a woman, however, even when divinely tutored, takes much longer to learn to read.

Mary, perhaps inspired by her role as teacher of Christ (and by the image of her mother St. Anne as a teacher), is often described in saints' lives as a tutor of Latin.[59] On occasion, Mary might also encourage ongoing illiteracy

Dame Press, 2006), 21–26; see also "The Life of Isabelle of France," in *The Writings of Agnes of Harcourt: The Life of Isabelle of France and the Letter on Louis IX and Longchamp*, ed. and trans. Sean L. Field (Notre Dame: University of Notre Dame Press, 2003).

57. "Circa undecimum annum aetatis suae didicit Psalterium suum; & quando legit, videbatur ei saepius, quod cum Dilecto loqueretur, & Dilectus cum ea. . . . Tunc increpavit eam Magistra sua dicens: Tu bene scis lectionem tuam; ipsa vero subticuit. O Deus quam bene illa scivit lectionem. Haec autem infra septem septimanis didicit Psalterium; Sponsum enim & ejus Angelos habuit institutores." *AASS*, June, IV, 431. For Christina [Christine] of Stommeln, see also "Epistolae," in *Other Middle Ages: Witnesses at the Margins of Medieval Society*, ed. Michael Goodich (Philadelphia: University of Pennsylvania Press, 1998), 164–68; see also John Coakley, "A Marriage and Its Observer: Christine of Stommeln, the Heavenly Bridegroom, and Friar Peter of Dacia," in *Gendered Voices: Medieval Saints and Their Interpreters*, 99–117, 229–35.

58. "Concessit autem divina Leonorio beato tantam gratiam, ut in primo die, literarum omnium nomina; in secundo, conjunctiones earum; in tertio, scribendi notitiam agnosceret. Deinde quotidie in scripturarum sententia & in laudibus Dei ita floruit, ut per omnem regionem laus & fama ejus exiret, & multitudo populorum frequenter ad videndum eum veniret, & multa munera ei deferret, quae accipiens, egenis, orphanis, viduis distribuit, & nihil ad usum suum retinuit. *AASS*, Jul., 1, 121.

59. On the subject of Mary as a teacher, Pamela Sheingorn comments that Mary's reading as depicted in images is almost always limited to the Psalter and serves as a model for female literacy. See Sheingorn, "The Wise Mother: The Image of St. Anne Teaching the Virgin, *Gesta* 32 (1993): 69–80; repr. in *Gendering the Master Narrative: Women and Power in the Middle Ages*, ed. Mary Carpenter Erler and Maryanne Kowaleski (Ithaca: Cornell University Press, 2003), 105–34, at p. 134. Mary's reading habits suggest that, whereas men may read theological texts, the *Psalter* or *Book of Hours* is all a woman needs to be able to read. However, as Claire Sahlin has argued, many medieval sources described Mary as the "teacher of the Apostles," because she told them "all things that they did not completely know about her Son." Theologians imagined Mary to be

and refuse to tutor a woman of low social order, as with the example of the illiterate cowherd Veronica of Binasco, who was excused from having to learn the alphabet. Veronica attempted to teach herself to read so that she could meet the entrance requirement of the Augustinian convent of St. Martha in Milan that she wished to join.[60] Compelled to apply herself to her domestic chores during the day, Veronica tried to study in the evenings on her own, without the benefit of a tutor. Unable to learn by her own devices, she prayed for help from God and the Virgin Mary, explaining that she was prohibited from learning by her frequent manual labor. Suddenly, the Virgin appeared to Veronica to give her a lesson. The lesson was quite abbreviated, however, for Mary promised that all Veronica need learn was three letters, which were to be understood allegorically as the qualities the young woman must possess. The Virgin declared:

> Do not fear, my daughter; nor should you try to learn the letters anymore. It is my wish that you know only three letters: the first is the color white, the second black, the third red. . . . Listen to the meaning of the three letters. The white letter signifies the purity of heart, the obtaining of which I order you to concentrate on with all the prayers of your soul. . . . The black letter teaches that you must never take upon any inducement to sin on account of the deeds of your fellow man. Although men may like to accomplish evil deeds, you however must always feel pity for the impious. . . . By the red letter, I order you to meditate daily as attentively as possible on at least part of the Passion of my son. If you are able to learn the other letters, that's fine; if not, may these three letters never pass from your mind.[61]

---

extremely learned in a number of subjects, "surpassing the knowledge of educated men," a knowledge she gained as a result of her pregnancy with Christ; Mary does not impart this knowledge, however, as it is "unbecoming a woman." Mary, therefore, is both extremely learned but discreet in her performance of her intellectual knowledge. See Sahlin, *Birgitta of Sweden and the Voice of Prophecy*, Studies in Medieval Mysticism 3 (Woodbridge, UK: Boydell, 2001), 97. Thomas Aquinas states that Mary "did not use wisdom by teaching since this was not thought becoming to a woman." *Summa Theologiae* 3, q. 27, a. 5, quoted in Sahlin, *Birgitta of Sweden*, 97 and 97n81.

60. For nuns needing to know liturgy in Latin, see Paul Lee, "Books, Learning, and Spirituality in Late Medieval Nunneries," *Nunneries, Learning, and Spirituality in Late Medieval English Society*, chap. 4. See also Lewis, *By Women, for Women, About Women*, chap. 8, "Love of Learning."

61. Translation mine. "Concepto religionis voto, assiduis precibus Veronica efflagitabat ab monasterij Diuae Marthae Matre sancto habitu indui. Cui suadebat Mater eadem litteras perdiscere. Satagebat itaque Virgo satis iussa Matris perficere. Quamobrem totam diem rebus domesticis cum a patre insistere cogeretur, nocte vigilans litteris perdiscendis intendebat. Precabatur

Through Mary, Veronica learns that reading is a kind of symbolic action and that the qualities or actions these three particular letters represent are more important to her as a pious woman than a mastery over the actual letters themselves.[62] Veronica's knowledge of the three letters proved a sufficient enough education for her to enter the monastic community as a lay sister; there she set herself to performing the most menial of duties, which she undertook without complaint. After living in the convent for a number of years, God finally granted Veronica the miraculous ability to both read and understand the Psalter as a reward for her humility. Her reward for years of pious expression through hard labor was that she could perform her devotions in a more textually oriented way.[63] Moreover, the vita claims that three years before her death Veronica was taught by an Angel of God the entire Divine Office, which she prayed and recited at the various hours, an ability that no doubt allowed her to participate more fully in her devotions alongside her companions.[64]

In other narratives, however, the Virgin Mother advocates literacy, espe-

---

vero Deum pientissimum Matremque beatissimam, quo sibi praesto adessent in litterarum acquirenda notitia, a qua prohibebatur frequenti manuum opere. Apparuit tandem Virgini Dei immortalis genitrix. . . . [Maria] dixit: Ne timueris filia mea: neque plurimum coneris litteras nosse. Meae nempe voluntatis est, trium tantummodo litterarum peritiam te habere: Prima coloris albi erit, secunda nigri, tertia rubei. . . . Audi vero trium litterarum significata. Album quidem elementum signat cordis munditiam, cui nanciscendae totis animi votis te incumbere iubeo. . . . Verum littera nigra docet, vt numquam scandalum sumas ab proximi operibus. Peragant licet homines opera mala, tu tamen impiis semper compatiere. . . . Quod ad elementum spectat rubricatum, iubeo te quotidie saltim partem passionis filij mei quam attentissime meditari. Si ceteras litteras perdiscere poteris, recte; sin minus, hae tre mente numquam excidant." AASS Jan., I, 890–91.

62. My thanks to the anonymous reader for pointing out that the colors are also the allegory of the manuscript page, with white representing the parchment, black the letters, and red the rubrics.

63. "Huius ancillae suae humilitatem respiciens summus Opifex, totum psalterium illam edocuit, tantoque munere diuinarum litterarum sapientiam infudit, vt psalmos quosque Dauid & legeret & intelligeret." AASS, Jan., I, 899.

64. "Mense Februario anni ab ortu Christi Maximi millesimi quadrigentesimi nonagesimi quarti, qui secundus annus fuit, quo Angelico pane Veronicam Deus aluit; Angelus Domini magna luce coruscus adueniens octo dierum spatio omne Romanae Curiae officium Virginem edocuit, ac varios mores religiosorum, qui Romanam sequuntur Curiam in diuinis laudibus persolvendis." AASS, Jan., I, 899. Veronica is also said to have composed a book, an "opus praeclarissimum," from a dictating Angel: "Composuit Veronica opus praeclarissimum Angelo dictante." AASS, Jan., II, 900. In exemplary literature, Mary often supports and values unlearned men and women, for she encourages the illiterate and appreciates their humble devotions for their intense pious focus. Descriptions of Mary found advocating meditation on certain letters as symbolic representations of Christ and herself can be found in other miracle accounts. For example, The Middle English Miracles of the Virgin includes a similar narrative with its devotional emphasis on the individual letters of Mary's name. See Beverly Boyd, ed. Middle English Miracles of the Virgin (San Marino, CA: Huntington Library, 1964), 54–55.

cially for women who are or will be at the head of religious communities. The vitae of three women, Bl. Sperandea of Cingoli (d. 1276), Bl. Christiana of Lucca (d. 1310), and St. Bridget of Sweden (d. 1373), claim that Mary either ordered them to learn Latin or that she actually taught them herself so that they could fulfill their monastic, visionary, or spiritual duties more fully. That hagiographers imagine or describe the leaders of women's monastic houses as receiving divine calls to literacy demonstrates how important literacy could be perceived to be in the convent.

The vita of Sperandea of Cingoli, a Benedictine nun and then abbess in Piceno, Italy, relates how the visionary was commanded to learn to read and then "taught" by Mary and Christ so that she could use her skills for the good of others. According to her vita, which describes the various heavenly visions she experienced, on the night of Easter, while she was standing before the cross and mediating on the passion of Christ, a certain light appeared, which her eyes were not able to bear. She then saw the Queen of Heaven light a lamp of great brightness, and the Virgin Mary commanded Sperandea to read the words that were written upon it. "I don't know how to read," responded the woman. Then Mary said to her, "My son and I will teach you"; then Sperandea read the writing, which said that she would perform acts of compassion among the poor. It is not immediately clear whether Mary has bestowed a gift of infused understanding of the written words (*scriptura* in this context may indicate either "written words," or Scripture), or if Sperandea is suddenly able to read these particular Latin words related to her ministry to the poor.[65]

The more detailed account of Christiana of Lucca (Cristiana of Santa Croce or Oringa) emphasizes the pious women's successful tutoring of others, having been encouraged and facilitated in her Latin learning by Mary. This account is fascinating for it gives divine sanction to women's literate efforts. Christiana was a Tuscan farm girl who fled an impending marriage to become a serving girl in Lucca. She later went on a pilgrimage, gathered a number of followers, and eventually founded an Augustinian convent at Castello di Santa Croce in the Arno Valley. According to her vita, one night Christiana had a vision of Mary seated, holding in her hand a book written with golden letters. With her expression "neither smiling nor severe," Mary held out the book to

---

65. "Etiam nocte Paschatis, dum stabat ante crucem, & meditabatur Christi passionem, apparuit ei quoddam lumen, quod oculi ejus sufferre non poterant. Vidit etiam Reginam lampadam magni luminis accedere [*sic*], quae dixit ei: Lege, quae in ea scripta sunt. Nescio, respondit B. Sperandea, legere. Tunc inquit illa: Ego & filius meus docebimus te: & legit scripturam, quae dicebat, ut operaretur misericordiam in pauperes." *AASS*, Sept., III, 902.

Christiana and commanded, "Read, Christiana!" Similar to Sperandea, Christiana, with a depressed spirit, protested, "I don't know how to read." But the Virgin insisted, repeating her order "again and again." Again and again Christiana repeated that she could not. Finally Mary stated, "I will bring it about that you are able to," and then she disappeared.[66]

Thus began Christiana's education, after she awoke. When Christiana returned to her senses, "she pondered the dream more carefully, considering the unsuitability of her advanced age [for learning to read], and nevertheless she decided that it would be opportune for the community if it had a head who knew how to read and by whom the others nuns could be taught." Opportunity came knocking at the door in the form of six nuns who were enlisted among the sisters. Two of these women "had at one time looked into a Psalter," and they began to teach the little that they had learned to the others. Next, they began to discuss the Breviary and stammer a bit from the Canonical Hours, "and thus their thirst for knowledge grew by the help of God." But the Latin abbreviations proved to be major stumbling blocks for the eager learners, and when they were seeking the help of a teacher, help came to one of the two modestly educated newcomers in the form of the old priest who had originally begun her instruction in reading and who came to her in her sleep and cleared up the problems. She in turn faithfully relayed this information to the sisters, and yet "many matters still escaped her and the others." And so after repeated but unanswered prayers, Christiana finally made a fervent prayer for enlightenment for the sake of the sisters. "Thereupon she took up the book and explained it to the sister next to her and in the same moment learned from her that of which both of them had previously been ignorant."[67]

66. "Quanti veto referat non omnino ineruditas esse monachas didicit Virgo a nocturno spectaculo. Sedebat Deipara eo in loco, vbi Christiana amicis extraneis praesentiam suam commodare, aut dare aures negotiosis solebat. Tenebat autem manu altera codicem aureis litteris perscriptum, quem Christianae in genua prouolutae obtulit, ore neque ridenti neque seuero, dicens: Lege Christiana. Ipsa vero, profunda cum animi demissione: Domina, nescio legere. Illa vero cum iussum suum iterum iterumque repeteret, Christiana iterum iterumque reposuit tria sua verba: Domina, nescio legere. Tum Deipara, Efficiam, inquit, vt scias. Simul haec dixit, disparuit." *AASS*, Jan., I, 658.

67. "Reddita sensibus suis Virgo, pensiculatius ruminauit hoc insomnium, examinando aetatis, quae ia non parua erat, ineptitudinem; & tamen iudicauit commode actum iri cum coenobio, si haberet gnaram litterarum Antistita, a qua reliquae virgines instrui possent. Ecce adest statim prae foribus desideratae commoditatis articulus. Sacris monasticis initiatae in album sanctimonialium adscribuntur sex puellae, quarum duae aliquando psalterium inspexerant, & pauxillum, quod in eo discendo libauerant, alias vicissim docere coeperunt: deinde facinus palmarium ausae, Romanum Breuiarium volutare, & de horis Canonicis balbutire aliquid. Eoque creuit, auctore Deo, scientiae cupido; vt, cum verba passim in compendium paucis litteris consonantibus contracta, magistri opem exposcerent, datus sit earum alteri a caelo doctor, Presbyter quidam venerabilis, a quo olim legendi initium hauserat, qui dubia ei dormienti exponeret, & difficiliores nodos expediret. Non potuisset vigilanti dari magister vigilantior. Omnia enim illius praecepta

Christiana's vita emphasizes that the power of God had created in the women the desire to learn; the actual learning, as it is described, was at first accomplished mostly on their own as the women tutored one another to the extent that they were able, and the more difficult questions were answered by a learned and patient cleric who appeared to one of the women in a dream. Ultimately, the leader Christiana became a tutor of the other women through a gift of divine knowledge, as she expounded and interpreted the textual meanings that still remained hidden to her. Mary insisted that Christiana educate herself and that she see to it that her own female followers were educated with the help of a cleric. The author of the vita also mentions that learning to read was not enough for this new monastic community; they also had to learn how to sing, which they did without being taught by man. Thus, all the women were then able to perform the Latinate liturgical duties required of them in the nunnery, a long process that first began with Mary encouraging, inspiring, and commanding Christiana to become literate.

Similarly, the vita of St. Bridget of Sweden presents a holy woman whose Latinity is encouraged and supported by heavenly figures; of all the women explored in this chapter, Bridget appears to gain the most proficiency in the Latin language. Bridget's miraculously acquired Latinity greatly exceeds the expectations of all around her and actually becomes an item of note in her canonization process. In her example, therefore, we see a woman whose actual literate practices are sanctioned and ordered by the Divine so that she may participate in her own translation.

Bridget's late fourteenth-century vita and other documents produced during her canonization process report that she was gifted with a miraculously accelerated rate of learning Latin, which she achieved after being commanded by Christ to learn Latin with the help and tutelage of St. Agnes.[68] These re-

---

tam studiose obseruauit, & retinuit fideliter, vt eadem dare sororibus, & apprime imprimere posset. Et tamen multa adhuc eam reliquasque latebant. Itaque Christiana pro omniscientia Deum Deiparamque frequenti, sed inani prece rogauit. Tandem ergo corde effusissimo sic exclamat: Regina mundi vtriusque & Sponsi mei optimi Mater optima, quando me hac, quam rogo gratiam, indignam video, agnoscoque; collubitum tibi sit, obsecro, vt minimum sororibus meis aperire, quod ancillae tuae absconditum esse placuit. Hoc dicto, codicem sumit, vicinae sorori explicat, discitque ab illa eodem temporis puncto, quod antea vtraque ignorauerant. Mundi ergo Domina respexit humilitatem ancillae suae, quod omnium magistra ad sui magisterium aequo animo sororum minimam admisisset." *AASS*, Jan., I, 658. Christiana's vita was included in "Vita della B. Oringa Cristiana fondatrice del venerabile convento di S. Maria Novella," in vol. 18, *Deliciae eruditorum: sue veterum anekdoton opusculorum collectanea*, ed. Giovanni Lami (Florence, 1769). For a brief biography in English, see Agnes B. C. Dunbare, *A Dictionary of Saintly Women* (London: Bell, 1904–1905), 2:124.

68. According to Bridget Morris, the earliest Latin vita of Bridget was written by the two Peter Olafssons, Swedish priests who accompanied Bridget to Rome. Well-known redactions were also written by the Archbishop Birger Gregersson and Nikolaus Hermansson. Morris, *St Birgitta*

cords are particularly concerned with how the Swedish saint practices and displays her Latinity, because they promote Bridget's form of miraculously acquired literacy as a way of asserting that she aided her confessors in their Latin translation of her visionary text, the *Revelations*, a compilation of visions she received between the 1340s and 1370s, which she either spoke or wrote in Swedish. These were then recorded and translated into Latin by several clerics. Her earliest recorder was the canon of Linköping Cathedral, Master Mathias Övidsson. When Bridget relocated to Rome two Swedish clerics accompanied her: Prior Peter Olafsson of Alvastra served as "principal translator" of the revelations, with the assistance of Master Peter Olafsson of Skänninge. Last, the Spanish hermit and former bishop Alphonso of Jaén compiled, translated, and edited the visions so that they could be circulated.[69] The canonization documents promote Bridget's practice of translation as a way of ensuring that the Word of God has been accurately transmitted from Swedish into Latin, while the Word's dissemination and translation remain firmly under the control of and subject to the approval of prominent ecclesiastical figures.

According to Article 38 of her canonization process, Bridget learned Latin with remarkable speed, having been completely unlearned in the language before she undertook the task. The article proclaims that the Swedish woman was very quickly able to understand and to speak the learned language well: "The lady Bridget, though she had reached forty years of age and was completely ignorant of any knowledge of Latin grammar, following the command of Christ began to study grammar so that she might be better able to understand sacred Scripture, and within a short while, because she had been well instructed in this knowledge and art, she made such progress that she understood those speaking grammatically, and she herself also spoke even long discourses grammatically with good Latin diction."[70]

---

of Sweden, 8. Several copies of Bridget's vita are extant in Middle English, including one in British Library MS Claudius B.i. The translation of the process vita is attributed to Thomas Gascoigne, Chancellor of the University of Oxford. For a modern English translation, see Birger Gregersson and Thomas Gascoigne, *The Life of Saint Birgitta*, trans. Julia Bolton Holloway, Peregrina Translation Series 17 (Toroton: Peregrina, 1991).

69. Sahlin, *Birgitta of Sweden*, 28–29. See also Roger Ellis, "'Flores ad fabricandum . . . coronam': An Investigation into the Uses of the *Revelations* of St Bridget of Sweden in Fifteenth-Century England," *Medium Aevum* 51 (1982): 163–86. According to Ellis, the two Peters "acted both as scribes and as translators, and they assembled the revelations into a 'great book,' to which they added each new revelation as it came" (164). The most significant role of editor and publisher of the *Revelations* is attributed to Alphonso. Ellis argues that Alphonso had a tremendous effect on the organizing of the visions into a coherent text and attributes to him the basic shape and order of the *Revelations*, as well as the gathering of the visions from Bridget's last years into one volume (164).

70. "Item quod dicta domina Brigida, dum esset totaliter rudis in sciencia grammaticali et iam esset seu attigisset xlmum annum etatis sue, vt melius intelligere posset sacram scripturam,

Just how Bridget achieved her literacy, however, was questionable. Whereas some witnesses emphasize that her confessor Master Peter served as her tutor while St. Agnes aided her as a "comfort," other accounts insist on the role of Agnes as tutor. According to the testimony of Domina Golicie [Golizia Orsini], Agnes herself served as Bridget's tutor: "The witness herself heard it said by the confessor of Bridget that . . . the blessed Agnes instructed her and taught her in grammatical knowledge, so that Bridget was speaking well and was holding forth long discourses in Latin."[71] The importance of Agnes over that of Bridget's confessor as a Latin teacher is also emphasized in the Middle English translation of the vita originally composed by Birger Gregersson, which traveled with the fifteenth-century British Library Claudius B.i. manuscript of the *Revelations*: "Fell þat when sho was went oute of hir awne cuntre sho was comforted with mani revelacions, and was biden hir þat sho shuld lere grammere, whare Saint Agnes oft time teched her, and within a litill time sho profeted so greteli þat sho couthe vndirstand and speke wele Latin."[72]

The miraculous rate at which the visionary learned Latin is emphasized for two reasons. First, it answers the need of *discretio spirituum*. It asserts that Bridget's Latinity is commanded by Christ and aided by Agnes, and not the devil, which we saw examples of earlier in this chapter; the divinely granted gift therefore proclaims the true source of Bridget's prophetic visions.[73] Second, it is promoted to assert Bridget's participation in the translation of the *Revelations*, a suggestion that has been put forth by Rosalynn Voaden but not fully explored.[74] Bridget's divinely tutored Latinity answers the need for the

---

cepit studere ex precepto Christi in grammaticalibus et infra non longum tempus ita profecit, quod in dicta scientia et arte predicta bene erat instructa, ita quod bene intellegeret grammaticaliter loquentes, et ipsa eciam cum bonis latinitatibus longos eciam sermones grammaticaliter loqueretur. Et hoc est verum, publica vox et fama." *Acta et processus canonizacionis beate Birgitte*, ed. Isak Collijn, Samlingar utgivna av Svenska Fornskriptsällskapet, ser. 2 (Uppsala: Almqvist & Wiksells, 1924–31), 24.

71. "ipsa testis audiuit dici a prefato domino confessore ipsius domine Brigide . . . quod beata Agnes eandem dominam Brigidam in eadem sciencia grammaticali instruxit et docuit taliter, quod ipsa domina Brigida congrue loquebatur et latino sermone longos [loquens] sermones faciebat." *Acta et processus*, 456.

72. Bridget of Sweden, *The Liber Celestis of St Bridget of Sweden: The Middle English Version in British Library MS Claudius B. i., together with a Life of the Saint from the Same Manuscript*, ed. Roger Ellis, vol. 1, Early English Text Society, o.s. 291 (Oxford: Oxford University Press, 1987).

73. For a discussion of the importance of the "testing of spirits" in late medieval women's lives, see Caciola, *Discerning Spirits*.

74. Rosalynn Voaden, *God's Words, Women's Voices: The Discernment of Spirits in the Writings of Late-Medieval Women Visionaries* (Woodbridge, UK: York Medieval Press, 1999). "It can be argued that one of the reasons she learned Latin in middle age was to maintain control over the translations made by the two Peters. A number of sources testify to Bridget's checking of

translation of the Word of God to be "exact" or purely equivalent, without trace of human interference. Other channels of the Divine Word, like Hildegard of Bingen or Elisabeth of Schönau, may voice their visions directly from God in Latin, but when the Lord speaks in the vernacular, steps need to be taken to ensure that the words are accurately transmitted and translated.

Bridget's *Revelations* also contain several visions in which the Virgin Mary or St. Agnes discuss Latin grammar with her. It could be argued that the canonization documents assert the prominent role of Agnes as a tutor because her visionary text includes these visions in which Mary and Agnes are encouraging (albeit strict) Latin teachers. In one vision, the two holy women model several parts of speech in a grammar exercise. After Agnes describes all the ways that Mary is like a flower, the text relates, "Then, when Mary appeared, she responded: Agnes, you have said the substantive; say now the adjective."[75] Although Bridget's visions are originally received in Swedish, the references to the terms *substantive* and *adjective* indicate that the holy women are using Latin grammatical terms. At another point in the *Revelations*, Mary instructs Bridget that she must not put aside her learning of Latin to visit the holy places in Rome;[76] the Virgin therefore insists that Bridget's learning Latin is just as, if not more, important than other devotional practices.

Although Bridget authenticates the translation of her visions, the documents are careful to assert that Bridget does not actually produce her own translation, for she acts appropriately by always deferring to clerical control and submitting her texts to her confessors' judgment.[77] As Claire Sahlin has

transcriptions and translations of her revelations; again, this is evidence of her desire for some control over the written revelations" (94).

75. "Tunc apparens Maria respondit: 'Dixisti, Agnes, substantiuum, adde et adiectiuum!' Cui Agnes: 'Si dixero "pulcherrima" vel "virtuosissima" hoc nulli de iure competit nisi tibi, que es mater salutis omnium.' Et respondit Mater Dei beate Agneti: 'Dixisti verum, quia ego potencior sum omnium, ideo addam adiectiuum et substantiuum, canalis scilicet Spiritus Sancti. Sed veni, canalis, et audi me! Tu doles ex eo, quod prouerbium istud vertitur inter homines: "Viuamus secundum libitum nostrum, quia Deus faciliter placatur. Utamur mundo et honore eius, dum possumus, quia propter hominen factus est mundus.'" Bridget of Sweden, *Revelaciones, Book III,* ed. Ann-Mari Jönsson, *Samlingar utgivna av Svenska Fornskriftsällskapet, ser. 2, Latinska skrifter 7:3 (Uppsala: Almqvist & Wiksells, 1998), 181.*

76. Book 6:105: "Mater loquitur sponse: 'Cur sic turbaris, filia?' Respondit illa: 'Quia, domina, non visito loca ista sancta, que sunt in Roma.' Et mater: 'Permittitur,' inquit, 'tibi visitare loca ista cum humilitate et deuota reuerencia, quia in hac Roma maiores sunt indulgencie, . . . Verumptamen, filia, non dimittas propter hoc scholas tuas in gramatica nec patris spiritualis tui tuam sanctam obedienciam'" (266) in Bridget of Sweden, *Revelaciones, Book VI,* ed. Birger Bergh, Samlingar utgivna av Svenska Fornskriftsällskapet, ser. 2 (Stockholm: Almqvist & Wiksell International, 1991). These two episodes featuring Mary's instruction in Latin are referred to briefly in Morris, *St Birgitta of Sweden,* 102.

77. For a discussion of spiritual guides and confessors as necessary for the authorization of

noted, whereas the *Revelations* describes the process of its Latin translation as one of rhetorically developing and augmenting the inner meaning of the Swedish visions, the vita describes the process of translation from Swedish to Latin as "word for word," with Bridget overseeing the work.[78]

One of Bridget's visions, *Revelaciones extravagantes 49*, emphasizes how the process of Latin translation involves augmentation and rhetorical polishing of the text. This vision was not published while Bridget or her confessor Alphonso was alive, suggesting that it offered an uncomfortable description of how the visions were revised and edited during the process of writing them down and translating them.[79] In this vision, Christ commands that Bridget's visions be circulated, and he instructs Bridget to give the written visions to Alphonso for his refinement:

> Now, therefore, that they [i.e., the words] may be serviceable to more tongues, give over all the books of the revelations of these same words of mine to my bishop, the hermit, who is to write them together and to elucidate obscure things and to hold to the Catholic sense of my Spirit. . . . For just as your heart is not always capable and warm for uttering and writing those things that you sense, but now you turn and turn them again in your soul, now you write and rewrite them, until you come to the proper sense of my words, thus with the Evangelists and Doctors my Spirit ascended and descended because now they put some things that had to be emended, now some things that had to be retracted.[80]

women visionaries, see Voaden's chapter on St. Bridget, "The Lady Vanishes: Bridget of Sweden, Exemplary Visionary," in *God's Words, Women's Voices*, 73–108.

78. For Bridget's relationship with her redactors, see Claire L. Sahlin, "Submission, Role Reversals, and Partnerships: Birgitta and Her Clerical Associates," *Birgittiana* 3 (1997): 9–41, and Sahlin, *Birgitta of Sweden*, 72–73.

79. Barbara Newman suggests that Alphonso suppressed *Reuelaciones extrauagantes 49*, which "described the human element in her writing more fully than any other text in her corpus" (39), in "What Did It Mean to Say 'I Saw'? The Clash Between Theory and Practice in Medieval Visionary Culture," *Speculum* 80 (2005): 1–43. Claire Sahlin notes that Alphonso "apparently rejected revelations that were controversial, difficult to interpret, or unflattering to Birgitta." Sahlin, *Birgitta of Sweden*, 29, and footnote 60; see also her discussion of this particular passage on p. 32.

80. Translation from *Birgitta of Sweden: Life and Selected Revelations*, ed. Marguerite Tjader Harris, trans. Albert Ryle Kezel (New York: Paulist Press, 1990), 66. "Nam sicut cor tuum non semper est capax et feruidum ad proferendum et scribendum illa, que sentis, sed nunc voluis et reuoluis ea in animo tuo, nunc scribis et rescribis ill, donec venis ad proprium sensum verborum meorum, sic spiritus meus cum euangelistis et doctoribus ascendebat et descendebat, quia nunc ponebant aliqua emendanda, nunc aliqua retractanda, nunc iudicabantur et reprehendebantur ab aliis" (166) in Bridget of Sweden, *Reuelaciones extrauagantes*, ed. Lennart Hollman, Samlingar utgivna av Svenska Fornskriftsällskapet, ser. 2 (Uppsala:: Almqvist & Wiksells, 1956).

Bridget must repeatedly reexamine her visionary experiences to access and accurately represent the truth of the words engraved on her heart. In desiring the visions to be corrected first in Latin by Alphonso so that they can be suitably translated into many vernacular languages, Christ thus recognizes the need for submitting the text to a respected Latin authority to assure its orthodoxy before dissemination in vernacular languages. To achieve the widest possible audience, the Lord insists that the sense of the visions should be made as clear and attractive as possible. He compares the basic Swedish text of the visions to a carpenter who chops down wood to carve and paint a statue. When the carpenter's friends see the statue, however, they realize it would be more beautiful if they were to incorporate their own colors as well.[81] Christ is suggesting that the visions—the basic Swedish wood—must be colored with Latin rhetoric and composed "to elucidate obscure things" in order that the visions may be successfully translated and received into other languages.

In sharp contrast to this description of how the visions are produced through a process of augmentation and rhetorical development, in Bridget's vita, however, the two Peters state that Bridget's text was created by a process that included her supervision over every word of their Latin translation:

> The words that were given her from God she wrote down in her mother tongue with her own hand when she was well and she had us, her father confessors, make a very faithful translation of them into Latin. She then listened to the translation with her own writing, which she herself had written, to make sure that not one word was added or subtracted, but was exactly what she had heard and seen in the divine vision. But when she was too weak she would call her confessor and another scribe, especially appointed as secretary, whereupon with great devotion and fear of God and sometimes in tears, she spoke the words in her native language in a kind of tense, ecstatic trance as if she were reading from a book; and then the confessor dictated these words in Latin to the scribe, and he wrote them down there in her presence. When the words had been written down

---

81. "Filius Dei loquebatur ad sponsam dicens: 'Ego sum similis carpentario, qui prescindens ligna de silua deportat in domum et inde fabricat ymaginem pulchram et ornat eam coloribus et liniamentis. Cuius amici videntes ymaginem, quod adhuc pulchrioribus coloribus ornari posset, apposuerunt et ipsi colores suos depingendo super eam. Sic ego Deus prescidi de silua deitatis mee verba mea, que posui in cor tuum. Amici vero mei redegerunt ea in libros secundum graciam eis datam et colorauerunt et ornauerunt illa," in Bridget of Sweden, *Reuelaciones extrauagantes* 49, p. 165.

she wished to hear them and she listened very carefully and atten-
tively.[82]

The redactors insist that Bridget recited her visions, reading from her own
written text or speaking "as if reading from a book," and then after her words
were translated, they were read back to her so that she could ensure that not
one word had been altered. The vita therefore claims that the text was created
through a kind of translation practice that enabled the word to be directly
transmitted, unchanged, from the Lord to Bridget to the redactors and therefore to the audience.

Bridget's example demonstrates how miraculously tutored Latinity can be
promoted to assure audiences that the recording and translation of a visionary
text is accurate. Bridget's Latinate practice and ability, however, does not quite
extend to that of her clerical confessors, for she is described as reading, speaking, and understanding well in Latin, but never writing down her visions in
Latin, or translating them herself from Swedish to Latin. From the point of
view of the canonization documents, an ability to write Latin would have
been unnecessary for Bridget, since she always submitted her visions to her
confessors for their approval and translation and could not have authenti-
cated the visions on her own. Thus, even Bridget, who comes closest to having
a clerical command of Latin literacy, must fall somewhat short to ensure that
her confessors and spiritual supervisors can monitor exactly what is being
transmitted and translated.

Bridget's experience of Latin xenoglossia differs from that of other xenoglossic women described in this chapter in several important ways. Unlike
other examples of holy women who gain only one ability—to understand and
translate a particular text through a gift of sapientia—the Swedish holy
woman acquires a high-level proficiency in speaking, understanding, and
reading Latin. Bridget's Latinate ability is not the result of infused knowledge
like that received by so many other late medieval holy women; rather, it is a

---

82. Translation from Morris, *St Birgitta of Sweden*, 3–5n12. "Vel illa verba divinitus ei data
scribebat in lingua sua materna manu sua propria, quando erat sana, et faciebat illa translatari in
lingua latina fidelissime a nobis confessoribus suis et postea ascultabat illa cum scriptura sua,
quam ipsa scripserat, ne vnum verbum ibi plus adderetur uel deficeret, nisi que ipsa in visione
diuinitus audierat et viderat. Si vero erat infirma, vocabat confessorem suum secretarium ad hoc
specialiter deputatum, et tunc ipsa cum magna deuocione et timore Dei et aliquando cum la-
crimis referebat ei verba illa in uualgari suo cum quadam attenta eleuacione mentali, quasi si
legeret in libro, et tunc confessor dicebat illa verba in lingua latina illi scriptori, et ille scribebat
illa ibidem in sua presencia, et postea cum erant verba conscripta, ipsa volebat illa ascultare et
ascultabat valde diligenter et attente." *Acta et processus*, 84. See also Morris, *St Birgitta of Sweden*,
5n12.

command of a range of literate abilities achieved through a combination of both miraculous tutelage and human effort. Certainly, this aristocratic woman's quasi-clerical command of Latin, which she uses to guide the translation of her visions under the supervision of her confessors, is a far cry from the three Latin letters taught by Mary to the cowherd Veronica of Binasco.

Conclusion

In this chapter, I have argued that gifts of sapientia and linguistic knowledge are an extremely important part of medieval holy women's claims of blessedness. Despite the attention to the gift, it is actually quite difficult to determine the extent of Latin literacy a woman gains from her miraculous gift of sapientia. In many cases, the gifts are surprisingly unmiraculous; the divine gift does not offer much more than a woman might have been expected to learn on her own. I have suggested that the mundane quality of many of the gifts can be explained by two impulses: hagiographers either described limited gifts because of the women's potential challenges to clerical power, or the miraculous was employed as a way to explain real, lived experiences of Latinity acquired through nontraditional means.

A central question of this chapter has focused on whether medieval women could translate and gloss Scripture and the Divine Word, and if so, how, where, when, and to whom? I have demonstrated that the range of responses to this question suggest that there is no easy answer. For visionaries like Hildegard of Bingen, Elizabeth of Schönau, and Umiltà of Faenza, God's Latin is said to come through them and to remain unaffected by them; for Bridget of Sweden, her miraculous Latinate ability ensures the translation of vernacular Swedish visions into Latin to help maintain the integrity of her revelations as they are being translated for a pan-European audience. For nuns in their convents, the narratives assert that women can translate for themselves and for the benefit of their spiritual advisors as well as other nuns, and occasionally for other male religious when the women are approached by them. For those outside an order (like the possessed girl from Nivelles), translating and glossing Scripture could be much more dangerous.

The last examples I considered, that of women commanded to learn Latin or who are miraculously tutored, form an important branch of this xenoglossic experience and demonstrate, that for some, actual linguistic practice was afforded by the gift. Miraculous tutelage supports women's efforts at learning and indicates that a certain level of literacy was necessary for those in prominent positions of power in religious communities. That xenoglossia could be an explanation for actual literate practices is picked up on and adapted in the literature of the later medieval England, the subject to which the second half of this book turns.

Whereas the first two chapters of this book have drawn from a wide range of hagiographic sources, the second half will focus closely on two texts from late medieval England: *The Book of Margery Kempe* and Geoffrey Chaucer's *Canterbury Tales*. Both Margery Kempe and Chaucer adapt the hagiographic tropes and concerns of xenoglossia in their texts and develop the figure of the miraculously translating woman to explore their own issues with writerly control and authority. Both are also intensely concerned with the mechanics of miraculous translation because xenoglossia for them is as much (if not more) the *message* as the *medium*, that women are particularly suited to claims of miraculous linguistic ability and can use these special claims to assert their authority to speak and to translate.

THREE

"AN ALIEN TO UNDERSTAND HER":
MIRACULOUS AND MUNDANE TRANSLATION IN
THE BOOK OF MARGERY KEMPE

The previous two chapters have explored hagiographic models of xenoglossia, the miraculous ability to speak, to understand, to read, or to write a foreign language, and have argued that gifts of vernacular and Latinate xenoglossia form an important part of the vitae of many later medieval holy women. Whereas miraculous vernacularity in women's vitae is somewhat rare, miraculous Latinity occurs with much more frequency and is usually the result of divinely infused knowledge of the Lord's Word, either Scripture or vision. Miraculous literacy allows holy women to become translators of Latin scriptural, liturgical, and devotional texts for themselves and their communities. This gift, however, does not generally provide mastery over the entire Latin language but rather the ability to understand the Latin of these particular texts. This limitation in scope is due to two impulses: first, hagiographers (and perhaps the women themselves) desired to present their female subjects as obedient and not challenging clerical spheres of authority; second, the miraculous often explains women's mundane, nontraditionally acquired literacy. Toward the end of the Middle Ages, however, a variation of xenoglossia develops—the miraculous tutelage of Latin—which does imagine xenoglossia as affording actual literate practices.

Material from this chapter has appeared in *Studies in Philology* 101 (2004): 270–98 as "Miraculous Translation in *The Book of Margery Kempe*," by Christine F. Cooper.

During the fourteenth and fifteenth centuries in England, the allure and influence of xenoglossia stretched beyond hagiographic texts, as writers of other religious genres recognized in xenoglossia an important model and metaphor for their own assertions of writerly authority and control. With its assurance that language can be translated perfectly and its claim of Divine approval, xenoglossia became an attractive model for English writers, particularly those exploring women's authority to speak. This chapter explores how Margery Kempe and her scribe adapt xenoglossic tropes in her *Book*, a combination visionary text, confession, and autohagiography. The *Book* includes episodes of miraculous translation that Margery and clerics share, which link the narrative quite closely with the accounts of vernacular and Latinate xenoglossia experienced by more renowned medieval holy men and women, as discussed in the first two chapters of this book. The *Book*'s use of xenoglossia, however, is more troubled than its earlier hagiographical models. Moreover, the *Book* focuses extensively on moments of mundane or everyday translation that occur while Margery is abroad on pilgrimage; however, these moments of mundane translation are infused with miraculous qualities and demonstrate that the tropes of xenoglossia have influenced their presentation as well. Miraculous and mundane translation, therefore, work together in the *Book* to form a larger argument about how translation works as both God's medium and message of blessedness.

There has been a substantial amount of scholarship on translation and the *Book*, particularly on how Margery translates Christ's life, hagiographic patterns, and scriptural and devotional themes absorbed from religious literature into her own life and text.[1] Two groundbreaking studies from the previ-

---

1. First and foremost, Margery is a translator of Christ's life, a pious laywoman practicing *imitatio Christi* in fifteenth-century Europe. Margery's own version of that imitation, in particular her claims of renewed chastity, her spreading of the Holy Word (including preaching), and her suffering of persecution, have been the focus of much scholarship in the past decade. Gail McMurray Gibson argues that Margery's *imitatio Christi* consists of physical experiences, including the wrenching of the body, being spit on and scorned, and forgiving those who cause her harm (278), in "St. Margery: *The Book of Margery Kempe*, in *The Book of Margery Kempe: A New Translation, Contexts, Criticism*, ed. and trans. Lynn Staley (New York: Norton, 2001), 276–84, originally published in Gibson, *The Theater of Devotion: East Anglian Drama and Society in the Late Middle Ages* (Chicago: University of Chicago Press, 1989), 47–66; see also Gibson, "St. Margery: *The Book of Margery Kempe*," in *Equally in God's Image: Women in the Middle Ages*, ed. Julia Bolton, Joan Bechtold, and Constance C. Wright (New York: Peter Lang, 1990), 144–63. Sarah Beckwith in "Margery Kempe's *Imitatio*" asserts that "the mimesis of Christ is at the very centre of Kempe's book" (284), with Margery's *imitatio* consisting of "her willing assumption of suffering, and the way she functions as an object of scorn to those around her" (286), in Staley, ed., *Book of Margery Kempe*, 284–87, excerpted from *Christ's Body: Identity, Culture, and Society in Late Medieval Writings* (New York: Routledge, 1993), 80–83. This last point is developed even more strongly in the article "Margery Kempe as Traveler," *Studies in Philology* 87 (2000): 1–28, in which Terence N. Bowers argues that Margery's descriptions of her travels abroad bring into

ous decade focus on translation in the *Book* in both its metaphoric and linguistic forms. In *Margery Kempe and Translations of the Flesh*, Karma Lochrie argues that translation is the most fitting metaphor for Margery's textual practice; she translates vision into writing, reads and translates Christ's body and passion into her own life and *Book*, and translates and manipulates Latinate textuality to "steal into [magisterium] language," by inserting her challenging, "laughing" voice into a culture and discourse that she is intent on subverting.[2] In *Margery Kempe's Dissenting Fictions*, Lynn Staley also asserts that translation is one of the larger issues that preoccupies Kempe in her *Book*. For Staley, Kempe the author and Margery the character function as metaphoric and literal translators, as they translate Christ's gospel (both his physical experience and Scripture) into fifteenth-century English life and the vernacular.[3] Staley argues that Kempe is very concerned with language in general, particularly while Margery is on pilgrimage because in criticizing the English who should (but do not) understand and appreciate Margery, Kempe is attempting to construct a wider Christian, Pentecostal community that speaks a "common language."[4] More recently, Terence N. Bowers has developed Staley's argument regarding Margery's pilgrimages in his essay "Margery Kempe as Traveler," examining how Margery relives and translates Christ's passion while abroad on pilgrimage, which "tends to give rise to other forms of community."[5] According to Bowers, Kempe, in elaborating on the *imitatio Christi* motif, is also using Margery's travels to demonstrate that those who understand and care for her despite the language barrier are meant by contrast to make the English who abandon and torment her resemble the Jews who were said to have persecuted Christ.[6]

sharp relief the Christ-like persecution she suffers from her fellow English, who enact the role of Christ's torturers; see esp. 18–21.

2. Karma Lochrie, *Margery Kempe and Translations of the Flesh* (Philadelphia: University of Pennsylvania Press, 1991). For her discussion of "stealing into language," see especially 7 and 124. For the complexities of *imitatio Christi*, see chapters 2 and 3 in Lochrie.

3. Staley refers to this *imitatio* as a kind of translation, asserting that Margery's "life is captured in the book that we read, the radical gospel of Margery Kempe, whose wanderings, uncomfortable sayings, and confrontations with authority 'translate' Christ's life into the English of Lancastrian England, where Margery's welcome is all too like that Jesus received from his countrymen" (153) in Staley, *Margery Kempe's Dissenting Fictions* (University Park: Pennsylvania State University Press, 1994). See also ibid., 170.

4. Ibid., esp. 151–55.

5. Bowers, "Margery Kempe as Traveler," 6, citing Victor Turner and Edith Turner, *Image and Pilgrimage in Christian Culture: Anthropological Perspectives* (New York: Columbia University Press, 1978).

6. Bowers writes, "By focusing on her countrymen's ill-treatment of her, Kempe's pilgrimage reenacts her predicament in England." "Margery Kempe as Traveler," 18. The English become like Christ's persecutors (19); Rome "confirms Kempe as a social as well as a spiritual being" (22).

Although translation in a larger sense (Margery's metaphoric translation of Christ's and the saints' lives, or the ways in which Latinate learning and Scripture are translated into the vernacular *Book* both openly and surreptitiously) is a focus of numerous scholarly works, many of the actual scenes depicting linguistic translation in the *Book* remain largely unexplored.[7] No one has discussed the specific episodes of miraculous and mundane translation together for what they reveal about how the *Book* imagines Margery's own performance of translation and Kempe's writerly authority.[8] In this chapter, therefore, I shall argue that the *Book* has been heavily patterned on experiences of xenoglossia in saints' lives while being adapted to fit particular cultural and religious circumstances of early fifteenth-century England. The *Book* recounts Margery's experiences of miraculous translation on two related levels: first, the Pentecostal-like gift of xenoglossia shared by Margery and clerics, and second, her own ability to translate and be translated perfectly into other European vernaculars. There is, however, a strong sense in which the mundane or ordinary pervades the miraculous, and the miraculous pervades the mundane. Margery's rather unmiraculous experiences of xenoglossia can be explained by several possible reasons: first, they could represent her actual, lived linguistic experiences of translation being interpreted in a miraculous way; second, Kempe and her scribe could be shaping the accounts to resemble lived experience, understanding that to be the model found in the vitae of other later medieval holy women; third, that Margery shares the miracle with clerics shows her to be firmly under the authority and guidance

---

7. For Latinate and vernacular textuality incorporated into the *Book*, see Charity Scott Stokes, "Margery Kempe: Her Life and the Early History of Her Book," *Mystics Quarterly* 25 (1999): 9–67, in which she writes of the *Book*'s "reliance on the authority of the scriptures, scriptural commentary, liturgical texts, devotional treatises, accounts of revelations, homilies and lives of saints" (24). See also Lochrie, *Margery Kempe and Translations of the Flesh*; Melissa Furrow, "Unscholarly Latinity and Margery Kempe," in *Studies in English Language and Literature: 'Doubt Wisely'; Papers in Honour of E. G. Stanley*, ed. M. J. Toswell and E. M. Tyler (London: Routledge, 1996), 240–51, and Cheryl Glenn, "Popular Literacy in the Middle Ages: *The Book of Margery Kempe*," in *Popular Literacy: Studies in Cultural Practices and Poetics*, ed. John Trimbur (Pittsburgh: University of Pittsburgh Press, 2001), 56–73. Just how the textuality is incorporated into the *Book* is questionable: some see it as the contribution of the second scribe, arguing that Margery's illiteracy prevents her from incorporating many of these materials; others attribute the textuality to Margery, and either question her claims of illiteracy or assume that she had access to these materials in oral form. For Margery's claims of illiteracy, see Josephine K. Tarvers, "The Alleged Illiteracy of Margery Kempe: A Reconsideration of the Evidence," *Medieval Perspectives* 11 (1996): 113–24.

8. Furrow does briefly discuss Margery's attempts to be understood while abroad, including her claim of vernacular xenoglossia, as part of a larger exploration of Margery's Latinate abilities; see Furrow, "Unscholarly Latinity and Margery Kempe," esp. pp. 246–50.

of those clerics. However, when Margery engages in day-to-day, mundane translation, she is too easily (indeed, at times perfectly) understood, and she often understands those who speak other languages in an almost miraculous way. Even when Margery procures translators for herself and claims she does not speak the language of the country through which she is traveling, the *Book*'s desire to shape and control Margery's representation and reception as a holy woman makes Kempe (or the scribe) translate the motives, words, and actions of those whom, practically speaking, Margery should not be able to understand.

The *Book* presents mundane and miraculous translation as functioning in similar ways. Both are evidence of Margery's divine favor (and offer witnesses to that effect) and her efforts to ensure access to religious experience and pious practice, including veneration of the saints, participation in confession, taking communion, and listening to sermons. In addition, the frequent, and at times excessive, attention paid to moments of translation in the *Book* indicate anxiety on the part of Kempe and the scribe concerning how Margery is being "read" and understood by others and indicates a desire to regulate the representation of the holy woman, both orally and in writing. The *Book*'s movement between heightened attention paid to translation, and translation that is at other times forgotten or ignored, emphasizes the role of successful translation not just functioning as the medium of communication and exchange but rather as the message of God's approval.

In arguing this, I must acknowledge the complex issue of authority in Kempe and the scribe's creation of the *Book*. Similar to many of the vitae discussed in Chapters 1 and 2, the *Book*'s situation is complicated because there are several layers of textual mediation. The *Book* claims that Margery dictated her text to a first scribe who died; she then approached a priest (the "second scribe"), who said he was unable to read the text, but eventually picked it up again, rewrote the first scribe's part, and added a second book. Scholarly arguments concerning the balance of control between Kempe and her scribe fall into a broad spectrum. There are those who attribute much editorial power and authorship to the second scribe.[9] However, there are those who assert Kempe's control over the shape and content of her text; a number

---

9. These include Anthony Goodman, "The Piety of John Brunham's Daughter, of Lynn," in *Medieval Women: Dedicated and Presented to Rosalind M. T. Hill on the Occasion of her Seventieth Birthday*, ed. Derek Baker, Studies in Church History, Subsidia 1 (Oxford: Blackwell, 1978), 347–58, and John C. Hirsch, "Author and Scribe in *The Book of Margery Kempe*," *Medium Aevum* 44 (1975): 145–50.

of these scholars stress the important role of "witnessing" lent by the scribe over "editing."[10]

Although it is tempting to imagine that Kempe herself insists on including and developing these scenes of translation in the text because *she* understands them to be particularly significant, we cannot ignore the possibility that the scribe himself could be focusing on these moments because *he* sees them as particularly illustrative of Margery's blessedness. Moreover, following Staley, I must draw the distinction between Kempe the author and Margery the subject, for although the text is presented as a kind of autobiography or spiritual memoir with the author (Kempe) using the third person to describe herself (the "creature," Margery), we must recognize that Kempe acts as a hagiographer, one who both consciously and unconsciously shapes the presentation of her female subject to emphasize her blessedness. Therefore, I use "Kempe and her scribe" whenever I am speaking of the creators of the *Book* and Margery when speaking of the subject.[11]

Part 1: Miraculous Translation in *The Book of Margery Kempe*

It is well recognized that the *Book* is patterned on sacred biographies and visionary texts like those of St. Bridget of Sweden and Marie d'Oignies, while at the same time diverging from its models quite significantly.[12] My aim in

10. Perhaps the most extreme argument for Kempe's control is voiced by Lynn Staley, who suggests that the scribe might have been created by Kempe herself: "Since Kempe stresses the amount of time Margery spent with her scribe (216), it is likely she exerted a good deal of control over the text itself: either she wrote it herself and created a fictional scribe, or she had it read back to her and was aware of exactly what was in the text." Staley, *Margery Kempe's Dissenting Fictions*, 33.

11. In this chapter, I am employing Staley's distinction, as set out in *Margery Kempe's Dissenting Fictions*, between Kempe the author and Margery the character; Staley sees the latter as a literary construct in much the same way as we distinguish between Chaucer the writer and Chaucer the pilgrim, and Langland the author and Will the pilgrim. I do not go as far, however, as to assert that the scribe is the creation of Kempe. For further discussion of the *Book's* authorship, see Nicholas Watson, "The Making of *The Book of Margery Kempe*," in *Voices in Dialogue: Reading Women in the Middle Ages*, ed. Linda Olson and Kathryn Kerby-Fulton (Notre Dame: University of Notre Dame Press, 2005), 395–434, and Felicity Riddy, "Text and Self in *The Book of Margery Kempe*," in Olson and Kerby-Fulton, *Voices in Dialogue*, 435–53.

12. As the lives and works of holy women, including SS. Bridget of Sweden and Elizabeth of Hungary, are translated to Margery by the priest (and of course she hears vitae in sermons and in other places), she in turn translates the lives and their visions of these women into her own experience. Scholarship on the *Book* has suggested that these women include Marie d'Oignies, Dorothy of Montau, Hildegard of Bingen, Christina Mirabilis, and Angela of Foligno. See, for example, Gibson, "St. Margery," 47–66; Kathleen Kamerick, "Art and Moral Vision in Angela

this section is to contribute to this growing body of scholarship by arguing that, in her practice of *imitatio sanctarum*, Kempe and her scribe translate into Margery's own life and text the experiences of vernacular and Latinate xenoglossia, as discussed in Chapters 1 and 2, while altering these experiences to fit her particularly difficult situation as a laywoman visionary trying to negotiate a holy life "in the world" rather than in the cloister. Margery claims to be an illiterate woman who receives visions as well as gifts of infused knowledge of Scripture; these gifts enable her, when accused of heresy and questioned by hostile clerics, to expound on and to translate the Gospel and the Divine Word.[13] Margery herself is gifted with vernacular xenoglossia that draws on the models described in the first chapter, and her experience of the gift makes possible an intriguing variation of the gift of Latin that enables her to preach in Latin through the mouth of a high-ranking cleric. The *Book*'s second scribe also adapts the xenoglossic trope in a novel way by claiming for

---

of Foligno and Margery Kempe," *Mystics Quarterly* 21 (1995): 148–58; Naoë Kukita Yoshikawa, "Veneration of Virgin Martyrs in Margery Kempe's Meditation: Influence of the Sarum Liturgy and Hagiography," in *Writing Religious Women: Female Spiritual and Textual Practices in Late Medieval England*, ed. Denis Renevey and Christiania Whitehead (Toronto: University of Toronto Press, 2000), 177–95. Margery's patterning on St. Bridget is especially noticeable; as A. C. Spearing declares, "She sees herself as an English St Bridget, a wife specially favored by God in a culture that downgraded marriage in favor of celibacy" (629) in "*The Book of Margery Kempe*: Or, the Diary of a Nobody," *Southern Review* 38 (2002): 625–35. See also Nanda Hopenwasser and Signe Wegener, "Vox Matris: The Influence of St. Birgitta's *Revelations* on *The Book of Margery Kempe*: St. Birgitta and Margery Kempe as Wives and Mothers," in *Crossing the Bridge: Comparative Essays on Medieval European and Heian Japanese Women Writers*, ed. Barbara Stevenson and Cynthia Ho (New York: Palgrave, 2000), 61–85; Hopenwasser, "The Human Burden of the Prophet: St. Birgitta's *Revelations* and *The Book of Margery Kempe*," *Medieval Perspectives* 8 (1993): 153–62, and Gunnel Cleve, "Margery Kempe: A Scandinavian Influence in Medieval England?" in *The Medieval Mystical Tradition in England: Exeter Symposium V; Papers Read at the Devon Centre, Dartington Hall, July 1992*, ed. Marion Glasscoe (Cambridge: D. S. Brewer, 1992), 163–78. For a more recent discussion of how the *Book* adapts hagiographic models, see Catherine Sanok, *Her Life Historical: Exemplarity and Female Saints' Lives in Late Medieval England* (Philadelphia: University of Pennsylvania Press, 2007), 116–44.

13. For example, when Margery's orthodoxy is questioned in York, the *Book* relates: "And þan a-non, aftyr þe Erchebischop put to hir þe Articles of owr Feyth, to þe whech God ʒaf hir grace to answeryn wel & trewly & redily wyth-owtyn any gret stody so þat he myth not blamyn hir" (125:7–10). When she is questioned in Lincoln, "þer sufferd sche many scoryns & many noyful wordys, answeryng a-ʒen to Goddys cawse wyth-owtyn any lettyng, wysly & discretly þat many men meruedled of hir cunnyng. Þer wer men of lawe seyd vn-to hir, 'We han gon to scole many ʒerys, & ʒet arn we not sufficient to answeryn as þu dost. Of whom hast þu þis cunnyng?' & sche seyd, 'Of þe Holy Gost. . . . for owr Lord Ihesu Crist seyd to hys disciplys, 'Stody not what ʒe schal sey, for it schal not be ʒowr spiryt þat schal spekyn in ʒow, but it schal be þe spiryt of þe Holy Gost.' And thus owr Lord ʒaf hir grace to answer hem, worschepyd mote he be" (135:22–36). For other mentions of Margery's divine inspiration, see also 17:19–20, 35:2–6, and 121:9–10. All quotations from *The Book of Margery Kempe* are from the Early English Text Society edition by Sanford Brown Meech and Hope Emily Allen, o. s. 212 (London: Oxford University Press, 1940; reprinted 1997) and are referred to by page and line numbers.

himself a gift of miraculous translation of the strange hybrid vernacular in which Margery's text was originally written. That the experiences of xenoglossia can also be explained plausibly by mundane reasons could reflect both lived experience and skillful manipulation of the hagiographic tropes of xenoglossia.

Margery's Translated Text: The Scribe's Gift of Vernacular Xenoglossia

In her article, "The Jerusalem Pilgrimage: The Centre of the Structure of the *Book of Margery Kempe*," Naoë Kukita Yoshikawa explores the Pentecostal imagery prevalent in the *Book*. When describing the writing of the treatise, the *Book* includes the Pentecostal image of fire, which suggests divine inspiration: "& oftyn-tymys þer cam a flawme of fyer a-bowte hir brest ful hoot & delectabyl" (219.3–4). The connection between Margery's inspiration and Pentecost is also made by the clerical scribe at the close of the *Book*, when he describes how Margery prays. She begins with a request that "God xulde illumynyn hir sowle, as he dede hys apostelys on Pentecost Day" (248.8–10).[14] While these passages certainly suggest that Pentecostal imagery is important to the *Book*, I argue that this aspect of the apostolic model actually informs the *Book* on a much deeper level, for both Margery and her scribe are described as receiving gifts of xenoglossia that serve to authorize their experiences and the composition of the *Book*.

Indeed, the very creation of the *Book* is made possible by an event of vernacular xenoglossia, when the priest (often called the "second scribe"), to whom Margery appeals to write her book after the death of the first scribe, receives a miraculous ability, brought about by his and Margery's prayers, to translate the hybrid vernacular language of the first draft into readable English. In claiming a language miracle for his visionary subject, the second scribe shares much in common with the scribes of other better-known visionaries; the main difference, of course, is that the scribe claims to take the central role in the miraculous experience and that the miraculous experience is a vernacular one, not Latinate.

The *Book* opens with an account of xenoglossia experienced by the priest whom Margery desires to edit and to rewrite the first, unfinished draft. The priest, who initially could not read the poorly written "neiþyr good Englysch

14. Yoshikawa, "The Jerusalem Pilgrimage: The Centre of the Structure of the *Book of Margery Kempe*," English *Studies* 86 (2005): 193–205, at pp. 203–4. For discussion of the apostolic model in the *Book*, see also Sarah Salih, *Versions of Virginity in Late Medieval England* (Woodbridge, UK: D. S. Brewer, 2001), esp. 191–94.

ne Dewch" (4.15–16) first draft of the *Book,* discovers to his surprise, after much prayer (both his own and Margery's), that the text is much easier to read than it was previously. He describes this episode in the two prologues or proems that introduce the *Book.* Although the miraculous quality of this event is not emphasized in the earlier version of the proem, when the proem is rewritten, the priest elaborates on the efficacy of Margery's prayers in bringing about the creation of her text. Indeed, two miracles of reading are described in the scene: the first a miracle of "inner sight" or comprehension (involving both reading and translation) and the second a miracle of physical sight, when the priest's vision is restored after his eyes have failed him.[15]

Although the earlier prologue does mention the "special grace" necessary to read the strange text, it does not describe the event as miraculous or attribute the priest's ability to read the text to Margery's efficacy. Instead, it focuses on why the priest decides to approach the text again:

> And þan ʒet it was wretyn fyrst be a man whech cowd neiþyr wel wryten Englysch ne Duch, so it was vn-able for to be red but only be specyal grace, for þer was so mech obloquie & slawndyr of þis creatur þat þer wold fewe men beleue þis creatur. And so at þe last a preste was sor mevyd for to wrytin þis tretys, & he cowd not wel redyn it of a iiij ʒere to-gedyr. & sythen be þe request of þis creatur & compel-lyng of hys owyn consciens he asyad a-gayn for to rede it, & it was mech mor esy þan it was a-for-tyme. (6.12–21)

When the priest retells the story in the second proem, however, which he wrote to "expressyn mor openly" the brief description of the text's creation, the scribe brings out both the miraculous quality of his ability to read the incomprehensible language as well as Margery's own role in the event. Having been influenced by slander against her, the priest tells her that he cannot read the book. Margery makes the same request of another man, who tries but cannot read the text "so euel sett & so vnresonably wretyn" (4.39–40). Then, "vexyd in his consciens," the priest tries again. In the description of the event that he retells in the later proem, attention is shifted onto the efficacy of Margery's prayers:

> Þan sche gat a-geyn þe book & browt it to þe preste wyth rygth glad cher, preyng hym to do hys good wyl, and sche shuld prey to God

---

15. For Lochrie's discussion of these two events as miracles of reading brought about by Margery's intercession, see *Margery Kempe and Translations of the Flesh,* 99–100.

for hym & purchasyn hym grace to reden it & wrytyn it also. Þe preste, trustyng in hire prayers, be-gan to redyn þis booke, & it was mych mor esy, and as hym thowt, þan it was be-forn-tym. & so he red it ouyr be-forn þis creatur euery word, sche sum-tym helpyng where ony difficulte was. (5.4–12)

Of course, there is a practical explanation for this ability of the second scribe to read the script. A number of scholars have suggested that the first scribe was actually Margery's son. The prologue relates how the first scribe was a man who was English by birth but lived in Germany with his wife and child, and who came to England and lived with Margery and copied down what she related to him.[16] The second scribe states that originally he had recommended another scribe to Margery, a man who had read letters from the first scribe while he was in Germany; this would certainly indicate that the first scribe was a relation of either the letter-reader or Margery.[17] The second book describes how Margery's son and his German wife came to stay with her; after the son died, Margery accompanied her daughter-in-law back to Germany. If Margery's son were the first scribe as evidence suggests, then his strange writing, in which "þe lettyr was not schapyn ne formyd as oþer letters ben" (4.16–17), could be the result of someone only partially literate or unpracticed at writing English, or writing in a mixture of German or English, or perhaps even writing in a merchant's shorthand.[18] The second scribe would then have simply learned to decipher or translate the son's idiosyncratic hand into readable English.

The second scribe presents this episode, however, as a moment of miraculous translation. While some have focused on the "ill script" mentioned by the scribe, and therefore read the miraculous event as the sudden ability to

16. "Than had þe creatur no wryter þat wold fulfyllyn hyr desyr ne ȝeue credens to hir felingys vn-to þe tym þat a man dwellyng in Dewchlond whech was an Englyschman in hys byrth & sythen weddyd in Dewchland & had þer boþe a wyf & a chyld, hauyng good knowlach of þis creatur & of hir desyr, meued I trost thorw þe Holy Gost, cam in-to Yngland wyth hys wyfe & hys goodys and dwellyd wyth þe forseyd creatur tyl he had wretyn as mech as sche wold tellyn hym for þe tym þat þe were to-gydder. And sythen he deyd" (4:2–12).

17. "Þan he cownseld hir to gon to a good man whech had ben mech conuersawnt wyth hym þat wrot fyrst þe booke, supposyng þat he schuld cun best rede þe booke, for he had sum-tym red letters of þe oþer mannys wrytyng sent fro be-ȝonden þe see whyl he was in Dewchland" (4:29–34).

18. For references supporting Margery's son as the first scribe, see Liz Herbert McAvoy, *Authority and the Female Body in the Writings of Julian of Norwich and Margery Kempe*, Studies in Medieval Mysticism 5 (Cambridge: D. S. Brewer, 2004), 33n19. For the writing as a possible "merchant's script," see Watson, "The Making of *The Book of Margery Kempe*," 398; for the timeline when the son must have written down the *Book*, see ibid., 398–400.

decipher very bad handwriting, we must realize that the scribe also states that the text is neither good English nor good German; the language, not just the letters, are confusing.[19] The exact nature of the problem is not entirely clear, but the scribe wishes to present this episode as a miracle to authorize the writing of her text. What is clear is that Margery's prayers "purchase grace" for the priest to be able to read the book; trusting in her prayers, suddenly he is able to read the unintelligible text and understand it, in effect to translate it back into good English for Margery and her future readers. This miraculous reading encourages the text to be written and encourages the cleric (and therefore the text's future audiences as well) to believe Margery's claims that Christ has commanded her to compose the text.[20] Margery in turn is able to have her words copied down firsthand by a clerical witness, thereby lending her written visions a certain ecclesiastical acceptance and authority.

This miracle appears to be modeled on the experiences of xenoglossia that are described in other late medieval hagiographic and visionary texts. On the simplest level, the priest experiences a miracle involving the translation and comprehension of reading. Because the gift is a divinely aided reading ability that allows him to have access to a divinely inspired or holy text, the priest's gift is therefore similar to the gifts of Angelo Clareno (who is enabled to read Greek) and those of holy women like SS. Bridget of Sweden and Catherine of Siena (who are granted gifts of miraculous Latinity that are used in part for the purpose of reading).[21] The miraculous ability experienced by the priest, however, does not allow to him to read the learned languages of Greek and Latin (the latter of which he already knows) but rather grants him the ability to read a strange hybrid vernacular, permitting him access to and correction of what he will come to regard as divinely inspired mystical conversations.

---

19. Rosalynn Voaden, "God's Almighty Hand: Women Co-Writing the *Book*," 55–65, in *Women, the Book, and the Godly: Selected Proceedings of the St. Hilda's Conference, 1993*, ed. Lesley Smith and Jane H. M. Taylor, vol. 1 (Cambridge: D. S. Brewer, 1995). For example, in "God's Almighty Hand," Voaden states, "Margery Kempe's second scribe became convinced that his task was pleasing to God when he was miraculously enabled to read the handwriting of her original scribe" (63). Lochrie describes how Margery's intercession (and the priest's faith in God's grace) allows the priest to read the "idiosyncratic script" of the first scribe's text. Lochrie asserts "Not only did it [the text] suffer from a mutilated syntax and grammar, but it was incomprehensible at the level of the letters. The 'evilly' written letters with their queer shapes must have wreaked havoc with the most basic level of language, that is, the literal meaning" (100). Spearing calls this incident one of the first scribe "forgetting his native language." "*The Book of Margery Kempe*," 625. Stokes deemphasizes the miraculous by stating that the second amanuensis is able to read the text "with Margery Kempe's help." "Margery Kempe: Her Life," 40.

20. See Voaden's discussion of the "divine call-to-write" of women visionary writers in "God's Almighty Hand."

21. For Angelo Clareno, Bridget of Sweden, and Catherine of Siena, see Chapter 2.

His xenoglossia, therefore, presents a kind of reversal of the gift of the languages of Scripture: rather than being granted a learned, clerical language, the cleric is endowed with the grace to read a strange mutant vernacular, a hybrid tongue that no "fully literate" man would write.[22] The scribe is thus quite similar to St. Vincent Ferrer, who was given the gift of xenoglossia to help Breton-speaking women and children, those made particularly linguistically vulnerable by their isolation.[23] In effect, the priest needs grace to access and assess the divine words that have been obscured by another mediator and to read a transcription of something so "orally" vernacular that it is utterly incomprehensible.

The second scribe's assertion of this miraculous event has much in common with assertions made by other clerical amanuenses regarding their female visionary subjects. Indeed, the *Book*'s account of this episode seems to be modeled on those instances in which the scribes/priests/confessors of women visionaries claim that the women have experienced miraculous gifts of language, as a way of proclaiming the holiness, authenticity, and authority of the women's voices as bearers of the Divine Word. For example, as described in Chapter 2, Umiltà of Faenza, Elisabeth of Schönau, and Hildegard of Bingen all were said to experience gifts of speaking or writing Latin to compose (or have composed) their visionary texts.

Rather than receiving a Latinate gift, however, Margery's gift is a vernacular one, for her "dalliances" occur in English and are not intended to be translated into Latin. There is, moreover, another striking difference, for the scribe claims for *himself* the experience of the miracle, as brought about through the efficacy of Margery's prayers. Instead of claiming a miracle of language experienced by Margery when she receives the visions from Christ, her scribe locates the moment of miraculous translation as occurring when she seeks to have them recorded. In other words, because of the complex circumstances of the *Book*'s composition, he displaces the timing of the miracle from the oral reception of the divine visions onto the actual writing of them, thereby shifting the experience of the miraculous from visionary to amanuensis.[24] In effect, Margery becomes the miraculous translation receiver of her own text.

22. For a discussion of Margery's use of expert and inexpert scribes and the orality of the first scribe's draft, see Glenn, "Popular Literacy in the Middle Ages," 62.

23. For Vincent Ferrer, see Chapter 1.

24. Lochrie argues, "It is only through Kempe's intercession and his reliance on God's grace that his eyesight is repaired. More importantly, his ability to read, and hence to write, has been brought about through Kempe's interdiction, that is, her insertion of her own voice between text and reader. This interdiction becomes her authorizing practice, which not only inaugurates the

It is also striking how the scribe chooses to rewrite the proem to bring out the miraculous quality of the text's creation. Perhaps over the course of writing the book, the priest learned to interpret the event as miraculous; the more he was convinced of Margery's veracity and blessedness, the more he interpreted his sudden ability to read the unreadable hybrid language as a miraculous moment. Although the priest is in part convinced of Margery's holiness by this event, he will still need further proofs that her experiences are divinely inspired, which he will discover by reading other accounts of female visionaries, including the vitae of Marie d'Oignies and Elizabeth of Hungary.[25] As the priest's doubts are silenced by recourse to these more accepted religious models, the audience's doubts are meant to be silenced as well.[26]

"An alien to understand her": Margery's Gift of Vernacular Xenoglossia in Rome

This miracle of xenoglossia that allows the text to be written is not the only example of xenoglossia shared with a priest in the *Book*. Margery's experiences xenoglossia with a priest in Rome whom she seeks out and petitions to listen to her visions and holy dalliances, when she cannot find an English-speaking priest willing to confess her. Through an interpreter, Margery approaches a high-ranking cleric in St. John Lateran, a German priest (later identified as Wenslawe) who knows no English. She encourages him to pray with her for the grace to understand her speech. After thirteen days of prayer, the priest is miraculously able to understand Margery's English (although he can understand no one else's), and she is able to understand him. Confronted by rumors that she is engaging in fraudulent confession, Margery arranges to display the miracle in front of a prominent English cleric, who witnesses the translation of Margery's English "sermon" by the German priest into Latin. By under-

---

book but resurfaces in the text whenever the scribe (or reader) loses faith in her authority." Lochrie, *Margery Kempe and Translations of the Flesh*, 100.

  25. The priest doubts Margery on several occasions. In *Secretaries of God: Women Prophets in Late Medieval and Early Modern England* (Cambridge: D. S. Brewer, 1997), Diane Watt argues, "On each occasion the scribe describes the resolution of doubts which he has felt concerning Kempe's piety and her devotions and thus confirms the validity of her sanctity and religious practices" (17). According to Watt, Margery's scribe's doubt (and later confidence) is similar to that experienced by Geoffrey of St. Albans, author of the vita of Christina of Markyate (29–30). See also Roger Ellis, "Margery Kempe's Scribe and the Miraculous Books," in *Langland, the Mystics and the Medieval English Religious Tradition: Essays in Honour of S. S. Hussey*, ed. Helen Phillips (Cambridge: D. S. Brewer, 1990), 161–75, for a discussion of how the scribe "finds support for Margery's tears and loud sobbings" in books (162). See also Janette Dillon, Margery Kempe's Sharp Confessor/s," *Leeds Studies in English* 27 (1996): 131–38.

  26. As Staley argues, "Taken together, the two proems serve to emphasize the authority of the record they introduce." *Margery Kempe's Dissenting Fictions*, 31.

standing Margery's account of xenoglossia in the context of the miraculous experiences of holy men and women discussed in earlier chapters, we can see more clearly how Kempe and her scribe are modeling both the text and Margery's behavior on patterns of late medieval sacred biography, while adapting them in ways that demonstrate Margery's desire for clerical support and access to confession, as well as Kempe's desire to regulate Margery's own reception as a visionary authority.

The xenoglossic miracle occurs when Margery first approaches the German priest through an interpreter. With Margery's encouragement, direction, and prayer (as well as the prayers of the priest's "friends"), Wenslawe prays and receives what Staley has called "a sort of Pentecostal gift";[27] he is able to understand her English, and she is able to understand him:

> Þan þe preste vndirstod non Englysch ne wist not what sche seyd, & sche cowde non oþer langage þan Englisch, & þerfor þei spokyn be an jnterpretowr, a man þat telde her eyþyr what oþer seyde. Than sche preyd þe preste in þe name of Ihesu þat he wolde makyn hys preyeris to þe blysful Trinite, to owir Lady, & to alle þe blissed seyntys in Hevyn, also steryn oþer þat louedyn owir Lord to preyn for hym, þat he myth han grace to vndirstondyn hir langage & hir speche in swech thyngys as sche thorw þe grace of God wold seyn & schewyn vn-to hym. . . . Þus þei preyd therten day[s]. & aftyr therten days þe preste cam a-geyn to hir to preuyn þe effect of her preyerys, & þan he vndirstod what sche seyd in Englysch to hym & sche vndirstod what þat he seyd. & ȝet he vndirstod not Englisch þat oþer men spokyn; þow þei spokyn þe same wordys þat sche spak, ȝet he vndirstod hem not les þan sche spak hir-selfe. (82.16–83.7)

Once the miracle has been granted, Margery confesses to Wenslawe and then shows him "þe secret thyngys of reuelacyonys & of hey contemplacyons" (83.11–12). The miraculous gift of translation ensures that Margery can speak and be heard, both for the purpose of confession, which is of such vital importance to her, and for the relation and discernment of her visions.[28]

There are several ways to explain this event without recourse to the mirac-

27. Ibid., 111.

28. The importance of confession to Margery has often been repeatedly observed in scholarship. Bowers see Margery's problems at the start of the book arising from her unconfessed sin and also arising "from her confessor, whose bullying silences her and triggers her descent into madness." "Margery Kempe as Traveler," 11. In many ways, this early scene is answered by what she experiences in Rome with Wenslawe.

ulous. Charity Scott Stokes has suggested that this account could reflect a degree of linguistic understanding on Margery's behalf, encouraged by trade between the English of East Anglia and the German spoken on the Frisian and Baltic Coast.[29] The account could also reflect actual mundane language learning, for it takes almost two weeks for the miracle to be experienced. In this time certainly Margery and the priest could have learned something of each other's language, especially if each was simply passively understanding the other's tongue and not having to speak or produce that language. In addition, the rather unmiraculous quality of the event might also be attributed to Kempe and her scribe's conscious patterning of the *Book* on saints' lives. If they were aware that hagiographic literature described women's xenoglossic experiences as quite limited in scope, Kempe and the scribe might have hoped to replicate that quality in the *Book* in an attempt to authenticate it.

Margery and Wenslawe's miracle of xenoglossia owes much to the models described in the first two chapters of this study. The miracle is shared privately between two people and experienced when one woman in need approaches a respected religious spiritual authority for advising. In this way, the miracle resembles that of the gifts of French attributed to SS. Lutgard of Aywières and Clare of Montefalco,[30] when they were approached by a despairing woman and a pious pilgrim, respectively, in their convents; Margery, herself a pious pilgrim in desperate need of confession and clerical support, desires the miracle so that she can tell Wenslawe of her visions and contemplations. As the miraculous translation is granted to both Wenslawe and Margery to facilitate pious conversation while on pilgrimage, the gift also shares some similarities with the xenoglossia experienced by St. Dominic and his companion Bertrand, who receive the gift of German to engage in spiritual conversation with German pilgrims over the course of several days.[31]

Because the miracle is one that is initiated by a pressing need for confession, it also resembles that experienced by St. Bridget of Sweden to pass on Christ's words to a desperate Finnish pilgrim in Rome, or more closely, that

---

29. Stokes argues, "From the account given of an occasion when the mutual understanding was tested by others, it seems that the pious dialogue was highly predictable on both sides. However, it is possible that the trade links between Lynn and the Baltic enabled the trading families of Lynn to achieve an understanding at least of the German spoken along the Frisian and Baltic coast not shared by speakers from other places and backgrounds. The fact that the first amanuensis of Margery Kempe's book, an English man who had spent many years in the Baltic lands, was said to write neither good German not good English (4/14–16) suggests that a fair degree of contamination, and presumably also of mutual understanding, could come about between the Germanic dialects of Norfolk and the Baltic." "Margery Kempe: Her Life," 33–34.

30. For Lutgard of Aywières and Clare of Montefalco, see Chapter 1.

31. For Dominic, see Chapter 1.

experienced by St. Pachomius, who prayed to God to be able to speak with and hear the confession of a monk whose language he did not understand.[32] There are some significant differences, however, between the xenoglossia experienced by Pachomius and by Wenslawe and Margery. First, there is the obvious difference in the amount of time and prayer it takes to receive the miracle. For Pachomius, it took just three hours of his own private prayer for him to learn all the languages of the world; for Margery and Wenslawe (who were aided by the prayer of their friends), it took almost two weeks. The length of time needed for the prayers to be answered has the effect of undermining the miraculous quality of it, for it is about as mundane or "nonmiraculous" as the gift of tongues can be; it could certainly be argued that in two weeks Margery could have learned some German, and Wenslawe some English. So why does the *Book* describe the miracle in this way, instead of as a sudden ability to speak another language? Certainly, no other saint's life describes a holy person needing to pray for so long before receiving a gift of vernacular xenoglossia.

However, as I discussed in the previous chapter, women saints are not always infused with Latin immediately; on occasion their gift is a drastic shortening of their lengthy study of Latin, as in the example of St. Bridget of Sweden who learned Latin rapidly under the tutelage of St. Agnes, or Christine of Stommeln, who learned her Psalter in seven weeks with divine aid. Margery could, therefore, have stories such as these in mind; two weeks of prayer to "learn" to understand each other in a vernacular tongue, therefore, would be quite short in comparison to learning Latin. In addition, although it is tempting to understand the length of time as a truth claim ensuring the *Book*'s accuracy (and that Kempe and her scribe do not exaggerate), there could be another explanation. It could also demonstrate how important a miracle this actually is, by showing that a very high-ranking priest is willing to spend almost two weeks seeking a way to communicate with Margery, and that he recognizes the value of his serving as her translation receiver.

The agency in this miracle account is also at stake. No other holy woman prays for the miracle of vernacular xenoglossia for herself or for a companion; a number of male saints, however, do pray for and receive the gift, both for themselves and for their other companions. Many holy women, however, do

---

32. For Bridget's account of possible Finnish xenoglossia, see Chapter 1. Although this episode does not appear in the extant Middle English *Revelations*, it is included in a number of Latin manuscripts. The similarity between Margery's experience of xenoglossia and that of Bridget's has been noted by Cleve, "Margery Kempe: A Scandinavian Influence," 169. For Pachomius, see Chapter 1.

pray to the Lord for Latinate gifts so that they can enter convents or understand scriptural and devotional texts. What could be interpreted as Margery's boldness and even presumption in praying for the vernacular miracle (a gift for which only renowned male saints ask) can therefore be understood as less presumptuous or perhaps even to be expected, if we see her prayers as being influenced by accounts of holy women requesting Latinate gifts.

Perhaps the most significant difference between this episode and descriptions of vernacular xenoglossia in later medieval saints' lives is that the miracle in the *Book* is a shared one. Both Margery and the cleric receive the presumably aural ability to understand the other (or to be understood by the other); everyone else is excluded from the gift. Whereas Pachomius is able to understand all the languages of the earth to aid as many of his followers as possible, in Margery and Wenslawe's case, the shared experience takes place on a more intimate level because they are only able to understand each other. Margery repeatedly emphasizes that Wenslawe is able to understand *her* alone, but she does not elaborate on her ability to understand him; she therefore concentrates on his reception of her words, and not vice versa. Just how Margery understands the priest is not explained: does he speak in German and she is able understand his language, or does he miraculously speak in English? (She is careful to assert, however, that she does not understand the German of others.)[33] Margery does not describe or ever mention again her own comprehension of Wenslawe, because what she gains from listening to him is not nearly as important as what he does for her; the priest who "had on of þe grettest office of any preste in Rome" (82.29–30) listens to Margery's visions and serves as a very prominent witness to her grace. In fact, she refers more often to this miracle than to any other single miracle in the text, thereby relying on it to make an important claim supporting her divine inspiration.

This sharing of the miracle is quite significant. In other hagiographic examples of vernacular xenoglossia, the saint (or his/her companions) receives the miracle in order to understand or be understood in situations of pressing need. To have both the seeker and the sought after (Margery and Wenslawe) pray for the miracle and to receive it indicates how necessary Wenslawe's words are to Margery, even though she does not elaborate upon what he says. Clerical witnesses are of the utmost importance in the *Book*, as Margery repeatedly seeks them out in order to have them support and pronounce upon the value of her words. Indeed, the *Book* appears quite defensive in

---

33. While in Rome after having experienced the miracle with Wenslawe, Margery bemoans her inability to understand some German-speaking preachers. When Margery visits the chapel of St. Bridget, however, it is not clear how she understands the preaching of a German priest.

this way, repeatedly emphasizing the support of clerics throughout.[34] Margery needs the clerics to share, to witness, and to pronounce the blessedness of her experiences. Kempe, therefore, is careful to describe how Margery approaches Wenslawe but then how *he* prays for the miracle, and how *he* is granted the ability to understand her.

The miracle becomes the center of an episode recounted several chapters later, when Margery returns to her experience of miraculous translation, in what amounts to a "trial" scene in which other clerics and pilgrims witness and proclaim the validity of the miracle. This episode is even more explicit in its description of Margery's desire for access to religious practice (in particular, her access to devout conversation with other clerics) and to correct how she has been received by unsupportive clerics and pilgrims. Through Wenslawe's translation of Margery's words, the visionary is able to sidestep Paul's injunction against women preaching and actually preach a sermon in Latin in front of an audience of clerics and other pilgrims. Margery triumphantly shows off the miracle for the glory of God and has her words translated into Latin, proving herself before her judges as being the recipient of a Pentecostal miracle and providing her miraculous experience with prominent clerical witnesses.

When an English priest confronts Margery with the rumor that she is being confessed by a priest who cannot understand her language, Margery organizes a dinner "trial" in which the English priest and his companions can observe the miracle. The *Book* develops the scene in some detail, describing how the English priest purposefully speaks in English to his companions and Margery to test whether Wenslawe can understand him:[35]

> At þe last, þe seyd creatur, seyng & wel vndirstondyng þat hir confessowr vndirstod not her langage & þat was tediows to hym, þan, in party to comfort hym & in party er ellys meche mor to preuyn þe werk of God, sche telde in hyr owyn langage in Englysch a story of Holy Writte whech sche had lernyd of clerkys whil sche was at hom

34. For the importance of clerical witnessing in the *Book*, see Dillon, "Margery Kempe's Sharp Confessor/s," and Dillon, "Holy Women and Their Confessors or Confessors and Their Holy Women? Margery Kempe and Continental Tradition," in *Prophets Abroad*, ed. Rosalynn Voaden (Cambridge: D. S. Brewer), 115–40. See also John W. Coakley, *Women, Men, and Spiritual Power: Female Saints and Their Male Collaborators* (New York: Columbia University Press, 2006).

35. "Þe Duche preste, a worthy clerke as is wretyn be-forn, confessowr to þe seyd creatur, satt al stille in a maner of heuynes for cawse he vndirstod not what þei seyden in Englysch les þan þei spokyn Latyn. & þei dede it in purpose, hys vnwetyng, to preuyn ȝyf he vndirstod Englysch er not" (97:24–29). I quote the scene in full in order to demonstrate the overly repetitive nature of the references to language.

in Inglond, for sche wolde spekyn of no vanyte ne of no fantasijs.
Than þei askyd hir confessowr ȝyf he vndirstod þat sche had seyd, &
he a-non in Latyn telde hem þe same wordys at sche seyd be-forn in
Englisch, for he cowde neyþyr speke Englysch ne vndirstondyn Englisch saue only aftyr hir tunge. & þan þei had gret meruayle, for þei
wist wel þat he vndirstod what sche seyd & sche vndirstod what he
seyd, & he cowde vndirstonde non oþer Englysch-man, so blyssed
mote God ben þat mad an alyon to vndirstondyn hir whan hir owyn
cuntre-men had forsakyn hir & wolde not heryn hir confessyon les
þan sche wolde a left hir wepyng & spekying of holynes. (97.29–98.9)

Margery's private miracle of confession and translation now takes on a public,
performative aspect. It has a clerical and lay audience who marvel at its miraculous quality, so Margery conveniently does not need to proclaim it as a
miracle herself. This miracle of translation, which earlier appeared like the
more private miracles of SS. Pachomius, Dominic, Clare of Montefalco, and
Lutgard of Aywières, now resembles public manifestations of xenoglossia experienced by popular preachers like SS. Vincent Ferrer and Norbert, the
founder of the Premonstratensians, albeit on a much smaller scale.[36] In effect,
the translation miracle allows Margery to preach openly to clerics and to pilgrims who previously would not have listened to her, while at the same time
refuting the slander of her fellow English pilgrims.

Essentially, Margery's words are translated into Latin through the benefit
of a miracle; even though the miraculous translation actually occurs between
German and English and Wenslawe translates with his own traditionally acquired clerical Latinity, the result is the same. The vernacular gift is transformed into a gift of Latinity (albeit experienced second hand) and therefore
shares something significant with the miraculous gifts of Latinity experienced
by holy women, as described in Chapter 2. Enabled by xenoglossia, Margery
is able to preach a story of Holy Writ in Latin to her clerical and lay dinner
companions. Thus she is able to take her place by the clerics at the table and to
take part in learned Latin discourse while still maintaining her wholly illiterate
stance. Through the tongue of Wenslawe, Margery speaks not the heretical
words of a Lollard but rather the orthodox Latin words of a highly respected
priest.[37]

36. For Norbert, see Chapter 1.
37. Much has been written about how Margery engages in public preaching and "speaking
openly," despite the Pauline injunction against women preaching. See Michael J. Wright, "What
They Said to Margery Kempe: Narrative Reliability in Her *Book*," *Neophilologus* 79 (1995): 497–

That Margery herself arranges this display of her xenoglossia for her own vindication (as well as to comfort Wenslawe) is yet another difference between her experience and that of more renowned holy women, for no other holy women needs to prove her vernacular miracle in such a way. However, several medieval women who receive gifts of Latin, like SS. Catherine of Siena and Bridget of Sweden, have their gift of language tested and examined quite closely by clerics.[38] In this way, Margery is enacting a scene perhaps inspired by Bridget, whom she venerates and imitates. Just as Bridget's Swedish words that she received from the Lord were translated into Latin by her confessors for wide dissemination, Margery's English words that she learned from a priest are translated by her confessor into Latin publicly, albeit for a somewhat smaller audience. We are not told, however, how Margery checks Wenslawe's translation to make certain that it is accurate.

What stands out in this episode is how conscious the *Book* is to prove this is a miracle. Interestingly, it is not clear whether Wenslawe himself decides to prove the miracle by speaking in Latin to the clerics, or whether Margery encourages him to do so. That the narrative also does not explain *how* Margery knows exactly what Wenslawe said in Latin emphasizes that either Margery could but does not want to claim a gift of miraculous Latin understanding at this moment or, more likely, that mundane translation has taken a "back seat" to the miraculous, as the clerics who formerly criticized her now are forced to become her translation receivers and users and repeat back to Margery her own words. This transformative moment exposes Margery's problematic and confusing linguistic agency. It allows her to maintain her complete illiteracy while effectively preaching a Latin didactic tale from Scripture; her use of Wenslawe emphasizes that she does not need a gift of Latinity directly, since priests can stand in for her.

In sum, this scene is brilliant because it shows Kempe adapting what is a miracle of Latinity once-removed (Margery speaking a story of "Holy Writ," i.e., Scripture in Latin, via Wenslawe) that proclaims Margery's divine favor, offers clerical witnesses to her miracle, vindicates herself to those who have doubts, and justifies her seeking out a confessor, while at the same time protecting her from any allegations or suspicions of Lollard preaching or literate ability on her part. The translation of her story of Scripture into Latin, via the

---

508, in which he claims that Margery "touch[es] upon the masculine preserve of preaching without actually transgressing the threshold" (504). See also Sandra McEntire, "The Dialogics of Margery Kempe and Her *Book*," *Mystics Quarterly* 26 (2000): 179–97, esp. 190, and Lochrie, *Margery Kempe and Translations of the Flesh*, 107.

38. For Catherine of Siena, see Chapter 2.

German priest, links Margery with the tradition of holy women who receive miraculous Latinity, as well as bringing her as close as possible to a miracle of xenoglossic preaching.[39] Thus, while clearly being modeled on those accounts described in the earlier chapters, the *Book's* episodes of miraculous translation demonstrate significant adaptations fitted to Margery's particularly difficult circumstances.

The two experiences of xenoglossia that Margery shares with priests—the creation of her text and her conversations with Wenslawe—are included in the *Book* because they are important moments of clerical witnessing of her grace, for they feature clerics who receive the gift of miraculous translation to aid Margery in the expression of her visions. Two desires are satisfied by the experiences of miraculous translation described in the *Book*. First, the mira-- cles speak to Margery's intense need and desire to submit herself to clerical control and receive clerical support for her visionary experience, a support that she seeks out constantly, both at home in England and abroad on pilgrimage. The tension between the desire for clerical support, and the need to seek a "higher" or divine support when the clerical support fails, is at the center of the episodes of miraculous translation included in the *Book*. When Margery complains that she cannot understand the teachings of the German-speaking priests in Rome, Christ tells her that he will teach her himself. After Margery has been forced out of the Hospice in Rome and unable to find another English-speaking confessor, the Lord sends St. John the Evangelist himself to hear her confession. Still, Margery in no way abandons, or is encouraged to wholly abandon, the authority of clerics. The Lord instead works through the clerics in order to accommodate Margery's needs. He grants the second scribe the miraculous ability to read the first scribe's incomprehensible text and grants the German priest and Margery the ability to understand one another's language. In this way, the miracle of xenoglossia, while initiated by clerical negligence (both the second scribe and her original English-speaking confessor in Rome are influenced by evil slander), actually reinscribes clerical authority, for the Lord grants these clerics the seemingly impossible, thus enabling Margery's needs to be fulfilled by them alone.

39. As Furrow points out, the audience in this trial scene sees that Margery understands what the priest says when he translates her words into Latin; Furrow argues that this is because Latin is the language in which Wenslawe speaks to Margery. Furrow, "Unscholarly Latinity," 247–49. Furrow states that the only way she would have been able to understand him was if her ability were miraculous, or "the language was not as exclusive and written as its reputation suggests" (249). While I do believe the *Book* intends this episode to be understood as a vernacular xenoglossic miracle, Furrow's suggestion that Margery is able to understand the priest's Latin translation is a valuable one, as it might indicate that Margery is claiming an ability to understand his Latin miraculously.

Kempe and her scribe use the model of xenoglossia to make an argument about Margery's blessedness and her dependence on clerics. There is, however, a startling difference between Margery's claims of xenoglossia and those in women's vitae discussed in the previous chapters. Although Margery does demonstrate on several occasions that she has been gifted with *sapientia* or divinely infused "deep" scriptural understanding (indeed, a number of clerics admire her deep understanding and claim that it is better than their own), unlike other holy women's vitae, the *Book* never mentions that the gift of infused understanding offers her any kind of miraculous Latin literacy. Certainly, a gift of Latin literacy of some sort, however limited, might almost be expected when a later medieval holy woman was granted a gift of infused scriptural understanding—we would assume, therefore, that Margery would display the ability on occasion to read the Gospels or the Psalms or to speak inspired words in Latin. However, the absence of miraculous literacy, in a text that is consciously patterned so heavily on the religious experiences found in later medieval vitae, is quite striking.

There are two possible reasons Kempe and her scribe do not claim any kind of gift of miraculous Latin literacy for Margery. The first is because demonstrating an ability to read and understand Latin Scripture as a fifteenth-century English laywoman would link Margery even more closely with the Lollards, an association she denies in the *Book*.[40] With the passing of Arundel's *Constitutions* in 1409, English clerics attempted to reestablish or maintain their control over Latin scriptural translation and interpretation. According to the *Constitutions*, the laity were not supposed to translate the Bible for themselves, or even to possess (without permission) a text of Scripture translated after the time of Wycliffe.[41] Because Kempe was composing her text at

40. For a consideration of Margery Kempe's relationship to Lollardy, see, for example, McAvoy, *Authority and the Female Body*, 179–85, and John H. Arnold, "Margery's Trials: Heresy, Lollardy and Dissent," in *A Companion to The Book of Margery Kempe*, ed. John H. Arnold and Katherine J. Lewis (Cambridge: D. S. Brewer, 2004), 75–93.

41. See Nicholas Watson, "Censorship and Cultural Change in Late-Medieval England: Vernacular Theology, the Oxford Translation Debate, and Arundel's Constitutions of 1409," *Speculum* 70 (1995): 822–64, for a discussion of the effect of the Constitutions on fifteenth-century Middle English devotional writings. "Article 7: Item, It is a dangerous thing, as witnesseth blessed St. Jerome, to translate the text of the holy Scripture out of the tongue into another; for in the translation the same sense is not always easily kept, as the same St. Jerome confessith, that although he were inspired, yet oftentimes in this he erred: we therefore decree and ordain, that no man, hereafter, by his own authority translate any text of the Scripture into English or any other tongue, by way of a book, libel or treatise; and that no man read any such book, libel or treatise, now lately set forth in the time of John Wickliff, or since, or hereafter to be set forth, in part or in whole, privily or apertly, upon pain of greater excommunication, until the said translation be allowed by the ordinary of the place, or, if the case so require, by the council provincial.

a time when knowing Latin could have furthered suspicions of Margery's involvement with Lollardy and spark even greater threats of persecution, she takes great pains to demonstrate that Margery's divinely infused knowledge does not afford her any kind of miraculous literacy.

This helps to explain Margery's confusing literacy, which has been remarked on by many scholars. Margery has a very fine line to walk. On the one hand, she insists that she is divinely inspired and has a deep understanding of scriptural texts and theological and doctrinal issues that rivals or surpasses the learning of clerics. On the other hand, to avoid Margery being labeled a Lollard, the *Book* must insist that her knowledge is completely vernacular and not gained from reading or study.[42] Because she lives "in the world" and not in the convent, and she is not recognized by many as a holy or even pious figure, if Margery were to have a gift of Latinity she would appear much more like an English version of the girl from Nivelles possessed by the devil than an English version of SS. Lutgard of Aywières or Bridget of Sweden.[43]

The second reason the *Book* does not mention a gift of miraculous Latin literacy is because Margery is firmly "in the world" and therefore her translation experience (both miraculous and mundane) is a vernacular one as well. Her *Book* effectively argues that a gift of Latinity is not really necessary or even particularly desirable for Margery because her experience of the Lord is almost entirely in the vernacular. Because of this, Margery's accounts of mundane translation, that is, the everyday occurrences of interpretation that take place between different language speakers, become an important way of showing her to be divinely inspired. Throughout her pilgrimages Margery appears to experience mundane translation in an almost miraculous manner, for she reports that foreign-speaking people can understand her perfectly well, and at times she can understand them. Margery's efforts at mundane translation, therefore, break down any barriers between languages, and at times she appears almost to exist in a world miraculously restored to its pre-Babelian state.

He that shall do the contrary to this, shall likewise by punished as a favourer of error and heresy." John Foxe, *The Acts and Monuments of John Foxe*, ed. George Townsend, (New York: AMS Press, 1965), 3:245, quoted in Watson, "Censorship and Cultural Change," 828–29n15.

42. Even quoting Scripture in English could be dangerous; as Lochrie points out, "Kempe's efforts to authorize her own voice are thus very politicized and dangerous. . . . If she tries to quote Scriptures, she again incriminates herself, for Lollards were said to have been able to read English translations of the Bible." Lochrie, *Margery Kempe and Translations of the Flesh*, 108–9.

43. For the possessed girl from Nivelles in the *Life* of St. Norbert, see Chapter 2.

Part 2: "By signs and tokens and in few common words":
Margery Kempe and Mundane Translation

In addition to describing experiences of vernacular xenoglossia, Kempe's *Book* includes many examples of how Margery translates and is translated for in everyday situations that take place during her pilgrimages to Jerusalem, Italy, and Germany.[44] In this section, I examine Margery's linguistic activities while on pilgrimage and argue that the *Book* promotes moments of successful vernacular translation to show Margery as a divinely gifted channel of God's Word and to offer witnesses to this effect. Just as there is a strong sense in which the mundane pervades the miraculous in her xenoglossia, there is also a sense in which the miraculous pervades her mundane experiences, for Margery is too easily (indeed, at times perfectly) understood, just as she often understands those who speak other languages. The *Book*'s desire to shape Margery's representation and reception as a holy woman makes her translate the motives, words, and actions of those whom, practically speaking, she should not be able to understand. Kempe and her scribe therefore model Margery's experiences of mundane translation in part on the hagiographical descriptions of xenoglossia to emphasize that translation is both the medium and the message of God's grace.

This section focuses on three kinds of translational experiences while Margery is abroad on pilgrimage. First, Margery as translated by others; second, Margery's use of interpreters, and third, Margery translating for herself. As previously mentioned, Lynn Staley has argued that the many scenes in which Margery's blessedness and practices of roaring and crying are understood by those who do not speak English suggest that the author Kempe is constructing a larger, Christian community for the character Margery, a community that serves to critique both the English people and English institutions. Indeed, Staley remarks that Margery is always understood while abroad;[45] just how she is understood, however, is not at all clear. I shall therefore redirect the

---

44. Much recent scholarship has focused on Margery's pilgrimages. See, for example, Diane Watt, "Faith in the Landscape: Overseas Pilgrimages in *The Book of Margery Kempe*," in *A Place to Believe In: Locating Medieval Landscapes*, ed. Clare A. Lees and Gillian R. Overing (University Park: Pennsylvania State University Press, 2006), 170–87; Liliana Sikorska, "Between Penance and Purgatory: Margery Kempe's *Pèlegrinage de la vie Humaine* and the Idea of Salvaging Journeys," in *Beowulf and Beyond*, ed. Hans Sauer and Renate Bauer (Frankfurt: Peter Lang, 2007), 235–57; Naoë Kukita Yoshikawa, "Jerusalem Pilgrimage," 193–205, and Anthony Goodman, *Margery Kempe and Her World* (London: Longman, 2002), 152–74.

45. Staley, *Margery Kempe's Dissenting Fictions*, 151, 189.

discussion of Margery's mundane translation by examining exactly *how* Margery imagines she is understood and understands because the extent to which the *Book* interprets Margery's own reception has yet to be fully appreciated.

Margery as Translated Text

Because Margery is monolingual and traveling in foreign (and at times hostile) lands with heartless fellow countrymen who ostracize and even abandon her, she is a woman constantly in need of being "translated" and translated for. The *Book* repeatedly calls attention to this fact. For example, when she is abandoned by her English companions at Constance on her first pilgrimage, Margery is left in the temporary care of a kindly papal legate. The Lord then sends an old man named William Weaver to accompany her on the pilgrimage, but she is loath to leave the legate, for she sees two dangers arising from this situation: "Sche toke hir leue wyth ful heuy cher & rewful, hauyng gret heuynes in-as-meche as sche was in strawnge cuntre & cowde no langage ne þe man þat xuld ledyn hir neyþyr" (65.3–6). The precariousness of the situation, heightened by her reliance on this man she does not know, is exacerbated because she cannot understand the language of the country through which she is traveling. "To know" a companion and "to know" a language, while being two very different kinds of knowing, are intimately linked at this moment because the lack of each makes Margery particularly vulnerable as she does not know how William will both "interpret" her actions and interpret her words for her.

Margery's monolingualism and subsequent vulnerability while abroad present not only a physical threat but also a spiritual one, for they have the potential to limit her participation in pious activities. Margery desires direct access to religious sites, sermons, confessors, and most of all, the Lord. Exclusion from public forms of worship, in particular sermons, is exceedingly painful for her; indeed, the *Book* describes a number of occasions during which she is denied access to English churches or preachers because of her disruptive emotive responses. Margery also experiences this discomfort while abroad, when she is excluded from sermons and pious practices because she knows only English.

Margery's monolingualism, however, proves not as great a limitation as one might imagine, for reasons that are attributed both to the Lord and to Margery herself. First, Christ repeatedly ensures that his friends will aid her while she is abroad, even though they do not speak her language; and second, Margery is adept at noticing and translating other kinds of communication, including nonverbal "signs and tokens" (that is, gestures and body language), procuring translators and interpreters, and even on occasion translating for herself. The *Book* repeatedly directs attention to the almost miraculous way in which she is understood; hence, her efforts at mundane translation take on a miraculous sheen, for Christ helps to erase linguistic barriers on a number of occasions.

The *Book* imagines a Christ who appreciates Margery's linguistic vulnerability and responds directly to the needs of his messenger by supplying translators for her. Christ tells Margery that her purgatory will be the experience of others' language: "I haue be-hygth þe þat þu xuldyst noon oþer Purgatory han þan slawndyr & speche of þe world" (51.14–15), meaning of course the slander, gossip, and evil words spoken against her, but also, in the context of her pilgrimage, unknown, alienating, and potentially threatening foreign language.[46] Christ promises translation as a remedy for this purgatory, for he has friends throughout the world who will help her, friends who comfort and guide her despite her lack of knowledge of alien tongues.[47]

Kempe and her scribe emphasize how people care for Margery and seem to "understand her," despite the language barrier. For example, when Margery is traveling to Rome with Richard, they meet two Grey Friars and a woman accompanying an image of Christ. The *Book* describes how despite the language difference, they treat her exceedingly well: "& non of hem cowde vndirstand hir langage, & ȝet þei ordeyned for hir euery day mete, drynke, & herborwe as well as he dedyn for hem-selfe & raþar bettyr þat sche was euyr bownden to prey for hem" (77.25–28). On another occasion while Margery is residing in Rome, an Italian woman named Dame Margaret Florentyne invites Margery to eat with her every Sunday. Both women seem to understand each other despite their language differences; Margaret recognizes Margery's innate goodness and seats her in the high position at the table, and Margery can interpret her placement at the table above that of her host as a place of honor, one that indicates Margaret's respect: "Þan þe lady comawndyd hir to etyn wyth hir euery Sonday & set hir at hir owen tabil a-bouyn hir-self & leyd hir mete wyth hir owyn handys. Than thys creatur sat & wept ful sor, thankyng owr Lord þat sche was so cheryd & cherisched for hys lofe of hem þat cowd not vndirstond hir langage" (93.28–33).[48]

---

46. Julian also instructs Margery to "feryth not þe langage of þe world" (43:14).
47. Christ promises, "& þerfor drede þe not. I haue frendys in euery cuntre & xal make my frendys to comfort þe" (93:3–4).
48. For the contrast between Margaret's kind behavior and that of the English who are awful to Margery, see Bowers, "Margery Kempe as Traveler," 22.

In addition to showing how she is appreciated and cared for by others who do not speak her own language, Margery's experience of translation in Jerusalem both ensures access to religious practice when other Christians have failed her and offers witnesses to her divine favor by suggesting that Muslims recognize her innate blessedness. When Margery's English companions refuse to help her ascend Mount Quarantine to see where Christ fasted for forty days, she is able to communicate through signs and tokens (and a little money) with a Muslim who just happens by: "And a-non happyd a Saraȝyn, a welfaryng man, to comyn by hir, & sche put a grote in hys hand, making to hym a token for to bryng hir on-to þe Mownt" (74.13–16).[49] The *Book* seems to suggest that this man is one of "Christ's friends" who he promised would help Margery when all others forsake her. The *Book* emphasizes that several other Muslims almost miraculously understand Margery to be a blessed person, for the account describes how they "mad mych of hir & con-ueyd hir & leddyn hir abowtyn in þe cuntre wher sche wold gon" (75.15–16). The *Book* attributes their providing her access to the sites where she has such intense and moving experiences of Christ's life to their appreciation of Margery herself, for they "make much of her" and no further payment is mentioned.

At other times, when no one "happens by" to help, Margery's inability to translate and to understand and therefore to take part in pious practice is answered by Christ, who offers to serve as her own teacher/translator in English. Even after receiving the gift of vernacular xenoglossia in Rome so that Wenslawe and she can communicate, Margery still laments that she cannot understand other German priests who she hears preaching in other churches: "Svm-tyme, whan þe forseyd creatur was at sermownys wher Duchemen & oþer men prechyd, techyng þe lawys of God, sodeyn sorwe & heuynes ocupy-ing hir hert cawsyd hir to compleyn wyth mornyng cher for lak of vndirston-dyng" (98.17–22). Christ's answer to Margery's lamentation that she cannot understand foreign preachers is to promise that he will fulfill her desires him-self: "I xal preche þe & teche þe my-selfe" (98.26), he insists; Christ therefore promises to serve as Margery's own personal vernacular translator and tutor, in much the same way that Mary serves as a Latin tutor for several holy women who claim they cannot read Latin, as we saw in the second chapter.

Christ's offer to teach Margery in the vernacular is immediately followed by another instance of semimiraculous translation. After Christ makes his

---

49. According to Bowers, by including the scenes of kindly Muslims who respect Margery as a pious person, the *Book* purposely is attempting to make the cruel English Christians look even worse than they already do. "Margery Kempe as Traveler," 20–22.

offer, what he shows her is so marvelous that she experiences a fit of "gret wepyng & gret sobbyng" (98.31) of the sort that normally would bring scorn on her in England. The women who witness her crying in the church do not ostracize her; instead, despite their lack of a shared language, they comfort and protect her:

> Þan meche pepyl wonderyd up-on hir, askyng hir what sche eyled, to whom sche as a creatur al wowndyd wyth lofe & as reson had fayled, cryed wyth lowde voys, "þe Passyon of Crist sleth me." Þe good women, hauyng compassyon of hir sorwe & gretly meruelyng of hir wepyng & of hir crying, meche þe mor þei louyd hir. & þerfor þei, desiryng to make hir solas & comfort aftyr hir gostly labowr, be syngnys & tokenys, for sche vndirstod not her speche, preyid hir and in a maner compellyd hir to comyn hom to hem, willyng þat sche xulde not gon fro hem. (98.33–99.6)

At first glance, this seems like a straightforward example of what Staley argues as Margery and women in Europe communicating "by using a truly universal system of signs."[50] But this scene actually presents a somewhat baffling account of language, when we consider exactly what and how the *Book* reports those around her as comprehending. In effect, Kempe and the scribe appear to be attributing motives and words to the women so that the women serve as valuable witnesses of Margery's grace.[51]

A central question in this scene is in what language communication occurs. Margery receives her crying fit after listening to the incomprehensible sermons of German priests. "Many people" witnessing her fit ask her what ails her, and she answers back in English, "The Passion of Christ slays me"; presumably, she can understand their questions either because they are asked in English or because she can read the facial expressions, gestures, and vocal tones of the inquirers. They in turn are assumed to understand her English answer. The good women, however, whose language Margery does not understand (and presumably they do not understand her English) are said to "love her all the more" and have "great marveling" at her crying; the *Book* therefore "translates" their motives to complement Margery's own positive reading of herself, as she interprets that they "desired to make her solace and comfort her." Margery understands their signs and tokens as them wanting her to go

---

50. Staley, *Margery Kempe's Dissenting Fictions*, 151.
51. We can, as Wright has suggested, interpret statements and reactions differently from Margery. "What They Said to Margery Kempe," see esp. 497–504.

home with them, and we can only assume it is a correct interpretation for no other interpretation is offered.[52] It could be quite possible, however, that these women thought she had recently lost a loved one, or was suffering some kind of illness that required rest. Because all these interpretations that the *Book* reports are either translations of nonverbal acts or gestures, or perhaps facilitated by "invisible" interpreters or undisclosed interpretive mechanisms, the *Book* describes what appears to be almost a kind of miraculous translation, for the text imagines Margery to be able to communicate on a deep and spiritual level with others who do not necessarily speak English.

Margery and Her Interpreters

By exposing the role of Margery's interpreters, the *Book* attests to the extent of her efforts to seek out and receive approval for her visionary experiences. The presence of interpreters emphasizes that she is a vulnerable, monolingual woman insisting on access to translation and the control of that translation. In fact, the *Book* only mentions that Margery procures interpreters in those scenes in which it is very important that she express herself to another. The *Book* does not mention translation and the need for interpreters, however, when Margery's own words are not of the utmost importance. For example, the mechanics of translation are not addressed for most of Margery's day-to-day life in Rome, during her months of begging and aiding the impoverished. In these situations, Margery's actions and not her words are paramount, and therefore the *Book* does not include details about how communication occurs. When Margery is understood and understands without the means of an interpreter, we are left to wonder whether it is because of a kind of miraculous translation or, more likely, the rendering invisible of the interpreter.

The *Book* pays most attention to an interpreter when, having been initially thrown out of the Hospice of St. Thomas of Canterbury because of accusations of slander, Margery must ask Richard to approach a priest of a church quite close to the Hospice, to ask him to serve as her confessor so that she can receive communion. The *Book* describes how Margery directs Richard to approach the priest at St. Catherine's and to inform him of her character and current plight. What is immediately striking is that the description is quite specific about both what she instructs Richard to say to the priest and how he

52. The *Middle English Dictionary* defines *token* as, among other things, "an action intended to figure a concept, condition, etc; also, an action intended to suggest a state of affairs" (def. 1b) or "a visible indicator of an inward state" (3a), as well as a "significant bodily motion" or "gesture" (5). A *signe* can also be defined as a "significant bodily movement" or "gesture" (3).

carries out her instructions, for the *Book* insists on repeating exactly what the interpreter tells the priest, although there is no way that Margery herself could have known what was being said:

> & sithyn sche clepyd on-to hir þe forseyd Richard wyth þe broke bak, preyng hym to go ouyr to a cherch a-ȝen þe Hospital & enformyn þe person of þe chyrche of hir maner of gouernawnce, & what sorwe sche had, & how sche wept for sche myth not be schrevyn ne how-selyd, & what compunccyon and contricyon sche had for hir synnes. Than Richard went to þe person & enformyd hym of þis creatur, & how owyr Lord ȝaf hir contricyon & compunccyon wyth gret plente of teerys, & how sche desired to be howseld euery Sonday ȝyf sche myth & sche had no preste to be schrevyn to. And þan þe person, heryng of hir contricyon and compunccyon, was ryth glad & bad sche xulde come to hym in þe name [o]f Ihesu & sey hir Confiteor, & he xulde howseln hire hys owyn self, for he cowde not vndyrstond non Englysch. (80.26–81.3)

The priest cannot understand any English, so presumably Richard (or perhaps even an "invisible" interpreter for Richard) must translate into the priest's language. Curiously, the *Book* includes both what Margery tells Richard to say, as well as exactly what Richard says to the priest. The specific information that Richard is reporting as relating to the priest responds exactly to and even amplifies those points that Margery has instructed him to say, even to the extent of including similar phraseology such as "contrition and compunction." There are two specific additions: one is the frequency of her desire to receive the sacraments (every Sunday), the other, the elaboration of her sorrow as a "great plenty of tears." Then, the *Book* reports, the priest "hearing of her contrition and compunction," or in other words, not just hearing but also taking heed, agrees to listen to her *Confiteor*.

Richard's position as intermediary and translator is of such prominence in this scene because he serves as yet another outside witness attesting to Margery's goodness, this time to a non-English-speaking cleric to whom she desires to confess. The insistence on including exactly what the interpreter says and how the priest receives and understands it points to Kempe and the scribe's desire to control exactly how Margery is being interpreted by her internal and external audiences. Since Margery could not logically have known exactly what Richard reported to the priest (unless a second interpreter stood by, translating Richard's words to the priest into English for

Margery's benefit), the *Book* includes this repetition in an effort to shape the response of both the priest and the *Book*'s audience. Margery's efforts at translation are ultimately rewarded with St. John coming to confess her himself, since the priest cannot.

The need for and reliance on an interpreter is what propels Margery to seek the gift of xenoglossia. After being confessed by St. John, Margery asks Richard to approach another priest, the German Wenslawe, to be her new confessor. This scene appears to involve two interpreters: first Richard, who requests that Wenslawe speak with Margery, and then another nameless interpreter who aids Margery's direct communication with the German priest. The *Book* states,

> þan sche preyd hir man wyth þe brokyn bak for to gon to þe preste & preyn hym to spekyn wyth hir. Þan þe preste vndirstod non Englysch ne wist not what sche seyd, & sche cowde non oþer langage þan Englisch, & þerfor þei spokyn be an jnterpretowr, a man þat telde her eyþyr what oþer seyde. Than sche preyd þe preste in þe name of Ihesu þat he wolde makyn his preyeris to þe blysful Trinite, to owir Lady, & to all þe blissed seyntys in Hevyn, also steryn oþer þat louedyn owir Lord to preyn for hym, þat he myth han grace to vndir-stondyn hir langage & hir speche in sweche thyngys as sche thorw þe grace of God wold seyn & schewyn vn-to hym. (82.14–26)

Both Richard and the interpreter drop out of the scene immediately after Margery meets Wenslawe. Obviously dissatisfied with this arrangement of approaching the high-ranking cleric through an interpreter, especially an interpreter who does not know her and possibly will not represent or translate her favorably, Margery has a better answer: she encourages Wenslawe to pray for a miracle of xenoglossia that will enable him to understand her speech. She desires to be in control of her own translation and be able to approach Wenslawe directly, without an interpreter. Margery's communication to the priest is paramount, and thus the *Book* records the interpreter's presence only as long as it is necessary to set up the miracle of xenoglossia, for he becomes invisible immediately after his introduction.[53] Therefore, his presence not only

---

53. This sudden disappearance of the interpreter in the account has not been fully appreciated by scholars. Stokes smoothes the transition by restating the scene to read, "After an initial period requiring an interpreter, they were able to understand one another." "Margery Kempe: Her Life," 33. The "initial period" described in the text is actually only their first conversation.

ensures Margery initial access to the priest, but it also helps set up the miracle of vernacular xenoglossia that she will experience.

Margery wishes to have access to Wenslawe without recourse to a translator, either because there is no translator available for the amount of time she intends on conversing with Wenslawe, or simply because she desires direct access to him, so that she can tell him herself of her dalliances with the Lord, without being interpreted by a third party. In this case, xenoglossia is granted not as a last-ditch answer when mundane translation has failed but rather because it provides better circumstances for the interaction Margery wishes to have. After all, it is not as if Margery has exhausted all the possibilities in trying to find an English-speaking confessor in Rome, for the *Book* mentions her approaching only one other priest before deciding that the German Wenslawe, one of the highest-ranking priests in the city, is the man she wants.[54]

Margery also describes her reliance on an interpreter in another Roman scene, one in which she seeks access not to a priest but to St. Bridget of Sweden's maid, who shows Margery the chamber where the holy woman lived. The inclusion of Margery's efforts to communicate with the maid shows her pursuance of pious practice, which is emphasized still further by her efforts at procuring a translator. This scene has attracted a fair amount of scholarly attention because of the information it provides about the Swedish saint and Margery's veneration of her.[55] In addition to demonstrating Margery's divine favor (indeed, Christ even compares her favorably with Bridget and is angry that the saint is so out of favor, as is Margery herself), the *Book* includes the presence of the interpreter to emphasize the effort Margery goes to venerate Bridget by seeking out her maid. The *Book* calls attention to the presence of the interpreter because of the importance given to what Margery communicates to the foreign-speaking woman; the interpreter immediately falls out of the scene when his usefulness for this particular purpose is over, even if he is still needed for further acts of translation:

Aftyrward þis creatur spak wyth Seynt Brydys mayden in Rome, but sche cowd not vndirstondyn what sche seyd. Þan had sche a man þat cowde vndirstondyn hir langage, & þat man tolde Seynt Brygiptys

54. Certainly, an English-speaking confessor would have been easier to find in Rome than a Finnish-speaking one, the difficulty described in St. Bridget's *Revelations*.

55. See, for example, discussion of Margery's "laughing cheer" and St. Bridget in Lochrie, *Margery Kempe and Translations of the Flesh*, chap. 5. See also Cleve for Margery's devotion to St. Bridget and her knowledge of the controversy surrounding Bridget's canonization process. Cleve, "Margery Kempe: A Scandinavian Influence," 168–69.

mayden what þis creatur sedye & how sche askyd aftyr Seynt Brigypt, hir lady. Þan þe mayden seyd þat hir lady, Seynt Brigypt, was goodly & meke to euery creatur & þat sche had a lawhyng cher. And also þe good man wher þis creatur was at hoste telde hir þat he knew hir hys owyn selfe but he wend lityl þat sche had ben so holy a woman as sche was, for sche was euyr homly & goodly to alle creaturys þat woldyn spekyn wyth hir. Sche was in þe chawmbre þat Seynt Brigypt deyd in, & herd a Dewche preste prechyn of hir þerin & of hir reuelacyonys & of hir maner of leuyng. (95.10–25)

This scene is included in the *Book* not so much for the information that Margery is given about Bridget as for the information Margery supplies to the maid about herself. The interpreter is rendered visible here and included in the recounting of the event because he contributes to the conversation by explaining how Margery asks after the neglected saint; in effect, the translator makes Margery's direct access to veneration possible. What he tells the maid on behalf of Margery is as, if not more, important than what she tells Margery in return, for the crux of the scene is that the English pilgrim is expressing her devotion to the Swedish saint. Indeed, Margery then translates or interprets the "tokens" of storm and lightning that the Lord sends as his anger that others in Rome are not venerating Bridget as they should. That Margery is both translated for and translates in this scene is proof that she is acting with the Lord's explicit approval.[56]

Moments later the interpreter drops from the scene, once Margery's own words are no longer needed. When she visits Bridget's room and hears a German preacher, we must ask how she understands that he is speaking of the *Revelations* and of Bridget's manner of living. Is he speaking in English, and therefore she can understand his words without the need of an interpreter? Is he speaking in German or Italian or another language that the inter-

---

56. This scene's successful translation, as experienced by Bridget's maid and Margery through an interpreter, directly echoes the scene that immediately precedes it, that of Margery's unsuccessful communication in English with her own former maid. When Margery is invited back to the Hospice of St. Thomas of Canterbury, she finds her original maid who had abandoned her in Constance at the start of the pilgrimage. The faithless maid is now prosperous and refuses to return to Margery, despite the scorn she has received. The contrast between Margery's interactions with the two maids is stark and carefully crafted. On the one hand, the vulnerable Margery tries to compel her faithless English-speaking maid to fulfill her duty and to help quell the world's hostile words against her; on the other hand, a supplicating Margery seeks, with some significant effort, to express her veneration for Bridget to the saint's faithful, devoted maid, who attests to her mistress's pious character. It is no simple coincidence that Margery is better able to communicate with Bridget's foreign-speaking maid than with her own.

preter must translate for Margery? Or, can Margery on her own discern particular words that might be spoken similarly in a number of languages, just as Ida of Nivelles recognized holy names when she looked at Latin Scripture?[57] The *Book* is not at all concerned, however, with describing *how* Margery knows what is being preached. Because the point of including her visit to the chamber is to show the pious Margery observing where the saint died, it is enough that the English woman listen; she need not speak to the priest. The interpreter therefore has vanished from this scene because the *Book* only includes references to Margery's interpreters when what she has to say is paramount, not when she needs them to translate others for her. Whereas Margery can understand Wenslawe through a gift of xenoglossia, her understanding of this particular German priest also seems quite miraculous, albeit probably because the translator has been rendered invisible.

Margery as Translator

Margery presents herself as an effective translator engaged in "feminine communication"; she is able to communicate spiritual concepts and be understood on a very "deep" level by a number of women who seem to appreciate her blessedness. For example, when she is staying overnight in a "good man's house" outside of Rome, the ring that Christ ordered her to have made in England goes missing. Unable to find her precious token, she effectively communicates the importance of what has been lost to the wife of the house:

> Þan had sche mekyl heuynes & compleyned to þe good wyfe of þe hows, seying in þis wyse, "Madam, my bone maryd ryng to Ihesu Crist, as ho seyth, it is a-wey." The good wyfe, vndirstondyng what sche ment, preyde hir to prey for hir, and sche chongyd hir cher & hir cuntenawns wondyrly as thow sche had ben gylty. Þan þis creatur toke a candel in hir hand & sowt al a-bowtyn hir bed þer sche had leyn al nygth, and þe good wyfe of the hows toke an-oþer candel in hir hand & bisyed hir to sekyn also a-bowte þe bed. & at þe last sche fonde þe ryng vndyr þe bed on þe bordys, and wyth gret joye sche telde þe good wyfe þat sche had fownden hir ryng. Þan þe good wyfe, obeyng hir, preyd þis creatur of forʒeuenes as sche cowde, "Bone Cristian, prey pur me." (78.30–79.8)

57. For Ida of Nivelles, see Chapter 1.

This episode is remarkable because of the inclusion of the limited yet strikingly effective attempts on both women's parts to translate into one another's language. The account includes the phrases "seying in this wyse," "as ho seyth," and "as sche cowde," indicating that both the Italian wife and Margery are consciously translating for the other's benefit.

What is heavily implied in this scene is that the wife has stolen the ring and is made to feel repentant to such an extent that she returns it. Margery has managed to communicate the spiritual value of the ring/token in such an effective way that the wife not only returns it but, recognizing Margery's efficacious powers, begs her to pray for her. Margery attempts to speak in a mixture of English and Italian, to express herself in words and concepts that the wife will understand. When she describes the ring, she calls it a "bone maryd ryng" (for "good marriage ring"); the concept of a "good marriage ring" to Christ is something that crosses cultural and linguistic barriers, and the *Book* assures us that the Italian woman "understands what she meant."[58] But how does Margery know that the woman actually understands her description of the ring and not just that a ring is missing? Margery assumes she does, for apparently feeling quite guilty, the wife begs Margery, in a mixture of Italian and English (and echoing the English woman's use of "bone"), "Bone Cristian, prey pur me." Margery then interprets this as the wife's asking for forgiveness "as she could."

The conversation is included in the *Book* for several reasons.[59] First, the wife serves as another lay witness of Margery's persuasive goodness, for the woman is "converted" by Margery's words away from sin and returns the ring, asking for her prayers. Second, Margery is demonstrating how resourceful she is to be able to communicate a spiritual concept so succinctly and easily, without the aid of an interpreter; both women understand fully what a "married ring" to Christ means and that this is a spiritual union that can be comprehended and appreciated without further recourse to spoken language. The ring itself is a token of interpretation, a representation of the cycle of translation that occurs between Christ, Margery, and her many various audiences. Margery states that Christ commanded her to have the ring made with

58. Furrow refers to Margery's words here as one of several "attempts at a kind of Europidgin." Furrow, "Unscholarly Latinity," 246.

59. According to Cleve, the ring indicates that Margery "felt a very special affiliation" for St. Bridget's Order of the Holy Savior, because the motto inscribed on rings of the Bridgettine nuns reads, "Amor meus crucifixus est." Cleve, "Margery Kempe: A Scandinavian Influence," 169–70. For the association of the inscription on Margery's ring with Richard Rolle's *Incendium amoris*, see Mary Morse, "Seeing and Hearing: Margery Kempe and the *mise-en-page*," *Studia Mystica* 20 (1999): 15–42, at p. 21.

the words "Ihesus est amor meus";[60] many chapters later, we are told that Christ tells Margery: "Dowtyr, þu mayst boldly seyn to me 'Ihesus est amor meus,' þat is to seyn, 'Ihesu is my lofe.' Þerfor, dowtyr, late me be al thy lofe & al þe joy of thyn hert" (161.5–8).[61] Just as Christ translates the ring's words from Latin into English for Margery, she translates the ring's message effectively for the Italian wife. The ring, therefore, is a token that demonstrates how Margery translates on both the literal and metaphorical levels, as she translates between languages and her life "translates" the message of Christ.

The ease with which Margery translates deep, spiritual concepts is revealed in yet another scene that occurs while she is residing in Rome. The episode describing Dame Margaret Florentyne and Margery's interchange about the latter's poverty is actually quite complex in its translational ambiguities, despite its simple dialogue. As the *Book* attempts to describe the communication between these woman, what emerges is a reading of how Margery is read by others. When Margery meets for the second time Margaret, who had initially accompanied her to Rome, through basic translation efforts the two women communicate quite effectively on a significant spiritual level: "& in schort tyme aftyr þis visyon sche met wyth a worshepful lady, Dame Margarete Florentyn, þe same lady þat browt hir fro Assyse in-to Rome. & neiþyr of hem cowd wel vndirstand oþer but be syngnys er tokenys & in fewe comown wordys. And þan þe lady seyd on-to hir, 'Margerya in pouerte?' Sche, vndirstondyng what þe lady ment, seyd a-ȝen, 'ȝa, grawnt pouerte, Madam'" (93.20–27). At the most basic level, the *Book* includes this interesting interchange to demonstrate that Margery is understood better by a pious Italian woman than by women of her own tongue. The two can communicate by "signs and tokens and a few common words," which are more than enough to express accurately Margery's difficult situation.

Once again, if we consider how the *Book* represents Margaret's understanding of Margery, the question of language becomes quite perplexing. If we imagine that the interchange could be taking place in either English or Italian, the scene clearly demonstrates Margery's attitude toward vernacular languages in general. The exchange could be occuring entirely in English, with Margaret attempting to comfort the wretched, linguistically and physically

---

60. See *The Book of Margery Kempe*, 78.12–15.

61. Christ and Margery's communication takes place mostly in the vernacular, but Margery does occasionally use some common Latin words and phrases in her mystical conversations. When Christ sends St. John to hear her confession, she says "Benedicte," and he answers "Dominus" (81.5–6). The Lord also gives Margery a token by which she may believe that it is God who speaks to her. "Þan fro þat tyme forwarde sche vsyd to seyn whan sche saw hem comyn, 'Benedictus qui venit in nomine domini'" (88.23–25).

vulnerable visionary by speaking to her in English, and with Margery responding in her own tongue. However, the exchange could be taking place in Italian, with "grawnt" a form of "grande" and "poverte" to stand for "povertá," thereby demonstrating that despite her desperate situation, Margery has learned some Italian and is successful at communicating with those from whom she is begging. Another possibility, perhaps more likely, is that each is attempting to translate for the other: Margaret to speak in English, and Margery to speak in Italian. Each woman, therefore, could be seen as trying to meet the other on her own "linguistic turf," so to speak.

Mutual comprehension is emphasized in this scene. Margaret chooses to speak in a simple sentence either because she is trying her hand at English, or because she realizes Margery will not understand more complex sentences in Italian. Margaret fully comprehends the extent of Margery's poverty—not only the physical state of her misery but also her spiritual practice of *imitatio Christi* that underlies it. Margery states that she understands what Margaret "means," and her answer confirms that she appreciates her Italian friend's limited English vocabulary, or she in turn is limited in her own Italian vocabulary. Margery's answer is in fact remarkably clever, for in four words she manages to confirm the woman's observation with "Ya" (English, or even German), capitalize on the extent of her poverty with the use of "grawnt" (English, Italian, or French), and demonstrate respect with the term "Madam" (English or French). The communication between the two women, informed by both a mutual understanding of the lived reality of poverty as well as the experience of *imitatio Christi*, is of particular significance despite its brevity. That the same conversation can be held in several languages indicates what Margery sees as Christian "roots" underlying these European vernaculars, which make them perfectly translatable.

With Margery's response of "Ya," we are reminded of Jordan of Giano's account of the first Franciscan mission to Germany, in which the friars only knew one word of German: "Ja." By answering "Ja," they received everything they needed, until they were asked if they were heretics.[62] The response to Margery's "Ya" is that Margaret Florentyne brings Margery home to dine and cares for her needs; it is Margery's own countrymen, not foreigners, who think her a heretic. This carefully crafted scene mirrors another, in which Margery has been told by Wenslawe to leave off wearing her white clothes, to which she answers simply, "Ya, syr." When the "wives of Rome" ask Margery facetiously if she has been robbed by a highwayman, she answers, "No, Ma-

---

62. For Jordan of Giano's account of the first Franciscan mission to Germany, see Chapter 1.

dame."[63] Margery's response to the Roman women could be taken as a sign of humility (she speaks only two words, just as she answered Wenslawe), as protective of herself (so as not to incur further ridicule), or even punishing of the women (for in this moment she is withholding her special knowledge of Christ). Her "No, Madame," could also be a sign of her limited linguistic ability in Italian, for perhaps it is too difficult to explain herself to the Romans. But just how she initially *understands* the question of the Roman wives is not at all clear; once again, in glossing over the mechanics of mundane translation, the *Book* calls attention to Margery's strangely miraculous ability to understand the languages of others while traveling in foreign lands.

Conclusion

Translation, both miraculous and mundane, is one of the most important ways that Margery knows and experiences Christ and forms a significant part of her identity as a visionary. Margery's gift of xenoglossia can be understood as either a divine gift granted to aid a linguistically vulnerable, monolingual woman, or as a laywoman's aggressive, successful pursuit of and participation in vernacular translation that might otherwise have been denied her. Similarly, the *Book*'s accounts of mundane translation can be explained as Kempe remembering the difficulties and successes of her pilgrimages, or Kempe and her scribe carefully crafting a way of including witnesses to Margery's blessedness, expressing her desires to have access to religious experiences and trying to control the way she is "read" and "translated" by others. In any case, the *Book* demonstrates the complex ways in which a late medieval English lay merchant–class visionary could translate and adapt the trope of xenoglossic translation and its related issues into her own life and text.

Much has been written about how saintly *imitatio* authorizes the *Book*.[64]

63. "Than þe good man, þe Duche preste þat sche was schrevyn on-to, thorw þe steryng of þe Englysch preste whech was hir enmye askyd hir yf sche wolde be obedient vn-to hym er not. And sche seyd, 'ȝa, syr.' 'Wyl ȝe don þan as I schal byd ȝow don?' 'Wyth ryth good wyl, sire.' 'I charge ȝow þan þat ȝe leue ȝowr white clothys, & weryth a-geyn ȝowr blak clothys.' & sche dede hys comawndment. . . . Than suffyrd sche many scornys of wyfys of Rome. Þei askyd hir ȝyf malendrynes had robbyd hir, & sche seyd, 'Nay, madame'" (84.32–86.5).

64. See, for example, Sarah Beckwith, "Problems of Authority in Late Medieval English Mysticism: Language, Agency, and Authority in *The Book of Margery Kempe*," *Exemplaria* 4 (1992): 171–99, and Catherine Sanok, who asserts that imitation of saints' lives is "often read as an attempt to 'authorize' a woman's devotional practices or spiritual identity." Sanok, *Her Life Historical*, 116. Sanok argues, like Staley, that this imitation can also be employed "to criticize the community she inhabits by comparing it to the social world depicted in traditional legends" (116).

In this chapter, I have explored an important and overlooked way in which the *Book* is heavily modeled on hagiographical tropes. But the xenoglossia found within the *Book* is profoundly complicated and troubled, for Margery must repeatedly justify herself in the face of doubt in a way that few other female holy women must. Social and political circumstances do not permit Margery to experience Latinate xenoglossia as other holy women do. Instead, she must share her miracle with a cleric, one who miraculously translates her vernacular speech into Latin, and another who claims for himself the moment of miraculous textual production. Margery is denied the basic xenoglossic model available to so many of her female models, and in its place the *Book* concentrates on mundane vernacular translation as a medium of God's message.

We can use the *Book*'s complex negotiation of miraculous and mundane translation as a way to look back on and better understand the confusing linguistic agency that we saw in women's saints' lives described in the first two chapters. For example, Margery's xenoglossic experience in Rome with Wenslawe, in which she prays for thirteen days and they achieve a mutual comprehension, offers us a way to understand claims made by Thomas of Cantimpré in his *Life* of St. Lutgard, that she was unable to learn French during the many years of her stay in the monastery at Aywières but was then able to converse with a despairing woman and a bishop who came to see her. First, we recognize in both texts the desire to interpret translation miraculously to emphasize the women's blessedness. We also see a desire to call attention to how the women are under clerical control: Lutgard converses with a bishop and Margery shares her miracle with a high-ranking cleric. If we also accept the *Book*'s account of miraculous translation as either representing, or being modeled on, lived experience of language being interpreted in a miraculous way, then Lutgard's experience can be understood in a similar light; although Lutgard was said to have not learned much more than being able to beg for bread, perhaps in certain circumstances, depending on the topic and how much listening versus speaking was expected of her, Lutgard could understand French.

Similarly, the *Book*'s attention given to the importance of everyday translation is both illuminated by and helps us to understand more fully the *Life* of Ida of Nivelles, who as we recall from Chapter 1, pointedly did not receive a gift of xenoglossia. Ida's linguistic struggles in the Dutch-speaking convent of Kerkom, and her gradual translational successes, emphasize her blessedness and bring her closer to God. Margery's translational struggles and her successes indicate similar impulses but are much more developed in the *Book*, either because there is more space to develop them or because being "in the world" rather than enclosed brings Margery up against potential linguistic impasses again and again. Moreover, perhaps the fifteenth-century English *Book* can imagine the Lord sanctioning and encouraging vernacular language in a way that the thirteenth-century Latin *Life* of Ida did not.

Thinking about how Kempe and her scribe are writers and hagiographers who construct the xenoglossic experiences of their female subject to assert the authority of the *Book* can also be illuminated by comparing the *Book* with another later medieval English work, the *Canterbury Tales*, a text that consciously explores how acts of mundane translation may appear miraculous when the translators are ignored or rendered invisible. The final chapter of this study turns from a woman's visionary text and autohagiography to a male author writing about women's xenoglossic experiences in a literary endeavor. In the *Canterbury Tales*, Chaucer discovers the usefulness of xenoglossia as a metaphor to describe how translators authorize their own vernacular works.

FOUR

WOMEN'S MIRACULOUS TRANSLATION IN CHAUCER'S *CANTERBURY TALES*

The last chapter explored how the late medieval English visionary writer Margery Kempe and her scribe masterfully adapt the hagiographic tropes of women's xenoglossia to support the authority of the *Book*. The *Book* mingles mundane and miraculous translation experiences in a way that emphasizes translation as both a medium and message of God's blessing. Acts of translation show Margery to be divinely blessed and ensure her access to religious and devotional practices; at the same time, the heightened attention paid to translation points to anxieties about how both Margery and the *Book* are being received by their audiences and to attempts to control their reception.

This final chapter examines a male literary author imagining female xenoglossic characters to discover how he adapts the hagiographic tropes of women's xenoglossia to explore his own issues of writerly control and authority. In his great translation experiment, the *Canterbury Tales*, Geoffrey Chaucer dramatizes the tension between miraculous and mundane translation in the *Prioress's Prologue* and *Tale*, the *Man of Law's Tale*, and the *Squire's Tale*. I argue that in these texts Chaucer wields the xenoglossic trope with Kempelike alacrity, employing the female xenoglossic woman as a metaphor for a translator's relationship to his authoritative sources. Chaucer's specific use of the Pentecost narrative in the *Summoner's Tale* has been noted by several scholars; in this chapter, I argue that xenoglossia is more important to Chaucer's wider work than has been previously acknowledged.[1]

1. For an examination of Chaucer's use of Pentecost in the *Summoner's Tale*, see Bernard S. Levy, "Biblical Parody in the *Summoner's Tale*," *Tennessee Studies in Literature* 11 (1966): 45–60; Alan Levitan, "The Parody of Pentecost in Chaucer's *Summoner's Tale*," *University of Toronto Quarterly* 40 (1971): 236–46; Roy Peter Clark, "Wit and Witsunday in Chaucer's *Summoner's*

There has been a tremendous amount of scholarship on Chaucer and translation, much of it quite recent, as translation has come to be seen as necessary to understanding Chaucer's accomplishments as a vernacular writer and his contribution to Middle English literature. The reevaluation of the importance of translation in understanding Chaucer has encouraged Glending Olson, in *The Cambridge History of Medieval English Literature*, to suggest that "thinking of Chaucer's achievement as a range of different kinds of translation is perhaps as valid as any single approach to the entirety of his work."[2] Scholarly approaches to Chaucer and translation include examining Chaucer's own translation theory and practices as well as how the "idea" of translation is central to many of his texts.[3]

In this chapter, I shall argue that Chaucer focuses on the mechanics of miraculous and mundane translation in the *Prioress's Prologue* and *Tale*, the *Man of Law's Tale*, and the *Squire's Tale*. Each text examines a woman's access to privileged language through a linguistic gift, as well as her practice and performance of her newly acquired linguistic knowledge. Chaucer explores how translation is imagined to function in different religious and secular genres, including the miracle of the Virgin, the saint's life, the chronicle history, and the romance. By creating narratives of miraculous translation in genres other than the vita, Chaucer raises a number of questions about the public assertions or "stances" that translators make about the relationship between their translations and their sources. By "public stances," I mean the translators' proclamations that describe their relationships with sources, rang-

---

Tale," *Annuale Mediaevale* 17 (1976): 48–57; Glending Olson, "The End of the *Summoner's Tale* and the Uses of Pentecost," *Studies in the Age of Chaucer* 21 (1999): 209–45; see also discussion of critical reception in John Finlayson, "Chaucer's *Summoner's Tale*: Flatulence, Blasphemy, and the Emperor's Clothes," *Studies in Philology* 104 (2007): 455–70, at pp. 455–57.

2. Glending Olson, "Geoffrey Chaucer," *The Cambridge History of Medieval English Literature*, ed. David Wallace (Cambridge: Cambridge University Press, 1999), 576, quoted in Roger Ellis, "Translation," in *A Companion to Chaucer*, ed. Peter Brown (Oxford: Blackwell, 2000), 443–58, at p. 443.

3. See Tim William Machan in "'Chaucer as Translator,' *The Medieval Translator: The Theory and Practice of Translation in the Middle Ages*, ed. Roger Ellis, assisted by Jocelyn Price, Stephen Medcalf, and Peter Meredith (Cambridge: Brewer, 1989), 55–67, in which he argues that "translation is indeed central to Chaucer's conception of himself as a vernacular writer" and calls for increased attention to "the ways in which this centrality [of translation] is evinced" in Chaucer's works, particularly those that do not articulate an obvious theory of translation (67). More recent studies have responded by considering the ways in which the idea of translation is at the core of many of Chaucer's *Canterbury Tales*, including those told by the Wife of Bath, the Summoner, and the Squire. See, for example, Susan Signe Morrison, "Don't Ask, Don't Tell: The Wife of Bath and Vernacular Translations," *Exemplaria* 8 (1996): 97–123; Fiona Somerset, "'As just as is a squyre': The Politics of 'Lewed Translacion' in Chaucer's *Summoner's Tale*," *Studies in the Age of Chaucer* 21 (1999): 187–207; Alan S. Ambrisco, "'It lyth nat in my tonge': Occupatio and Otherness in the *Squire's Tale*," *Chaucer Review* 38 (2004): 205–28.

ing from statements describing themselves as humble, ineffectual translators who cannot hope to reproduce their authoritative sources, to bold, confident translators who claim to be translating both the "word and sense" of the sources. In all three tales, Chaucer envisions the translator who translates "perfectly" or miraculously to be a woman, in large part because he imagines it is her particularly passive or *gentil* nature that makes her especially receptive to another's words.

In the *Prioress's Prologue* and *Tale*, Chaucer creates a female speaker who claims to be the blankest of all slates—an infant who is practically speechless. Her tale, however, is focused on the little clergeon's rote learning of a Latin song and presents a miracle of speech that is not xenoglossia but rather the regeneration of speech organs. In this *Prologue* and *Tale* Chaucer examines two stances that religious translators or authors may take: they can claim complete lack of control over the text and assert that they are merely a conduit for the text, or they can claim a divinely enhanced ability of their traditionally acquired learning. In the hagiographic romance of the *Man of Law's Tale*, Chaucer imagines a xenoglossic preaching woman whose native tongue is Latin; her gift is not one of miraculous Latinity but of miraculous vernacular- ity, as she is translated into the Saxon language of the Northumbrians. The ambiguous nature of the xenoglossic gift, however, calls attention to the care- ful combination of genres (vita, chronicle history, and romance) that Chaucer is working with in the tale, as he imagines how translation functions in each of these related genres. Last, in the romance of the *Squire's Tale*, Chaucer explores how ludicrous the idea of purely equivalent translation can be when experienced not in a religious context (by two pious people, for example) but rather by a woman and a jilted bird. Canacee becomes the translator who translates both word and sense, without effort; the absurdity of understanding as free from linguistic constraints is exposed by the juxtaposition of her mi- raculous translation with the first part of the tale, in which the narrator's repeated humble assertions argue that equivalent translation is impossible.

Part 1: Miraculous Speech in the *Prioress's Prologue* and *Tale*

In the *Prioress's Tale*, a female narrator relates the tale of a young clergeon who, having learned to sing his *Alma redemptoris* by rote, is then murdered by Jews and hidden in a privy, only to be discovered because of his miraculous singing made possible by the Virgin Mary. The *Tale* is closely linked with the

Prioress's Prologue in that the narrator of the *Prologue* calls on Mary to aid her speech because human *science* or learned discourse cannot express Mary's grace. Many critics understand the Prioress as wanting to model her own pious speech on that of the little clergeon. They note the relationship Chaucer draws between the Prioress's humble claims of linguistic insufficiency as she likens her expression to infant speech in her *Prologue*, and the focus on the purity of the little clergeon's song.[4] Indeed, Lee Patterson has asserted, "the tale establishes the clergeon's song as a model of linguistic innocence, a privileged speech that the Prioress seeks to imitate."[5] It is not surprising that the Prioress would want to model her speech on that of the clergeon; it is certainly a common religious trope for adults to imagine children as their pious models, especially as Christ asserted that men and women must be like children if they wish to gain the kingdom of heaven.[6]

What scholarship has failed to appreciate fully, however, is that Chaucer describes two different models of miraculous speech in the *Prologue* and the *Tale*: the gift of infant tongues and the miraculous ability to speak when the organs of speech have been severed. Whereas in the *Prologue* Chaucer imagines the Prioress asking for a gift of infant tongues, which asserts her complete lack of linguistic agency, the tale assigned to the Prioress actually focuses *more* attention on the clergeon's mundane, rote learning of Latin than on the linguistic miracle. What the clergeon is gifted with is the miraculous ability to articulate speech and song after his throat has been cut, a gift that emphasizes that Mary rewards his efforts at learning. I argue that the *Prologue* and

4. For example, Helen Cooper has argued that the *Prioress's Prologue* and *Tale* speak to "the relationship of language to meaning," because "the words most acceptable as worship may be the babblings of an infant or the uncomprehended Latin of an anthem beyond a child's rational grasp" (296), in Cooper, *The Canterbury Tales*, 2nd ed., Oxford Guides to Chaucer (Oxford: Oxford University Press, 1996).

5. Lee Patterson, "'The Living Witnesses of Our Redemption': Martyrdom and Imitation in Chaucer's *Prioress's Tale*," *Journal of Medieval and Early Modern Studies* 31 (2001): 507–60, at p. 508.

6. Matthew 18:3 ("Truly, I say to you, unless you turn and become like children, you will never enter the kingdom of heaven") and Matthew 19:14 ("Let the children come to me, and do not hinder them; for to such belongs the kingdom of heaven.") *The New Oxford Annotated Bible with the Apocrypha: Revised Standard Version*, expanded ed., ed. Herbert G. May and Bruce M. Metzger (New York: Oxford University Press, 1977). The Douay-Rheims Bible records the following: Matthew 18:3 ("And [Jesus] said: Amen I say to you, unless you be converted, and become as little children, you shall not enter into the kingdom of heaven.") and Matthew 19:14 ("But Jesus said to them: Suffer the little children, and forbid them not to come to me: for the kingdom of heaven is for such."). *The Holy Bible: Translated from the Latin Vulgate, diligently compared with the Hebrew, Greek, and other editions in divers languages. The Old Testament first published by the English college at Douay, A.D. 1609, and the New Testament first published by the English college at Rheims, A.D. 1582* (Rockford, IL: Tan Books, 1971).

Tale examine two different approaches that a writer may take when composing or translating religious and devotional writings. In the *Prologue*, Chaucer explores how a feminine speaking position can be useful when writing and translating religious texts because, as we saw in the earlier chapters of this book, women may claim for themselves complete illiteracy or even speechlessness, thereby abdicating linguistic control and asserting that they are only a vessel of the Divine Word. In the *Tale*, however, Chaucer explores how the voice of the clergeon, with his first tentative steps toward Latin literacy, mirrors the voice of the writer or translator who claims a divine gift that enhances the little he has already learned on his own.

In the *Prologue* to the *Prioress's Tale*, the female narrator imagines herself in an extremely passive linguistic position: she compares herself to a babe, twelve months or less, who can scarcely articulate a word.[7] Professing she has not enough knowledge or learning to express Mary's graces, she calls on the mother of God to aid the articulation of her hymn and, by extension, her storytelling:

> My konnyng is so wayk, O blisful Queene,
> For to declare thy grete worthynesse
> That I ne may the weighte nat susteene;
> But as a child of twelf month oold, or lesse,
> That kan unnethes any word expresse,
> Right so fare I, and therfore I yow preye,
> Gydeth my song that I shal of you seye.
> (VII. 481–87)[8]

In the face of the divine presence, the narrator is infantilized or rendered (scarcely) unable to speak, and therefore humbly requires Mary's aid to help her articulate her pious tale in a worshipful manner. Mary must become a mother coaxing and modeling language for her child, or a voice that can be channeled through her speechless vessel. The *Prologue*'s narrator clearly privileges *sapientia* over *scientia*, divinely given wisdom over that learned through study. "Thy vertu and thy grete humylitee / Ther may no tonge

---

7. Both the *Prologue* and the *Tale* include "quod she" (454 and 581), which clearly indicate Chaucer intended his audience to imagine a female speaker, if not the Prioress herself. For discussion of the problematic relationship between tale and teller, see C. David Benson, *Chaucer's Drama of Style: Poetic Variety and Contrast in the Canterbury Tales* (Chapel Hill: University of North Carolina Press, 1986), esp. chap. 1, "Beyond the Dramatic Theory," 3–25.

8. Geoffrey Chaucer, *The Canterbury Tales*, in *The Riverside Chaucer*, ed. Larry D. Benson, 3rd ed. (Boston: Houghton Mifflin, 1987). All quotations of Chaucer are from this edition.

expresse in no science" (475–76), she exclaims; by referring to the inability of scientia to articulate Mary's ineffable graces, the narrator is arguing what fertile ground she is for the Divine Word. The use of this "inexpressibility topos" emphasizes the narrator's rejection of any literacy or learning that she might possess, since she suggests that Mary and the Lord are most pleased by a woman's uneducated devotion.

The narrator is actually asking for something more than the ability to articulate Mary's praise, something that emphasizes still further her desire for complete lack of linguistic agency. Chaucer opens the *Prologue* by imagining his female narrator actually requesting a gift of infant tongues. The Lord is invoked with the following passage drawn from the canonical Hours and the Little Office of the Virgin:

> O Lord, oure Lorde, thy name how merveillous
> Is in this large world ysprad—quod she—
> For noght oonly thy laude precious
> Parfourned is by men of dignitee,
> But by the mouth of children thy bountee
> Parfourned is, for on the brest soukynge
> Somtyme shewen they thyn heriynge.
>
> (453–59)[9]

How do babes sucking at the breast perform praise?[10] This opening stanza suggests that while men perform praise through speech, babes perform through nursing. This certainly could refer to a great number of medieval legends involving miracles at the breast. For example, it was said of St. Nicholas that he refused to nurse on Wednesdays and Fridays in honor of the Lord; a variation of this miracle records that St. Cunegund practiced abstinence by only drinking from one breast on those two days. Some babes refused to suck on sinful women: St. Catherine of Vadstena, the daughter of St. Bridget of Sweden, rejected a sinful wet-nurse, as well as her own mother's breast when Bridget had had sexual relations with her husband.[11]

9. For the liturgical uses of these lines, see Chaucer, *The Riverside Chaucer*, 914n1, and Laurel Broughton, "The Prioress's Prologue and Tale," in *Sources and Analogues of Chaucer's Canterbury Tales*, ed. Robert Correale and Mary Hamel (Cambridge: D. S. Brewer, 2002–2005), 2:583–647, at pp. 584–86.

10. William Orth, "The Problem of the Performative in Chaucer's Prioress Sequence," *Chaucer Review* 42 (2007): 196–210.

11. For St. Nicholas, see Ann S. Haskell, *Essays on Chaucer's Saints* (The Hague: Mouton, 1976), 47–57. For miracles of babes at the breast, see Donald Weinstein and Rudolph M. Bell, *Saints and Society: The Two Worlds of Western Christendom, 1000–1700* (Chicago: University of Chicago Press, 1982), 24–25.

The *Prologue*'s linking of men's laudatory speech with infants' mouths suggests another kind of miracle arising from the mouths of infants: the very popular miracle of infant speech. The Bible contains several scriptural verses that suggest babes might miraculously open their mouths and speak; verses such as Psalms 8:1–2 ("Thou whose glory above the heavens is chanted by the mouths of babes and infants thou hast founded a bulwark because of thy foes") and Matthew 21:16 (in which Jesus asks, "have you never read, 'Out of the mouth of babes and sucklings thou hast brought perfect praise?'") seem to have encouraged this popular genre of miracle in the Middle Ages.[12] Miraculous infant speech is closely related to xenoglossia in that it is a gift of a language previously unlearned; in the case of infants, their xenoglossia is taken one step further, for the miracle imagines the gift of language being granted not only to someone who does not have the physical ability to articulate words (mutes or those lacking actual tongues, for example) but also to one who has not yet learned any language or even appears aware that language exists. Although it could always be suggested that xenoglossic women gained their linguistic ability or scriptural knowledge through traditional means (and therefore the hagiographers and visionaries are careful to show how they were not formally educated), it is impossible to imagine that infants achieve this linguistic knowledge by their own means without divine intervention.

Miraculous infant tongues occur in a number of later medieval saints' lives and miracle collections. In general, there are two kinds of miraculously speaking infants: those saintly infants who exhibit precocious speech as a mark of their blessedness to come (the *puer senex* or *sacra infantia* motifs), and those ordinary babies whose sudden verbal outcries serve as witnesses to others' sanctity.[13] Accounts of *sacra infantia* include saintly fetuses shouting out from

12. *New Oxford Annotated Bible*, May and Metzger. The Vulgate records: "ex ore infantium et lactantium perfecisti laudem propter inimicostuos ut destruas inimicum et ultorem." *Biblia Sacra iuxta Vulgatam Versionem*, ed. Bonifatius Fischer et al., rev. Robertus Weber, 4th ed. (Stuttgart: Deutsche Bibelgesellschaft, 1994), Psalms 8:3; the Douay-Rheims translates this as, "Out of the mouth of infants and of sucklings thou hast perfected praise, because of thy enemies, that thou mayst destroy the enemy and the avenger." "Iesus autem dicit eis utique numquam legistis quia ex ore infantium et lactantium perfecisti laudem." *Biblia Sacra*, Mathew 21:16; the Douay-Rheims records, "And Jesus said to them: 'Yea, have you never read: Out of the mouth of infants and of sucklings thou hast perfected praise?'" The passage in Chaucer is related to the Mass of the Holy Innocents; see Patterson, "Living Witness," and Marie Padgett Hamilton, "Echoes of Childermas in the *Tale* of the Prioress," *Modern Language Review* 34 (1939): 1–8.

13. For the topos of *puer senex*, see, for example, Shulamith Shahar, *Childhood in the Middle Ages* (London: Routledge, 1990), 15–16; Ernst Robert Curtius, *European Literature and the Latin Middle Ages*, trans. Willard R. Trask (New York: Pantheon, 1953), 98–105, and Patricia Healy Wasyliw, "The Pious Infant: Developments in Popular Piety During the High Middle Ages," in *Lay Sanctity, Medieval and Modern. A Search for Models*, ed. Ann W. Astell (Notre Dame: University of Notre Dame Press, 2000), 105–15, esp. 106. For *sacra infantia*, see István P. Bejczy, "The

the womb, like SS. Fursey and Isaac,[14] or infants proclaiming their religious faith; for example, St. Peregrinus responded "Amen" at his baptism and then proceeded to repeat the Lord's Prayer and the Creed.[15] Popular legends also recounted that infants could declare their faith in the face of pagan torturers. The *Life* of the Martyr Maximus describes how the saint had a three-month-old baby brought to the governor so that the infant might proclaim the truth of the Christian faith. The babe then commanded the governor to listen to his words and to believe in Christ. When questioned how he had such knowledge, the infant responded by asking what teacher could possibly have taught him, unless it was God himself? The governor had the baby tortured, and when he asked for a drink of water from his mother, she instructed him to drink the waters of heaven.[16] Infants could also expound Scripture, the most

---

sacra infantia in Medieval Hagiography," in *The Church and Childhood: Papers Read at the 1993 Summer Meeting and the 1994 Winter Meeting of the Ecclesiastical History Society*, ed. Diana Wood, Studies in Church History 31 (Oxford: Blackwell, 1994), 143–51. Bejczy discusses in some detail the problematic nature of the term *puer senex*, as well as other terms used for this topos in hagiographic literature.

14. The *Acta Sanctorum* records the following for St. Fursey: "Cognouit ergo Phyltanus Gelgehen coniugem suam clam patre suo: quae mox concepit, vt rei exitus probauit, puerum dignum Deo. Nec multo post ad patrias aures fecunditas filiae peruenit: qui ferocitate animi commotus in iram vehementius exiliit; filiamque suam igni cremandam adiudicauit. Quod intelligens puerulus adhuc materno vtero clausus, cunctis qui aderant obstupescentibus, furibundo auo infit: Indignu(m) est certe cuiuscumque ditionis homini filiam suam tradere igni, nisi probabili caussa exigente & rationabili." *AASS*, Jan., II, 45. For Isaac the *Acta Sanctorum* records: "Tribus namque vicibus una die, paulo antequam nasceretur, visus est loqui: cujus rei novitate perrerrita mulier, pene mortua, vim verborum nequaquam potuit intelligere." *AASS*, June, I, 325.

15. According to the vita of the fifth-century bishop St. Exuperantius, at the age of eighteen days, he opened his mouth and thanked the Lord, who caused him to be born. Later, at the age of three, he was said to have prayed to God in quite an articulate manner, well beyond the speech patterns of a typical child. "Post dies vero natiuitatis suae decem & octo B. Exuperantius locutus est, dicens: Gratias ago Domino meo Iesu Christo, qui me fecit nasci." *AASS*, Jan., II, 1148. In addition, the forty-day-old infant St. Sigebert recognized the significance of his baptism; a version of his story is related in *An Alphabet of Tales*, a fifteenth-century exemplum collection "We rede ex 'Gestis Beati Amandi' how þat when þe kyng of Fraunce had no chylde, he made a grete prayer vnto Allmiȝty God, & God sent hym one. And when it was born, he vmthoght hym whome he mot make to baptys it. And so þis Amandus come in his mynde & he made hym to baptis it. And when it was namyd & crystend, þe childe answerd þat all myght here, and said, 'Amen!'" (264, number 382) in *An Alphabet of Tales: An English 15th Century Translation of the Alphabetum Narrationum of Etienne de Besançon*, edited by Mary Macleod Banks, Early English Text Society o.s. 126–127 (London: Kegan Paul, Trench, Trübner, & Co., 1904, 1905). The vita of St. Peregrinus also records that at his baptism, the baby responded "Amen" when the priest said the Lord's prayer, "and then proceeded to repeat the prayer, followed by the creed, 'ac si fuisset uiginti annorum'" ("as if he were 20-years-old"), quoted in *Three Eleventh-Century Anglo-Latin Saints' Lives: Vita S. Birini, Vita et miracula S. Kenelmi and Vita S. Rumwoldi*, ed. and trans. Rosalind C. Love (Oxford: Clarendon Press, 1996), clxx. See also *AASS*, Aug., I, 77.

16. "Puer autem respondens, dixit Praesidi: 'Infelix et miser, non sentis opera Christi, cum sim infans trium mensium, quem necdum decet aetatem loqui? Quis magistrorum me potuit discere vel docere? Vel quis doctor qui linguam meam poliit, nisi Deus omnipotens, qui dat innocentibus astutiam, puero autem juniori sensum et cogitationem?' Praeses vero cum haec

famous being St. Rumwold, who, at three days old, preached a long sermon after his baptism and then died.[17]

Miraculously speaking infants who give witness to others' blessedness include those who exclaim the sanctity of saints, like the babe at the death of the thirteenth-century achoress St. Verdiana, who announced that the servant of the Lord was dead.[18] Infants could also explain how a saint had protected them from harm, as did a ten-month-old child in the legend of St. Martin of Tours, when its mother feared that the baby would die without being baptized. She placed him on St. Martin's tomb, and when he woke up, he laughed and called out, "Come here" to his mother and asked her to bring him some water.[19] Even more strikingly, infants could on occasion expose their true

---

audisset, jussit infantem torqueri; et cum torqueretur, dixit matri suae: 'Mater, da mihi aquam bibere.' Mater vero ejus dixit ei: 'Fili, noli jam istam aquam bibere, sed aquam illam bibe caelestem, ubi sunt omnes innocentorum animae, qui pro Christi nomine passi sunt.'" *AASS*, Oct., XIII, 322. The *Legenda aurea* includes a similar account of an infant defender of the faith in the life of the fourth-century martyrs SS. Quiricus and Julitta. Jacobus reports that in one version of the legend the infant Quiricus, when he saw his mother Julitta tortured because she refused to make a sacrifice, resisted the pagan prefect by crying out, "I am a Christian!" "In quadam autem legenda inuenitur quod Quiricus tyrannum blandientem eque ut minantem paruipendens christianum se esse confitebatur, secundum quidem tempus elinguis infantulus, sed in eo loquebatur spiritus sanctus. . . . Qui cum cederetur clamabat: "Christianus sum!" Jacobus de Voragine, *Legenda aurea*, ed. Giovanni Paolo Maggioni, 2nd ed., 2 vols. (Tavarnuzze-Firenze: Sismel, Edizioni del Galluzzo, 1998), 1:533.

17. The most extreme example of infant speech and proclamations of faith occur in the legend of the seventh-century Northumbrian St. Rumwold. According to his vita, after his birth Rumwald announced in a clear voice, "I am a Christian" three times. During the first three days of his life (after which he died), he requested to be baptised, even indicating a stone to be used as the font. He then insisted that a mass be celebrated so that he could receive communion, and afterward to his parents and those others standing by he preached a sermon full of scriptural references. He ended his long discourse by describing the locations where his body should rest after his death. See the *Life* of Rumwold (alternatively in English Rumwald, Rumald). *AASS*, Nov., I, esp. 685–90. For an English translation of his life, see *Three Eleventh-Century Anglo-Latin Saints' Lives*, 91–115; for the vita as a description of the elements of baptism, see Appendix F, "The baptism of St Rumwold," 135–38.

18. The child, "not yet capable of speech, still carried in his mother's arms," was heard to have pronounced these words clearly: "The servant of the Lord, Verdiana, is dead." "Fertur praeterea infantulus, necdum loquelae capax, adhuc maternis vlnis gestatus clare isthaec pronuntiasse verba: Famula Dei Verdiana mortua est." *AASS*, Feb., I, 260. Similarly, Raymond of Capua reports that when St. Agnes of Montepulciano died, local babies began to repeat that the holy Sister, Prioress Agnes, had passed away: "Statim enim ut Sancta decessit de mortali hoc corpore, pueri parvuli, qui in stratibus cum suis erant parentibus, subito excitati divinitus, coeperunt ore lactenti ac infantili sanctae Virginis laudem perficere, parentibus suis sic dicendo: Soror Agnes, Priorissa monasterii S. Mariae novellae, quae est Sancta, modo migravit de corpore." *AASS*. Apr., II, 808.

19. For example, the life of the thirteenth-century St. Cunegund describes how a two-year-old child, suffering from an ocular malady, called upon the holy woman to intercede for him. Afterward, wishing to be released from his mother's grasp, he told her, "Now, dear mother, don't hold me, since I am well, and my eye has been opened"; in this case, his mouth was opened as well. ". . .voce alta clamavit infans: Deus adjuva me, S. Cunegundis, intercede pro me; quo dicto,

parentage when they were abandoned on the church steps or when holy men were falsely accused of fathering them. The vitae of SS. Simon and Jude, Bridget of Ireland, Martin, Goar, and Vincent Ferrer include accounts of newborn infants who suddenly speak, usually to exonerate innocent men who have been accused of fathering them, or to identify the guilty men who did.[20]

Many of these narratives of miraculous infant tongues emphasize how the pious behavior of the young babe, often just days, weeks, or months old, is meant to be a model for adults. The direct receiver of the miracle may be an infant, but in most circumstances, the miracle's focus is on the adult audiences surrounding the infant and the ways they are enlightened, informed, and corrected by the child. Miraculously speaking infants become the teachers of piety and devotional practices for adults, for their complete lack of formal education makes them extremely desirable as receptacles for heavenly teachings.

---

subjunxit ad matrem: Jam, cara mater, non teneas me; quia sanus sum, & oculus apertus est." *AASS,* Jul., V, 763. In the *Miracles of St. Martin,* Gregory of Tours relates how an unbaptized tenth-month-old child was close to death. Fearing that he would die without baptism, the mother placed him on the tomb of Martin. The infant then awoke with a laugh and called on his mother, demanding "Come here!" and asked her to bring him some water. Afterward, he "returned to the first wailings of infancy, and never spoke again until he reached that age at which children are accustomed to loosen their tongues in speech." Quoted in Edward James, "Childhood and Youth in the Early Middle Ages," in *Youth in the Middle Ages,* ed. P. J. P. Goldberg and Felicity Riddy (York: York Medieval Press, 2004), 11–23, at pp. 17–18, from *Gregory of Tours: Life of the Fathers,* trans. E. James, 2nd ed. (Liverpool: Liverpool University Press, 1991), 15–16.

20. I term these episodes "paternal outings," in which abandoned or orphaned babes identify their true parents. The point of these oft-repeated narratives is that the most vulnerable of the flock, an infant, can identify what another more powerful person refuses to say and expose the crimes of the guilty so that they can be punished accordingly. The life of St. Goar, a sixth-century anchorite, describes how the hypocritical Bishop of Trier, Rusticus, ordered Goar to determine the father and mother of a newborn infant who had been abandoned before the gates of the church. When the holy man asked how old the child was and learned it was only three days old, he prayed in the name of the Trinity that the baby could declare the identity of his parents. The baby then spoke, "The Bishop Rusticus is my father, and my mother is called Flavia." The bishop then fell at Goar's feet, and the holy man laid down a penance. "Iste est pater meus Rusticus episcopus et mater mea Flavia nuncupatur" (649–50) in "Vita Sancti Goaris Auctore Wandalberto," 639–54 in Jacques-Paul Migne, ed., *Patrologia Latina* 121 of 221 vols. (Paris, 1844–1866). See also Walter Berschin, *Biographie und Epochenstil im lateinischen Mittelalter* 3 (Stuttgart: Anton Hiersemann, 1991), 71–74. A paternal outing miracle featuring St. Brice appears in Gregory of Tour's sixth-century *The History of the Franks,* trans. O. M. Dalton (Oxford: Clarendon, 1927); 2:36–37. The exemplum collection *An Alphabet of Tales* contains another version of the miracle with SS. Simon and Jude; see *An Alphabet of Tales,* 264, no. 383. For the account of SS. Simon and Jude in the *Legenda aurea,* see Jacobus de Voragine, *Legenda aurea,* 2:1084–85. The version in the *Life* of St. Brigid of Ireland, however, has the baby both exonerating the bishop and exposing his real father. See Seán Connolly, "Vita Prima Sanctae Brigitae: Background and Historical Value," *Journal of the Royal Society of Antiquaries of Ireland* 119 (1989): 5–49. See also *Bethu Brigte,* Celt: Corpus of Electronic Texts, http://www.ucc.ie/celt/published/T201002/index.html (chapter 40), accessed August 28, 2008.

In the Prioress's *Prologue*, Chaucer imagines a woman who desires to model her religious experience on that of an infant rendered suddenly able to proclaim the praises of the Divine. Chaucer depicts a woman who gives up all linguistic agency and desires to be a "blank slate" on which language can be written or the vocal passage through which the Lord or Mary can speak. As we recall from Chapter 2, many vitae of holy women who were said to have received gifts of sapientia go to great lengths to demonstrate their subjects' formal Latin illiteracy. Chaucer is similar to those hagiographers who explore how women reject traditional efforts at learning or scientia and imagine their female subjects as either being wholly unteachable except by divine illumination (like St. Catherine of Siena or Veronica of Binasco), or as even requesting a gift of not-learning (like St. Lutgard of Aywières), because a woman's unilluminated efforts might be more pleasing to God and ultimately more rewarding than her divinely infused knowledge.[21] Claims of miraculous Latinity are particularly important for those women who speak their visions fully or partly in Latin, for ongoing illiteracy reassures audiences that the women have not affected the Latin message in any way. Chaucer pushes this typical hagiographic motif of the illiterate woman to its extreme. The Prioress can suggest to her audience that her vernacular tale has not only been divinely inspired, but it is divinely articulated; since she cannot deny that she knows English, she declares herself an infant to proclaim the divine origin of her English tale.

If we are meant to associate the narrator of the *Prioress's Prologue* with the pilgrim described in the *General Prologue* (although it is not at all clear that we are), then Chaucer presents us with a woman schooled in the manner of Stratford atte Bowe (I. 125)and heading a convent not only claiming illiteracy or a lack of scientia but also claiming to be infantilized with no vernacular linguistic ability whatsoever. Chaucer is therefore imagining an educated woman who in turn imagines that the simple assertion of illiteracy (like that asserted by a number of xenoglossic women and their hagiographers, as discussed in the second chapter) is not sufficient for her; she prefers to imagine herself in a prelinguistic state in which any utterance must be guided by God.

Much has been made of how the Prioress wishes to model her speech on that of the little clergeon in her tale. Surprisingly, however, the Prioress does *not* tell a tale of miraculous infant speech. Rather, the tale describes a very different kind of gift: the clergeon's ability to sing after his throat has been cut, a regeneration of the speech organs. Moreover, the close of the tale suggests a

---

21. For Catherine of Siena and Veronica of Binasco, see Chapter 2; for Lutgard of Aywières, see Chapter 1.

gift of sapientia or divinely infused wisdom has enlightened the boy's understanding. Even more significantly, whereas the Prioress's *Prologue* denies all formal education and focuses on how an infant is the best model for miraculous speech, the tale focuses on how a seven-year-old boy learns his Latin through rote memorization and mundane effort. The tale, therefore, suggests that the extreme "blank slate" called for by the Prioress in the *Prologue* is not necessary, for Mary appreciates educative efforts.

The tale is not about a babe unable to speak, but it is about an older *infans* (a seven-year-old boy on the border of *pueritia*, or boyhood) learning by rote to sing a Latin antiphon, the *Alma redemptoris mater*, of which he does not understand the literal meaning.[22] Many have noted the clergeon's young age, which is usually attributed to Chaucer's desire to heighten the tale's sense of pathos.[23] Despite the narrator's attempts to compare the clergeon to the Holy Innocents, Chaucer emphasizes that the clergeon is definitely *not* an infant with miraculous speech; the boy already has mastered the power of speech and has entered school. When he is given his miraculous ability to sing out loudly after having his throat cut, he shares more in common with those saints who expose their attackers by speaking after their tongues have been cut out or their heads have been severed (like SS. Edmund and Cecilia), than with infants who suddenly burst forth in speech.

The tale pays much attention to the clergeon's mundane learning of the *Alma redemptoris* and his inability to translate the words he learns. The narrator repeatedly asserts that little clergeon has no formal education in Latin; the

---

22. According to the stages of life as defined by Isidore of Seville and others, the first stage of *infantia* actually lasted from birth to seven years, at which point *pueritia*, or "boyhood/childhood," began. For discussion of the medieval stages of childhood, see Shahar, *Childhood in the Middle Ages*, esp. 21–31. Further distinctions were sometimes made between the ages when speech was thought to begin (age two), and when speech was considered no longer ill-formed and incorrect (age five). For these substages, see Shahar, *Childhood in the Middle Ages*, 23. Many scholars point out that the lengths of the stages of *infantia*, *pueritia*, and *adolescentia* are not firmly defined during the Middle Ages; see, for example, James, "Childhood and Youth in the Early Middle Ages," 11–23, and Rob Meens, "Children and Confession," in *The Church and Childhood*, Wood, 53–65, esp. 53–54. For terminology related to *infantia*, see Didier Lett, *L'enfant des miracles: Enfance et société au Moyen Âge (XIIe-XIIIe siècle)* (Paris: Aubier, 1997), 42–56; for his discussion of children's speech, see especially 77–82 and 103–13. Chaucer's clergeon, therefore, is on the cusp or border between "infancy" and "childhood," on the verge of leaving the first state behind, as he moves from inarticulate *infantia* to fully aware and articulate *pueritia*, the age at which children were typically considered capable of sin. Graham Gould's "Childhood in Eastern Patristic Thought: Some Problems of Theology and Theological Anthropology," 39–52, in *The Church and Childhood*, Wood, discusses medieval debates over the capacity of religious understanding in infants.

23. See Robert Boenig, "Chaucer and St. Kenelm," *Neophilologus* 84 (2000): 157–64. Denise L. Despres has argued that the tale draws on the image of bleeding-child as host; see "Cultic Anti-Judaism and Chaucer's Litel Clergeon," *Modern Philology* 91 (1994): 413–27, at pp. 416–17.

boy can only say his *Ave Maria*, which he learned by rote and performed whenever he saw an image of Christ's mother (505–8). In mentioning how the clergeon wished to learn and did not forget his *Ave Maria*, the narrator invokes St. Nicholas (as she did in the *Prologue*), by stating, "But ay, whan I remember on this mateere, / Seint Nicholas stant evere in my presence, / For he so yong to Crist dide reverence" (513–15). Nicholas was famous for his remarkable early manifestations of blessedness as well as for his "precocious learning" as a child.[24] He did not experience a gift of Latin xenoglossia but rather a gift of divinely facilitated learning.

To invoke the divinely gifted Nicholas at this moment in the tale is somewhat startling, for the narrator before and after this stanza insists on the wholly unmiraculous, mundane way in which the clergeon memorizes his Marian hymns. We are told that while the clergeon is learning his Latin primer, he comes across the *Alma redemptoris*, a text he heard sung, "And as he dorste, he drough hym ner and ner, / And herkned ay the wordes and the noote, / Til he the firste vers koude al by rote" (520–22). There is nothing miraculous about the little clergeon's learning by rote the first Latin verse, or indeed, his rote learning of the remaining verses. In comparing the clergeon's dedication to worship with that of a truly divinely gifted learner, Nicholas, the narrator asserts that even one's wholly unmiraculous, pious efforts to learn devotional texts are appreciated by God and Mary.

The narrator is also careful to insist that the clergeon does not know the literal meaning of the Latin words he sings; nor does he have a gift of sapientia, which could afford literate knowledge or scientia. He is, however, attracted to the innate worshipful quality of the verses, which leads to him to seek out their translation:

> Noght wiste he what this Latyn was to seye,
> For he so yong and tendre was of age.
> But on a day his felawe gan he preye
> T'expounden hym this song in his langage,
> Or telle hym why this song was in usage;
> This preyde he hym to construe and declare
> Ful often tyme upon his knowes bare.
>
> (523–29)

24. For the "Boy Bishop" St. Nicholas, see "St. Nicholas and the Prioress's Calendar" and "St. Nicholas and the Prioress's 'cursed Jewes,'" in Haskell, *Essays on Chaucer's Saints*, 46–57.

The clergeon therefore appeals to an older boy either to translate and gloss the song into his own vernacular language or to explain the purpose of the verses. The older boy replies that he cannot translate the meaning because he has little grammar, but he does explain the song's purpose to the best of his ability:

> "This song, I have herd seye,
> Was maked of our blisful Lady free,
> Hire to salue, and eek hire for to preye
> To been oure help and socour whan we deye.
> I kan namoore expounde in this mateere.
> I lerne song; I kan but smal grammeere."
>
> (531–36)

Even the potential translator does not know the literal meaning of the words; he can, however, explain their use in a way that is understandable and appealing to the clergeon. It is significant that the clergeon has no other authoritative translators to appeal to; he does not seek out a teacher, for example, who could tell him what the verses mean in his own tongue (indeed, he is afraid of being beaten by his teacher for concentrating on memorizing it!). The clergeon approaches one who appears more authoritative than he is, an older boy, who understands enough to be able to tell him the significance and value of the text, which is all the younger boy need know.

In focusing in some detail on the little clergeon's determination to learn the hymn, as well as on how he actually accomplishes that learning through hard work, the narrator emphasizes still further the boy's mundane and wholly unmiraculous way of learning. The clergeon declares he will memorize the *Alma redemptoris* by Christmas, "Though that I for my prymer shal be shent / And shal be beten thries in an houre, / I wol it konne Oure Lady for to honoure" (541–43). The older schoolboy then tutors him on their way home from school until the clergeon has learned it by heart:

> His felawe taughte hym homward prively,
> Fro day to day, til he koude it by rote,
> And thanne he song it wel and boldely,
> Fro word to word, acordynge with the note.
> Twies a day it passed thurgh his throte.
>
> (544–48)

Why does this short tale place so much emphasis on the clergeon's rote learning of the hymn? Indeed, the stanzas that describe his study and schooling number over a quarter of the entire poem. The narrator repeatedly asserts that the boy has no comprehension of the actual Latin he is singing, for what matters is his dedicated performance of that hymn. Certainly, this would be a powerfully attractive idea for nuns, who often did not understand the actual liturgical verses they were singing, although they did understand the purpose of those verses.[25] The position of the clergeon, therefore, is similar to the position of adult worshippers who did not necessarily understand the Latin they were practicing; the tale promises that their diligent and patient performance will be rewarded. After all, miracle accounts demonstrate that Mary often rewarded the single-minded piety of the unlearned. Popular miracle collections recorded how illiterate lay and religious men and women could receive special grace through their concentrated prayers. Many medieval exempla and miracle collections, for example, include accounts describing how an unlearned man who prays the Ave Maria devoutly is then found, after death, to have a lily growing from his mouth.[26]

The miraculous gift that the child *does* receive in the tale is not a gift of language per se but rather the ability to voice a Latin song he had already learned by rote. When the clergeon's mother searched for him, "He *Alma redemptoris* gan to synge / So loude that al the place gan to rynge" (612–13), which draws the Christians to his body. The child is then carried to the church, "syngynge his song alway" (622); as he is about to be buried and holy water is sprinkled upon him, "Yet spak this child, whan spreynd was hooly water / And song O *Alma redemptoris mater!*" (640–41). It is not clear when the child initially stopped his singing, since he sang all the way to the church; presumably, he ceased and then began once again. That this is unclear is quite remarkable, when compared with the anxious specificity in the description of the clergeon learning the hymn. There seems nothing miraculous about the clergeon's actual song, unless we are to understand that the loudness of it is extraordinary; the clergeon's gift pointedly does not

---

25. According to Katherine Zeiman, "Reading, Singing, and Understanding: Constructions of the Literacy of Women Religious in Late Medieval England." "The Prioress champions singing explicitly characterized as illiterate as the purest form of piety" (107). Moreover, "the *litel clergeon* is the perfect choice to further this opposition to formal, institutional knowledge: whereas the Prioress might be excluded from these institutions, the clergeon, as a male, pre-cleric, does have access to them, but chooses to shun them" (107). In Sarah Rees Jones, ed., *Learning and Literacy in Medieval England and Abroad*, Utrecht Studies in Medieval Literacy 3 (Turnhout: Brepols, 2003), 97–120.

26. For "lily miracles," see Broughton, "The Prioress's Tale," 2:592–94.

appear to be a gift of Latin song or heavenly music, like that experienced by Christina Mirabilis so that she could sing the *Te Deum* with the nuns of Sint Truiden.[27]

However, the tale does give much attention to the actual mechanics of the miracle of speech, which mirrors the attention given to the mechanics of mundane learning. When the abbots asks the clergeon to relate how he is able to sing, the little boy explains in some detail:

> "And whan that I my lyf sholde forlete,
> To me she cam, and bad me for to synge
> This anthem verraily in my deyynge,
> As ye han herd, and what that I hadde songe,
> Me thoughte she leyde a greyn upon my tonge.
>
> "Wherefore I synge, and synge moot certeyn,
> In honour of that blisful Mayden free
> Til fro my tonge of taken is the greyn;
> And after that thus seyde she to me:
> 'My litel child, now wol I fecche thee,
> Whan that the greyn is fro thy tonge ytake.'"
>
> (658–68)

Chaucer dedicates two stanzas to the mechanics of the miracle. As I shall argue in later sections of this chapter, Chaucer is particularly concerned with how translation, miraculous or mundane, happens. He focuses attention on the miracle's medium (a grain of sand, seed, or even piece of the Eucharist), an intense focus that in turn becomes the message of the miracle: illiteracy or some learning is not an impediment to enlightenment.[28] On the contrary, when combined with intense devotion, it can offer a path to special grace.

The clergeon's speech to the abbot and all those listening also suggests that the boy may have been given a gift of *sapientia* or divinely infused wisdom. Although he does not understand the Latin of the *Alma redemptoris* before his attack, he does appear to become aware of its inner meaning afterward. His rhetoric in the church before burial reflects his new adultlike sophistication;[29] the little clergeon now points to scholarly or scriptural texts ("But Jesu

27. For Christina's miraculous Latin song, see Chapter 2.

28. For discussion of the nature of the *greyn*, see Albert B. Friedman, "The Mysterious 'Greyn' in the *Prioress's Tale*," *Chaucer Review* 11 (1977): 328–33.

29. "This single example of positive speech in the tale has been correctly seen as symbolizing intellectual growth in the child." Benson, *Chaucer's Drama of Style*, 138.

Crist, as ye in bookes fynde, / Wil that his glorie laste and be in mynde" 652–53), and his speech reflects his understanding of the Virgin Mother as a mercy-giver and guide to Christ, important aspects of the *Alma redemptoris*.[30] This description of the gift of sapientia, however, is not developed; it is not at all clear if he has received any access to Latinity, or simply if he knows that books contain information that he was never able to read and now no longer needs to.

Whereas both the *Prologue* and *Tale* suggest that single-minded devotion to Mary may be rewarded, each approaches linguistic agency from a different perspective. The *Prologue* imagines the female narrator abdicating all personal linguistic agency; the *Tale* suggests that some linguistic agency, afforded by mundane learning, is favorable. I would like to suggest that Chaucer is using the female narrator and the clergeon in the *Prologue* and *Tale* as a way of exploring a writer's authority to speak. Adopting the speaking persona of the Prioress in the *Prologue* allows Chaucer to imagine the writer or translator who claims to be a simple vessel through which language passes, much like the visionaries SS. Hildegard of Bingen or Elisabeth of Schönau are said to be simple conduits who in no way affect the form or content of their divine visions. Chaucer goes to extremes, however. It is not sufficient to insist that the Prioress is an uneducated woman, for she is already proficient in her vernacular tongue; claims of illiteracy, therefore, while asserting her lack of scientia, would do nothing to negate her mastery of English, the vehicle of her tale. To emphasize her role as heaven's vernacular mouthpiece, she must envision herself as an infantilized babe.

With the clergeon, Chaucer represents the writer who claims a divine enhancement of his traditionally learned ability, the beginnings of scientia enhanced by sapientia. Many writers throughout the Middle Ages asserted that their traditionally acquired learning was illuminated by divine grace. Whereas the clergeon is, of course, formally illiterate and cannot truly represent scientia, having only just started his schooling, he does represent the first forays into literacy as he learns his Latin prayer by rote. Even after having his throat slit, he is still textually focused and refers to learned books as a way to "know" Christ. Mary encourages his mundane efforts at learning and rewards him. Just as adults are encouraged to use miraculously speaking infants for models

---

30. Robert Boenig argues that the focus on the *Alma Redemptoris* is significant, for in other analogues the boy sings *Gaude Maria, Ave Regina*, or *Sancta Maria*. Boenig argues that Chaucer changes the song to something a child might be able to sing, thereby emphasizing the clergeon's youth. "*Alma Redemptoris Mater, Gaude Maria*, and the *Prioress's Tale*" *Notes and Queries* 46 (1999): 321–26.

of piety, male religious writers can turn to miraculously speaking women and children as models for their pious translations.

That we are unsure how to read the *Prioress's Tale* is part of the interrogation of the claim of divine inspiration. Whether or not the pilgrims believe the tale to be so inspired is unclear, for their reactions are not elaborated on beyond the statement that they were "sobre" (692), an ambiguous response at best. Even Chaucer the pilgrim stares down at the ground, either in reverence or embarrassment. Are we meant to read the tale as an aesthetically pleasing, positive testament of Mary's mercy? Or are we meant to be critical of the Prioress, to be horrified by her callousness and brutal anti-Semitism? Claiming the position of simple vessel allows an author or translator not to accept personal responsibility for what emerges. Elsewhere in the *Canterbury Tales* Chaucer explores how claims of lack of writerly control function as a protection against blame. For example, in the *General Prologue*, Chaucer the narrator asks that his readers not blame him for what the pilgrims say, for he merely copies down their words.[31] Similarly, in *Prologue* to the *Miller's Tale*, he instructs the audience to skip over the tale if they may be offended; "Blameth nat me if that ye chese amys. / The Millere is a cherl; ye knowe wel this" (I. 3181–82) he states, attempting to relieve himself of any responsibility. Reading these passages in the context of the *Prioress's Prologue* would suggest that Chaucer appreciates the usefulness of claiming the abdication of writerly control but is also critical of these claims, for authors may only imagine that fictional characters have full agency and speak on their own behalf. The *Prioress's Tale* explores the question, What happens when an assertion of miraculous speech actually produces something that is less than miraculous, something that is violent, vitriolic, and unfortunately all too human? It is not surprising that Chaucer pokes fun at the Prioress's claims of inspiration with the tale that follows, *Sir Thopas*, which claims no other inspiration than a rhyme Chaucer the pilgrim learned long ago, but which still manages to parody the miracle of the clergeon.[32]

---

31. "Whoso shal telle a tale after a man, / He moot reherce as ny as evere he kan / Everich a word, if it be in his charge, / Al speke he never so rudeliche and large, / Or ellis he moot telle his tale untrewe" (I. 731–35). See Michael P. Kuczynski, "Don't Blame Me: The Metaethics of a Chaucerian Apology," *Chaucer Review* 37 (2003): 315–28, and Alcuin Blamires, "Chaucer the Reactionary: Ideology and the *General Prologue* to *The Canterbury Tales*," *Review of English Studies* 51 (2000): 523–39.

32. For *Sir Thopas*'s relationship to the *Prioress's Tale*, see Alan T. Gaylord, "The 'Miracle' of *Sir Thopas*," *Studies in the Age of Chaucer* 6 (1984): 65–84, and E. S. Kooper, "Inverted Images in Chaucer's *Tale of Sir Thopas*," *Studia Neophilologica* 56 (1984): 147–54.

Part 2: Translating Custance: Latinate and Vernacular Xenoglossia in the *Man of Law's Tale*[33]

In the *Prioress's Prologue* and *Tale*, Chaucer's intense focus on the mechanics of mundane and miraculous translation calls attention to a woman's deliberate lack of control over that translation and language in general. In the *Man of Law's Tale*, Chaucer explores similar issues from a different perspective, as he purposefully mutes the mechanics of miraculous translation to experiment with what happens when one imagines a gift of xenoglossia in a hybrid genre, the hagiographical romance, which owes its attitudes toward language to the saint's life, the romance, and the history chronicle.

Within the *Man of Law's Prologue*, *Tale*, and *Epilogue*, Chaucer covers a range of approaches to literary and cultural translation. The work is full of moments of successful and unsuccessful translation, as well as translation that is at times highlighted, and at other times ignored or suppressed.[34] I shall focus on one instance of translation in particular, the strange occurrence of Custance's being understood when she arrives in Northumbria. I argue that in rewriting Custance from his sources, Chaucer creates a monolingual, Latin-speaking woman whose words are translated into English by means of a miracle usually experienced by medieval saints, the gift of xenoglossia. Custance's experience of xenoglossia, however, is not openly declared a miracle, and her ability to be understood by the Saxons in Northumbria has several possible explanations. This purposeful ambiguity on Chaucer's part points to larger issues of translation in the tale and in Chaucer's work in general, specifically his ongoing exploration of how translation is imagined to function through

---

33. A version of this section on the *Man of Law's Tale* has appeared as Christine F. Cooper's "'But algates therby was she understonde': Translating Custance in Chaucer's *Man of Law's Tale*," *Yearbook of English Studies* 36 (2006): 27–38.

34. In the *Prologue*, the Man of Law presents Chaucer as a wholly successful literary translator, one who has even surpassed his Latin authority, Ovid. The tale the Man of Law tells is not, however, an English translation of a Latin Ovidian romance or history, as we have been led to expect by the *Prologue*, but rather a tale the Man of Law claims was told to him by merchants, one that Chaucer actually translates from a French chronicle. The tale opens with a detailed description of merchants traveling to sixth-century Rome and bringing back to the Sultan of Syria reports of Princess Custance's beauty and renown. These reports represent successful, lived experiences of translation, which mediate between languages and cultures. Unsuccessful translation is figured by man's inability to translate the prophetic message of "the book of the stars" to see Custance's fate, for man is not learned enough to know the stellar tongue. Translation ignored or suppressed is seen when Custance, her family, and entourage arrive in Syria for her wedding and attend the banquet; no mention is made of any linguistic difference between the Romans and Syrians, and we are left to wonder how they understand one another, if they do understand one another at all.

various means, mundane or miraculous, depending on the genre of the text at hand. Moreover, because Chaucer elsewhere employs the metaphor of a man in a boat that he is unable to steer as a figure for the translator at the mercy of his authoritative sources, Custance, who is "translated" about the Mediterranean and Atlantic in a rudderless boat she cannot steer, therefore, in addition to being a figure of the translated text from Latin to English, becomes an apt figure for the translator him/herself, who is outwardly passive, seemingly at the mercy of seas and sources, but surreptitiously active, quietly "steering" his or her way through the source material to form a new kind of text.

When Custance's rudderless boat is cast upon the shores of Northumbria after "yeres and dayes" (II. 463) at sea and she is found by the local constable, the Roman princess begs for mercy in her own tongue, which is identified as a kind of "corrupt Latin." As a number of scholars have noted, in having Custance speak Latin, Chaucer has made an important change from his source, the fourteenth-century Anglo Norman *Les Cronicles* of Nicholas Trevet:[35] rather than being learned in many languages and able to speak Saxon to the constable, Custance speaks only her own language, which is nevertheless understood by the Northumbrians. During this encounter, the narrator calls particular attention to Custance's native tongue:

> *In hir langage* mercy she bisoghte,
> The lyf out of hir body for to twynne,
> Hire to delivere of wo that she was inne.
> *A maner Latyn corrupt was hir speche,*
> *But algates therby was she understonde.*
> (516–20, emphasis added)

---

35. Of Custance's language skills, Trevet states, "Et [ele] lui respoundi en Sessoneis, qe fu langage Olda, come cele q'estoit aprise en diverses langages . . ." (lines 129–30), in Nicolas Trevet, "De la noble femme Constance," 296–329 in *Sources and Analogues of Chaucer's Canterbury Tales,* Correale and Hamel, 2:303. Studies on the sources of the *Man of Law's Tale* generally agree that Chaucer's tale is a translation and adaptation of this work, with some additional borrowing from Gower's *Confessio Amantis,* II. 587–1707. For Chaucer's adaptations see Edward A. Block, "Originality, Controlling Purpose, and Craftsmanship in Chaucer's *Man of Law's Tale,*" *PMLA* 68 (1953): 572–616, and Robert Correale, "Chaucer's Manuscript of Nicholas Trevet's *Les Cronicles,*" *Chaucer Review* 25 (1991): 238–65. According to most critics, Chaucer's version borrows from Gower and not vice versa. Peter Nicholas argues that Chaucer is more dependent on Gower's version than on Trevet's: see Nicholson, "Chaucer Borrows from Gower: The Sources of the *Man of Law's Tale,*" in *Chaucer and Gower: Difference, Mutuality, Exchange,* ed. R. F. Yeager, English Literary Monograph Series 51 (Victoria, Canada: University of Victoria and English Literary Studies, 1991), 85–99, and Nicholson, "*The Man of Law's Tale*: What Chaucer Really Owed to Gower," *Chaucer Review* 26 (1991): 153–74.

In contrast to Trevet's educated woman who can speak Saxon, Chaucer's Custance is a monolingual Latin speaker who can communicate only by having her language understood by the Saxon Northumbrians.

Many critics have attempted to explain why Chaucer alters Custance's language abilities. Some, including J. A. Burrow and A. C. Spearing, argue that Chaucer was trying for "historical verisimilitude" by reflecting what he understood to be the early medieval linguistic situation as Latin evolved from classical to "corrupt" Latin or Italian, which was spoken in Italy or possibly throughout Europe as the *lingua franca* of merchants.[36] Others assert that Chaucer intended the mention of "corrupt Latin" to signal a significant language barrier between Custance and the early British, and that it therefore serves a thematic purpose by reflecting on Custance's character and/or heightening her experience of vulnerability and outsidedness.[37] David Raybin suggests that Custance's language contributes to making her "the consummate outsider" as her speech is "foreign-sounding and difficult to the inhabitants of northern England. . . . Existing without name, without provenance, without her hosts' language, and without prescribed status, Custance is, in essence, the unaccommodated woman, idealized as untainted constancy, form, and spirituality."[38] For Kathryn Lynch, Custance's serious language barrier in Northumbria makes England seem a place more foreign and strange than even the East.[39]

36. J. A. Burrow, "A Maner Latyn Corrupt," *Medium Aevum* 30 (1961): 33–37, argues that "corrupt Latin" was a phrase used in medieval sources to characterize the language of late antiquity (34). Either Chaucer knew that Custance, during the antique period, would have spoken corrupt Latin (as gleaned from Isidore of Seville) or "he simply brazened it out, relying, perhaps, on the unrealistic language-conventions of romance" (37). Burrow quotes H. J. Chaytor, *From Script to Print: An Introduction to Medieval Vernacular Literature* (Cambridge: Heffer, 1945), who argues that corrupt Latin was the *lingua franca* of merchants, and Burrow therefore suggests that Chaucer was trying to reflect accurately the important presence of trade in the early Middle Ages. Chaytor, *From Script to Print*, 28, cited in Burrow, "A Maner Latyn Corrupt," 36–37. A. C. Spearing, in "Narrative Voice: The Case of Chaucer's *Man of Law's Tale*," *New Literary History* 32 (2001): 715–46, asserts: "That sense of historical change in language, coordinated with a larger setting in which northern Britain had been invaded by pagan Saxons who had driven the Christian Britons into Wales, is not at all characteristic of pre-Chaucerian saints' lives" (740). That Chaucer realized that language changes over time is supported by the Proem from Book 2 of *Troilus*, lines 22–26.

37. R. A. Shoaf, "'Unwemmed Custance': Circulation, Property, and Incest in the *Man of Law's Tale*," *Exemplaria* 2 (1990): 287–302, asserts that the mention of her corrupt Latin, added "for the sake of verisimilitude," followed by the reassurance that she was understood [algates], "insists that corruption really has not affected Custance" (288).

38. David Raybin, "Custance and History: Woman as Outsider in Chaucer's *Man of Law's Tale*," *Studies in the Age of Chaucer* 12 (1990): 65–84, at p. 70. There is, however, no indication that Custance's language is difficult for the Northumbrians to understand.

39. Kathryn L. Lynch, "Storytelling, Exchange, and Constancy: East and West in Chaucer's *Man of Law's Tale*," *Chaucer Review* 33 (1999): 409–22, at pp. 418–19. Lynch's main point is that

No one, however, has suggested that Custance's strange linguistic situation results from the tale's heavy reliance on the genre of the saint's life.[40] In having Custance being understood in Latin by the Saxon-speaking Northumbrians, Chaucer is very clearly implying that she receives a gift of xenoglossia, a miracle of language that is described in a number of late medieval vitae and visionary texts. Because Chaucer makes the point that Custance's Latin is understood "algates" ("nevertheless," or even "entirely" or "continuously") by the Northumbrians, it seems that we are meant to find it remarkable, if not miraculous.[41] In translating and adapting Trevet's chronicle, Chaucer rewrites his source to suggest that the saintly Custance (whose holiness he also chooses to emphasize in comparison with his sources) experiences a gift of miraculous translation, much like those xenoglossic gifts that allow a number of medieval holy men and women to be received and understood by foreign-speaking audiences in order that they may preach the word of God (if they are men), give spiritual counseling, and engage in pious conversation and devotional practices. Because this tale owes much of its form and content to the saint's life and incorporates into the narrative a number of hagiographic tropes, including the performance of miracles and the conversion of pagans, an occurrence of xenoglossia would be quite fitting, perhaps even expected.[42]

As I have argued in Chapter 1, vernacular xenoglossia is relatively common in later medieval men's saints' lives. This allows the holy men either to be understood in the language of their listeners (an aural miracle) or to be able to speak a language they have never learned (an oral miracle). The gift of miraculous vernacular translation enables these men to engage in preaching and missionary work; in addition, it also facilitates pious conversation, spiritual guidance, and confession. In comparison with holy men, however, relatively few medieval women receive gifts of vernacular xenoglossia. The women's gifts are never granted for the purpose of public preaching but rather for individual spiritual guidance, often when the women are approached by

---

"both the Islam of the Syrians and the paganism of the Northumbrians are made shockingly alien and "Other" in the *Man of Law's Tale*" (410).

40. Elizabeth Robertson comes closest to this point in "The 'Elvyssh' Power of Constance: Christian Feminism in Geoffrey Chaucer's *The Man of Law's Tale*," *Studies in the Age of Chaucer* 23 (2001): 143–80, in which she argues, "As an agent of conversion, Constance is translatable, despite her foreignness" (165).

41. In translating *algates* as "nevertheless," I am following Larry Benson's gloss in the *Riverside Chaucer*. The *Middle English Dictionary* also defines *algates* as, "In all ways, in every way or respect; entirely, altogether," as well as "all the while, unceasingly, continually . . . at all times, on all occasions, under all circumstances" (def. 1a, 2a, and 2c).

42. See Michael Paull, "The Influence of the Saint's Legend Genre in the *Man of Law's Tale*," *Chaucer Review* 5 (1971): 179–94.

another in need. However, as I argued in Chapter 2, gifts of miraculous Latinity appear far more frequently than vernacular xenoglossia in medieval holy women's vitae, and these gifts enable the women to read scriptural texts, engage in more literate forms of pious practice, and participate in liturgical activities.

Custance's experience draws from these patterns and tropes of xenoglossia in later medieval vitae, while incorporating some striking adaptations. One similarity is that holy women are often granted the gift of vernacular translation when they are in vulnerable situations. That Custance can be understood means that, marooned on some strange shore and at the mercy of its inhabitants, she can be taken care of by others. Her situation can be compared with those of later medieval holy women. For example, as we recall from Chapter 1, St. Colette of Corbie was granted the ability to speak the language of her attackers when she and her fellow nuns were threatened by thieves while traveling in a strange land. And, as I explored in Chapter 3, Kempe and her scribe claim a xenoglossic miracle for Margery when, thrown out of the Hospice of St. Thomas of Canterbury in Rome, she must seek out another English-speaking priest to whom she could confess and express her mystical dalliances. In other vitae, the gift allows a holy woman to help someone in need, as with the Flemish-speaking St. Lutgard of Aywières, who brought a despairing woman back to sanity after conversing in French with her for a short time, or St. Bridget of Sweden, who aided a Finnish-speaking pilgrim when he could not find a confessor in Rome.[43] Custance's gift, however, does not, as with these other women, last for a short period, but rather (I assume) for the length of time she stays in England, or at least until she learns the Saxon language, an event that is never actually referred to.

Whereas later medieval holy women gifted with xenoglossia are either vernacular speakers who receive the gift of speaking or understanding another vernacular language to engage in private, spiritual conversation, or are women given literacy in Latin without ever having studied it, by contrast Custance is a woman whose mother tongue is Latin. In effect, she is the only medieval example of a xenoglossic holy woman who possesses a complete mastery over Latinity. As she speaks Latin, her words are presumably received by the English inhabitants in their own language; it therefore appears to be some kind of aural miracle facilitating the vernacular translation of Latin that occurs in the ears of the listeners, rather than in Custance's mouth.

Custance's Latinity, however, is not a clerical or scriptural variety but

43. For Lutgard's and Bridget's xenoglossia, see Chapter 1.

rather a vulgar or common one learnt "at the knee," a corrupt form of classical Latin that is fast approaching vernacular Italian. In this way, Custance's
native tongue represents an ambiguous, difficult-to-define state of linguistic
development and modification, as she herself hovers halfway between
"learned" Latin and vernacular language. Thus, her speech partakes of both
the Latin and vernacular worlds, while strictly belonging to neither. Chaucer
imagines Custance's language as existing at a time before clerics were relied
on as the authoritative translators and glossers of Latin Scripture in England.
Therefore, by imagining Custance as taking part in the early Christianization
of England, Chaucer can imagine a Latin-speaking woman who is able to
preach and teach in Latin without appearing in any way heretical. She is Latinate, but not too Latinate; she is authoritative, but not too clerical.[44] In this
way, Chaucer is quite similar to Margery Kempe, as they both find a way for
their female characters to preach in Latin by means of xenoglossia, while
deftly avoiding charges of heresy.

Custance's inability to speak the Saxon language, but nevertheless (or continuously) being understood while speaking Latin, is an example of unidirectional translation, that is, communication that is entirely (and only) effective
in one direction, speaker to audience. The "text" (Custance's words) is received by the Northumbrians, influencing their culture and initiating change
within it, without Custance herself being affected. Custance's ability to create
change in the Northumbrians is emphasized throughout the tale, for her prayers and pious example create new converts to Christianity. Yet what is the
Saxons' effect on her? Nothing, for she remains "unwemmed" (924), as Shoaf
points out. Indeed, it is never clear whether she learns the language of the
Northumbrians, or how she comes to understand them, because the important thing in the tale is not that she *listens*, but that she *speaks*, for there is
nothing that the Northumbrians have to say to her that is more important
than what she can say to them. In this way, the *Man of Law's Tale* shares
another thing in common with *The Book of Margery Kempe*, which relates
Margery's pilgrimage travels to Rome and Jerusalem and chooses to elaborate
only on Margery's own ability to be understood by foreign-speakers, rather
than on how she herself understands others.

Custance's experience of unidirectional xenoglossia is similar to that of a
number of holy men, such as SS. Anthony of Padua and the early Welsh
missionaries David, Padarn, and Teilo, whose words are miraculously trans-

---

44. As Robertson argues, "By placing Constance firmly in the past, Chaucer avoids directly
affirming a woman's ability to preach, while at the same time he is able to allude to a controversial issue of his day." "The 'Elvyssh' Power of Constance," 170.

lated into the language of their audiences; in these instances, the holy men's own ability to understand those to whom they are preaching is never mentioned, because it is perceived as unimportant.[45] What this unidirectional miracle indicates is the importance of the holy person's words being translated and received by others in need. Custance therefore receives the linguistic miracle so that her pious words can be translated like an authoritative text from Latin into the vernacular.

Xenoglossia enables Custance to preach and teach like famous later medieval holy men who are granted gifts of miraculous translation in order to preach to and convert large audiences. However, Custance is shown as converting just one person through preaching alone; in other instances, it is *both* her actions and her words that convert people. In this way, her preaching miracle granted for the sake of conversion resembles the more intimate, private xenoglossic experiences of holy women, experiences that are usually shared between the woman and only one other person.

The importance of Custance's proselytizing words is revealed in the first speech she makes after settling in Northumbria. In this scene, Chaucer redirects attention away from the miraculous curing of a blind man in order to focus on Custance's role as a xenoglossic preacher converting the local pagan constable. When a blind man confronts Hermengyld and Custance while they are "romen to and fro" (558) one day and begs for the return of his sight, Custance encourages her friend to perform the miracle and then explains the laws of Christianity to the surprised constable until the sun goes down:

> "In name of Crist," cride this blinde Britoun,
> "Dame Hermengyld, yif me my sighte agayn!"
> This lady weex affrayed of the soun,
>
> . . . .
>
> Til Custance made hire boold, and bad hire wirche
> The wyl of Crist, as doghter of his chirche.

> The constable weex abasshed of that sight,
> And seyde, "What amounteth al this fare?"
> Custance answerde, "Sire, it is Cristes myght,
> That helpeth folk out of the feendes snare."
> And so ferforth she gan oure lay declare

45. For the xenoglossic experiences of Anthony of Padua, David, Padarn, and Teilo, see Chapter 1.

That she the constable, er that is was eve
Converteth, and on Crist made hym bileve.

(561–74)

Although the implication is that Hermengyld returns sight to the blind man
when urged to do so by Custance, the passage never actually states that this
happens. The miraculous return of the blind man's vision, which is described
in detail in Chaucer's sources, is glossed over, "under-described," and even
neglected in the *Man of Law's Tale*.

Indeed, a comparison between Trevet's version and Chaucer's underscores
the latter's startling changes. Trevet focuses on the healing of the blind man:
"And Hermengild, before Olda and his retinue which followed him, in good
and firm faith made the holy cross on the eyes of the blind man, and said to
him in her Saxon language, 'Blind man, in the name of Jesus, slain on the
cross, have thy sight.' And he was immediately given sight and saw well and
clearly. When Olda had seen this, he wondered greatly where his wife had
learned her admirable skill."[46] In Chaucer's rewriting, however, after Custance
makes Hermengyld "bold" through her verbal encouragement, the focus immediately shifts to Custance's verbal persuasion of the constable through her
"lay declaring" or explication (and hence translation) of Scripture and Christian doctrine. In addition, the household that accompanies Elda, as described
in Trevet, has been completely eliminated in Chaucer's version; Custance
preaches only to the constable, discreetly, without an audience.

To deemphasize and "sidestep" the miracle of restored sight is quite an
interesting move on Chaucer's part. After all, medieval vitae and miracle accounts focus without exception on the miracles themselves. That Chaucer
avoids describing the actual miracle has caused some critical comment. In his
essay "Miracles in *The Man of Law's Tale*," William C. Johnson, Jr., argues
that Chaucer avoids directly attributing several miracles to God to highlight
the human agency involved in the events.[47] Whereas Johnson sees this side-

46. "Trevet, De la noble femme Constance," in *Sources and Analogues of Chaucer's Canterbury Tales*, Correale and Hamel, 2:306. "Et Hermegild, devaunt Olda et sa meine qe lui sui, de
bone foi et ferme fist sus les euz de lui enveuglé la seinte croiz et lui dit en sa langage Sessoine:
'Bisne man [in] Jhesu name in [rode] yslawe, have thi siht.' Et sil [meintenaunte] fu aluminé et
regardoit bien et clerement. Quant Olda avoit ceo veu, mult s'enmerveilla ou sa femme avoit
aprise sa bele mestrie" (2:307, lines 183–88).

47. For example, in John Gower's version the blind man prays to Hermengyld, who hears
his prayer and then tells him to "See"; he regains his sight and Elda concludes "That he the feith
mot nede obeie" (line 778), in *Confessio Amantis*, from John Gower, "Tale of Constance," 330–50
in *Sources and Analogues*, ed. Correale, 2:333, quoted from *The Complete Works of John Gower:
The English Works*, ed. G. C. Macaulay (Oxford: Clarendon, 1901; reprinted Grosse Point, MI:
Scholarly Press, 1968) 2:146–73.

stepping of the miraculous event as Chaucer emphasizing the human doubt that arises regarding "what we can feel and what we can understand" about an event,[48] I see Chaucer making the miraculous ambiguous for two very different reasons: first, because he chooses to focus on Custance's verbal activity instead of what many have identified as her utter passivity, and second, because he is experimenting with the implications of xenoglossia in genres other than the "pure" saint's legend.

Chaucer obscures the miraculous because he wishes to focus on Custance as an active agent in conversion. Deemphasizing the miraculous scenes calls attention to Custance's persuasive verbal activities. Whereas many critics see her as a figure of utter passivity, subject to male authority, both earthly and divine, as she is translated across the Mediterranean and Atlantic in a rudderless boat and likewise unable to control her own path on land, I argue that the implication of xenoglossia emphasizes her importance, not as a passive listener but rather as an active preacher, much like renowned xenoglossic holy men.[49] Chaucer refocuses the scene with the blind man so that the most prominent event is that Custance speaks and is heard by both Hermengyld and then the constable, who is converted by her after listening to her explications for hours. It is not important that Custance herself hears and understands; what matters is that she preaches persuasively and her language is ingested. Custance's words of Latin Scripture and spiritual explication are understood and fully appreciated by the constable; if we imagine a gift of xengolossia is occurring, then her Latin words of Scripture and explication are miraculously translated into his Saxon vernacular, a pure and equivalent "word and sense" translation that persuades the man to convert. Whereas in the early fifteenth century Margery Kempe can preach the Latin words of Holy Writ only by having them miraculously translated from English into Latin in the mouth of a cleric, as a saintly figure from the remote English past, Custance is able to preach and be translated for the sake of conversion without the worry of being labeled a heretic.

But there is another good reason why Chaucer "muffles the miraculous" in the tale, never directly referring to Custance's ability to be understood

---

48. William C. Johnson, Jr., "Miracles in *The Man of Law's Tale*," *Bulletin of the Rocky Mountain Modern Language Association* 28 (1974): 57–65, at p. 64.

49. For Custance's passivity, see, for example, Carolyn Dinshaw, "The Law of Man and its 'Abhomynacions,'" *Exemplaria* 1 (1989): 117–48, in which she states that "Constance's minimal self-awareness allows her no more than passivity" (141); Susan Schibanoff, "Worlds Apart: Orientalism, Antifeminism, and Heresy in Chaucer's *Man of Law's Tale*," *Exemplaria* 8 (1996): 59–96, esp. 62–63. According to Robertson, however, "Whether or not Constance can be called active or passive . . . seems indeterminate." "The 'Elvyssh' Power of Constance," 161.

while speaking Latin as a miracle and offering both a divine and a mundane explanation for each miraculous event. This is, of course, because Chaucer is not writing a strict saint's life. As many scholars have argued, several genres are at work in this tale, specifically the (vernacular) saint's life, the romance, and the chronicle history, which combine to form a "hagiographic romance" or "homiletic romance."[50] Events are not clearly described as miracles, as in a saint's life, because Chaucer is exploring places where the expectations of romance, vita, and history overlap and diverge; one such place is how the practice of translation and the ability to communicate between languages are conceptualized.[51] Much as she acts like one, Custance is not truly a saint; she becomes a married woman who must have sex as good wives do and can follow a religious life only after being released from the duties of marriage by widowhood.[52] Because she belongs to the literary worlds of history, romance, and vita, Custance's xenoglossia cannot be fully developed as it is in the vitae of medieval saints. Generic overlapping in the tale explains how she can be xenoglossically gifted and an example of "historical verisimilitude," her "corrupt Latin" at the same time a linguistic barrier and no barrier at all. Just as she exists between classical Latin and vernacular language, Custance is both a translator and no translator at all.

The ambiguity of Custance's xenoglossic situation urges the tale's readers to consider how linguistic communication and translation are imagined to operate and function in different genres. To think of the tale as a vita allows us to see her ability to be understood "algates" as a miracle of xenoglossia, something to marvel at because it lies beyond normal human capability; the claim of xenoglossia also attests to the pious speech of the holy woman and affirms her words as supported by God. If we consider the tale to be a chronicle history, then Custance's ability to be understood can be interpreted as commenting not so much on her own personal state as on the mundane

50. For the term "homiletic romance," see Helen Cooney, "Wonder and Immanent Justice in the *Man of Law's Tale*," *Chaucer Review* 33 (1999): 264–87. Cooney borrows this term from Dieter Mehl, *The Middle English Romances of the Thirteenth and Fourteenth Centuries* (London: Routledge, 1968), 120–22; Mehl quoted in Cooney, "Wonder and Immanent Justice," 264. Many reflect on the mixed genres of the tale; see, for example, Dinshaw, "The Law of Man," who states, "The *Tale* is a mixture of hagiography, romance, and chronicle history, in which Constance plays roles of saint and romance heroine that prove finally contradictory in the narrative" (117).

51. Of course, Chaucer's mixing of genres has been noted by many. See, for example, Derek Pearsall, "Chaucer's Religious Tales: A Question of Genre," in Benson and Robertson, *Chaucer's Religious Tales*, 11–19.

52. The example of St. Bridget of Sweden and other married saints would suggest that married women could become saints in the later Middle Ages, either after the death of their spouses or when the husbands had entered a monastery and released their wives from their spousal duties.

linguistic abilities of the Northumbrians and the situation of Latin comprehension in early medieval Britain; either Chaucer is imagining that the Saxon's language is quite similar to Custance's and can therefore be mutually understood, or that the Northumbrians are actually bilingual, since Latin was the *lingua franca* of merchants, or that perhaps there was an interpreter on hand, one rendered invisible in the annals of history.[53] If we consider the tale to be a romance, we can, as Burrow has suggested, imagine that Chaucer was relying "on the unrealistic language-conventions of romance" that ignore natural linguistic divisions, and therefore we may interpret her being understood as a comment about neither her own language nor that of the Northumbrians but rather as a way of calling attention to how mundane translation is often ignored in romance literature.

In all of these cases, Chaucer is exposing the narrative conventions of different genres that allow foreigners to speak and be understood through different means. Indeed, the references to translation that occur throughout the tale (like the book of the stars that no one can read because their "wittes ben so dulle" [202–3]) mean that we must also puzzle over the fact that no interpreters are mentioned when Custance attends the banquet in Syria or when Alla travels to Rome, even though the merchants are such conspicuous translators at the opening of the tale. In these moments, we are forced to wonder whether communication occurs through the conventions of historical narrative, romance, or saint's life: is there an invisible interpreter (historical narrative), a gift of xenoglossia (saint's life), or an ignored linguistic barrier (romance)? Is the difficulty so great that it must be magically or miraculously surmounted, or else humanly conquered (through learning), or is it no difficulty at all? I believe that by not clearly defining how Custance is understood in Northumbria, Chaucer intends his audience to consider other moments in the poem to explore the questions of just what can and cannot be translated, and by whom, in which genres. Just as Chaucer's frequent claims of "word for word and sense for sense" translation draw our attention to how his works are *not*, moments of actual, difficult, or miraculous translation in the tale draw our attention to those places were translation is not mentioned at all, or to those places in which translation is purposefully ambiguous, such as the inclusion of the Briton Gospels, a text that could either be Latin or English.[54]

---

53. For more on the invisibility of translators in certain genres (including travel literature), see Lawrence Venuti, *The Translator's Invisibility: A History of Translation* (London: Routledge, 1995).

54. For the question of the language of these Gospels, see Andrew Breeze, "The Celtic Gospels in Chaucer's *Man of Law's Tale*," *Chaucer Review* 32 (1998): 335–38.

These difficult and intriguing questions about language and translation in the tale, therefore, suggest that Custance herself becomes a figure for the vernacular translator's complex relationship to his authoritative, Latinate sources. In the Proem to Book II of *Troilus and Criseyde*, the narrator claims to be at the helm in a boat, at the mercy of the tempestuous waves of his matter and sources:

> Owt of thise blake wawes for to saylle,
> O wynd, O wynd, the weder gynneyth clere;
> For in this see the boot hath swych travaylle,
> Of my connyng, that unneth I it steere.
> This see clepe I the tempestous matere
> Of disespeir that Troilus was inne.
>
> (II. 1–6)

Chaucer imagines the translator at the mercy of his respected, Latinate sources, which dictate to him what he must say; theirs is a force almost too great for him, for he can scarcely ("unneth") steer the boat (i.e., his translation) through the violent and powerful matter. He therefore excuses himself: "Disblameth me if any word be lame, / For as myn auctour seyde, so sey I" (17–18). Claiming to be at the mercy of matter he has no control over, the translator appears almost completely helpless; similar logic is included at the beginning of Book IV, when the narrator states, "And now my penne, allas, with which I write, / Quaketh for drede of that I moste endite" (13–14). Chaucer presents the translator as a humble interpreter of language, unable to control his sources and compelled to write exactly what they say; he simply renders one language into another, attempting to translate "word for word and sense for sense." This is a familiar stance adopted by medieval translators, for it both excuses their work and asserts the translations' authority as direct models of their sources. Of course, Chaucer is doing anything but "slavishly" following his source in *Troilus*, and it is precisely at those points where he claims to be translating exactly that he is most experimental.[55]

In the *Man of Law's Tale*, Chaucer joins the image of the translator in a boat at the mercy of his authoritative sources with that of the Christian soul afloat in the sea of the world (representing the pilgrimage of man on earth),

---

55. See Wogan-Browne et al., "Authorizing Text and Writer," in *The Idea of the Vernacular: An Anthology of Middle English Literary Theory, 1280–1520*, ed. Jocelyn Wogan-Browne, Nicholas Watson, Andrew Taylor, and Ruth Evans (University Park: Pennsylvania State University Press, 1999), esp. pp 3–14. See also Ellis's discussion of *Troilus* in "Translation," 452–53.

as well as the boat as the Christian Church with the soul of man within it.[56] Custance, who repeatedly travels the seas in her rudderless boat, can be read as a metaphor for the position of the translator at the mercy of his or her authoritative sources. She is a figure of both the translated Latin text (she is translated physically over the seas, her words are translated miraculously or mundanely into Saxon) and the translator, appearing entirely passive, at the mercy of her sources, traveling out and returning again and again to her "Latin source," Rome.[57]

Chaucer identifies the public position of the humble Middle English translator, the *fidus interpres*, with the figure of the female translator in the *Man of Law's Tale*. As Jocelyn Wogan-Browne et alia have argued, "when he [Chaucer] chooses to identify one of his own texts as dependent on a source, he tends to emphasize passivity, and such passages are usually attached to works that themselves have a particularly passive, receptive, or suffering protagonist whose situations are mirrored in the narrator-translator's passivity, lack of free will, and powerlessness to change the preordained plot."[58] By identifying Custance as a figure for the outwardly passive stance of the translator, the position of the translator, therefore, becomes somewhat feminized. But just as the translator in *Troilus*, although admitting to having only a "little steering" actually charts new territories with his translation, Chaucer's Custance, although outwardly passive and tossed about on the waves of seas and sources, is subtly active in her xenoglossic preaching, charting new religious territories for pagan England.

Whereas late medieval English laymen and women, like the Shipman in the *Epilogue* to the *Man of Law's Tale*, may have had to protect themselves from accusations of Lollardy by claiming they had "but litel Latyn in my mawe" (1190), Custance, however, as an early English historical, saintly, and romance figure, is permitted to have *only* Latin in hers, although she must still walk a fine line between public preaching and private teaching. How different an experience from that of Margery in *The Book of Margery Kempe*, who must claim to possess absolutely no Latin in her maw or be accused of heresy, or Chaucer's Prioress, who prefers to imagine herself as an infant without any language at all.

---

56. See V. A. Kolve, *Chaucer and the Imagery of Narrative: The First Five Canterbury Tales* (Stanford: Stanford University Press, 1984), 297–358.

57. Chaucer also uses the image of traveling to Rome by diverse paths as a metaphor for translation in his *Treatise on the Astrolabe* (lines 25–40). For more on this image, see Ellis, "Translation," 447.

58. Wogan-Browne et al., *Idea of the Vernacular*, 9.

Part 3: "The Pyns and Gyns" of Miraculous Translation in the *Squire's Tale*

Whereas the hagiographic romance the *Man of Law's Tale* purposefully glosses over how miraculous translation functions in a tale that borrows from saint's life, history, and romance, the *Squire's Tale*, similar to the *Prioress's Prologue and Tale*, is highly invested in the mechanics of miraculous and mundane translation. In this tale, Chaucer focuses on just how translation is and is not imagined to take place in the genre of romance. Its intense attention paid to the mechanics of miraculous translation actually points to how romances typically *ignore* issues of translation. I shall argue that with the figure of Canacee as translator with her translator ring, Chaucer is critiquing (and poking fun at) the assumptions that lie behind claims of "word for word and sense for sense" translation, a fantasy of equivalence that imagines that a bird and a woman can perfectly understand one another and share exactly the same realms of experience.

That the *Squire's Tale* has a wider idea of translation at its core has been discussed at length by a number of critics. A mysterious knight sent by the King of Araby and India brings the Mongolian Court of King Cambyuskan four gifts, all of which function as some aid to translation, as John Fyler has noted. The first is a magical horse that will bear the rider wherever he wishes to go, a kind of physical *translatio*; the second is a magical ring that enables the wearer to understand bird speech and to be understood by birds; the third and fourth gifts, a mirror that enables the person who looks into it to see the true nature of others and a sword that mends wounds as well as creates them, are "also aids to translation, if in a less direct sense: like the horse and ring, they close gaps, recover unities, pull together what has been dispersed."[59] The four gifts, therefore, all seem to offer the miraculous (and therefore humanly impossible) ability of perfect and effortless translation of physical, linguistic, and mental states. The only gift actually employed in the tale, however, is that of the ring, which the princess Canacee uses to understand a conversation

59. John M. Fyler, "Domesticating the Exotic in the *Squire's Tale*," *ELH* 55 (1988): 1–26, at p. 3. Shirley Sharon-Zisser in "*The Squire's Tale* and the Limits of Non-Mimetic Fiction," *Chaucer Review* 26 (1992): 377–94, argues, "The strange knight's gifts all offer dissolution of what the court conceives to be the ultimate horizons of human capabilities." The ring "erases the boundaries imposed on human perception by the medium of language," and the mirror "is a heuristic device which makes it possible to penetrate beyond the bounds of the present moment and of other minds" (379). In "Chaucer's Strategies of Translation," *Chaucer Yearbook* 4 (1997): 1–19, Paul Beekman Taylor writes that "the Squire's style draws particular attention to the convergence of art and nature in acts of translation, most of which pertain to the gifts that the king of Araby and India sends Cambyuskan for his birthday" (16).

with a love-sick falcon, whose pain she comprehends not only because she magically speaks bird language but also because she is a noble woman and identifies with the experience of the noble bird wounded by her false lover. Furthermore, Paul Beekman Taylor's essay, "Chaucer's Strategies of Translation," examines how the gifts' abilities to translate "will and thought to speech and deed" point to Chaucer's translation process in general, for "Chaucer is not concerned with simply finding English equivalents for foreign words, but with mediating literary contexts and the ideas they inform. . . . Like Canacee's ring, Chaucer's translations constitute an interpretation of language."[60]

A number of critics have also noted how the tale falls quite distinctly into gendered halves, each offering a different approach to language: part one introduces the masculine realm of the court with Cambyuskan and the knight, and part two the feminine realm of the garden with Canacee and the falcon.[61] In an attempt to reconcile the seemingly disparate halves of the tale, Shirley Sharon-Zisser asserts that there are two kinds of literary modes at work. The first part presents the rhetorical or metafictional mode, and the second, the magical or fantastic mode. According to Sharon-Zisser, the two modes are in stark opposition, for the rhetorical encourages the audience to look closely at language and textual operations, whereas the magical encourages the audience to ignore textual operations.[62] More recently, Alan Ambrisco has argued that, whereas the first part of the tale claims difficulties in description and translation, the second is a "fantasy of complete linguistic competence for the English language" or a "fantasy of perfect communication" for a "language whose suitability as a medium of translation was far from being universally acknowledged."[63] Both of these studies call attention to the strikingly different treatment of language and translation in the two halves of the tale; it is precisely this difference that I would like to examine further.

In this tale, Chaucer is exploring the public stances that a translator can take regarding the relationship between a translation and its source(s). Although romances typically ignore linguistic difficulties and, according to J. A.

---

60. Taylor, "Chaucer's Strategies of Translation," 17.

61. A number of critics have noted the change from masculine to feminine space between these sections. For example, in "Chaucer's *Squire's Tale*: The Poetics of Interlace or the 'Well of English Undefiled,'" Carol Heffernan argues, "The falcon episode in Part Two of the *Squire's Tale* is fully female and thus contrasts sharply with the maleness of Part One" (39), in *Chaucer Review* 32 (1997): 32–45. In a similar vein, Lynch, "East Meets West in Chaucer's *Squire's* and *Franklin's Tales*," sees the latter section as focusing on the feminine, specifically with Chaucer imagining the east as a locus of female sexual power, while the former focuses on masculine courtly power. *Speculum* 70 (1995): 530–51.

62. Sharon-Zisser, "*The Squire's Tale* and the Limits of Non-Mimetic Fiction."

63. Ambrisco, "It lyth nat in my tonge," 215, 219.

Burrow, rely on "unrealistic language-conventions,"[64] Chaucer is deliberately setting two kinds of public stances of the translator against one another and gendering each stance. In the first part, the masculine realm of the court, the translator is represented by the narrator, who presents himself as a humble and ineffectual conveyor of both the tale and the speech he is reporting; he is an active yet impotent translator who cannot hope to reproduce his authoritative, learned sources, whether they are written or spoken. In the second half of the tale, the feminine realm of the garden and bedroom, Chaucer presents perfect, "word for word and sense for sense" translation, with Canacee as the translator who can ignore all linguistic differences and erase all translational difficulties. He uses Canacee to represent the myth of perfect equivalence, of the effortless ability to render one experience into the language of another, without distortion or alteration. The tale as a whole, therefore, purposely explores the possibilities and impossibilities of translation. In comparing and contrasting these two different public stances of the translator (the humble, ineffectual, translator who cannot hope to translate authoritative sources, and the bold, confident translator who claims to translate both word and sense and that perfect equivalence is possible), Chaucer links miraculous translation with the feminine and questions the underlying assumptions of xenoglossia when introduced into genres other than the religious.

In the masculine realm of the court, equivalent translation appears not at all possible as the narrator reflects on the hierarchies of language possessed and expressed by himself, the court, and the foreign knight. His inability stems from his not being a "rhetor"; he lacks the necessary education to approximate his source. As a number of critics have noted, the narrator suffers a failure of authorship,[65] for on several occasions, he claims that his English is not up to the task of telling this particular story; he cannot describe the beauty of Canacee nor "climb the stile" of the foreign knight's rhetorical excellence. He cannot tell of the dances at the court and engages in the rhetorical device of *occupatio* by refusing to tell of the elaborate feast. These remarks have been explained diversely by critics as the utterances of the immature, rhetorically ineffectual Squire, or as a statement about the insufficiency of English as a literary vehicle at this time. Fyler, for example, interprets this inexpressibility topos as the Squire protecting "the innocence and elegance of his exotic world,"[66] while Craig Berry argues that, because the *General Pro-*

64. Burrow, "A Maner Latyn Corrupt," 37.

65. See Robert Edwards, "The Failure of Invention: Chaucer's 'Squire's Tale,'" in *Ratio and Invention: A Study of Medieval Lyric and Narrative* (Nashville: Vanderbilt University Press, 1989): 131–45.

66. Fyler, "Domesticating the Exotic," 4.

logue states that the Squire "koude songes make and wel endite" (I. 95), it is English itself that *"is* insufficient when describing the marvelous details of romance."[67] All too often, however, these statements are attributed to the Squire as dramatic persona and are not interpreted in view of the tale as a whole.[68]

Translation in this section is presented as difficult, competitive, and imperfect. The narrator promises to relate an exotic story of the strong, noble King Cambyuskan and his family, yet he immediately admits his inability to describe Canacee:

> But for to telle yow al hir beautee,
> It lyth nat in my tonge, n'yn my konnyng;
> I dar nat undertake so heigh a thyng.
> Myn Englissh eek is insufficient.
> It moste been a rethor excellent
> That koude his colours longynge for that art,
> If he sholde hir discryven every part.
> I am noon swich, I moot speke as I kan.
>
> (V. 34–41)

By stating that he will not be able to translate the physical or linguistic scene for his readers, the tale, which promises to describe a wonder in "Sarray, in the land of Tartarye" (1), will thwart our very desire to see and understand its foreignness because of the narrator's own perceived lack of linguistic ability.

Indeed, the position of this narrator in the face of his material is analogous to how medieval vernacular translators often appeared to approach their classical sources, from the position of inferiority. This "humility topos" is quite common in late medieval English translations. In a number of texts, translators claim that they cannot hope to copy the grandeur and effect of the original source. Late Middle English examples of such include John Walton's *Translation of Boethius,*[69] Thomas Usk's *Testament of Love,*[70] John Lydgate's

---

67. Craig Berry, "Flying Sources: Classical Authority in Chaucer's *Squire's Tale,*" *ELH* 68 (2001): 287–313, at p. 288.

68. Lesley Kordecki, "Chaucer's *Squire's Tale*: Animal Discourse, Women, and Subjectivity." *Chaucer Review* 36 (2002): 277–97, argues that Chaucer is interested in seeing whether animal magic can help to develop the voice and subjectivity of the Squire (282).

69. "Insuffishaunce of connyng and wytte, / Defaute of langage and of eloquence / This werke fro me schulde have be holde yytte / But that youre heste hath do me violence / That nedis moste Y do my diligence / In thyng that passeth myne abilite." (1–6); John Walton, in his early fifteenth-century translation of *Boethius,* quoted in Wogan-Browne et al., *Idea of the Vernacular,* 35.

70. "Sothely, dul wytte and a thoughtful soule so sore have myned and graffed in my spyrites

Troy Book,[71] and John Metham's *Amoryus and Cleopes*.[72] What is the point or purpose of these claims of insufficiency? On the one hand, they can point out the hierarchical differences between languages and express fears of inferiority. On the other hand, according to Ruth Evans et alia, the humility topos must be read and understood with caution because an attitude of deference toward source and patron can actually mask a process of cultural aggrandizement, as English invents itself through *translatio studii et imperii* and imagines new audiences and new purposes for older texts.[73]

Why then does the narrator call attention to his own insufficient translation? First, he is claiming that he cannot do the very thing he is doing. For example, when the narrator refuses to describe another scene at the court, this one of dancing, by pointing out the untranslatable qualities of the tale, he is actually translating them, not in their words but in their sense:

> Who koude telle yow the forme of daunces
> So unkouthe, and swiche fresshe contenaunces,
> Swich subtil lookyng and dissymulynges
> For drede of jalouse mennes aperceyvynges?
> No man but Launcelot, and he is deed.
>
> (283–87)

By calling attention to what he cannot tell, the narrator again is reinforcing the understanding that exact translation is impossible for anyone; this he does also when he refuses to tell of the banquet, "Ther nys no man that may reporten al" (72).

The narrator emphasizes his inability to translate accurately when he describes the entrance of the foreign knight and focuses quite heavily on his linguistic interruption. As Sharon-Zisser argues, "the knight's appearance voids the court of ordinary speech: upon his sudden entrance, in 'al the halle

---

that suche craft of endytyng wol not ben of myn acqueyntaunce"; from the prologue to *The Testament of Love*, quoted in Wogan-Browne et al., *Idea of the Vernacular*, 29.

71. See Wogan-Browne et al., *Idea of the Vernacular*, 43–48.

72. "And the sempyl wryter besechyth off supportacion / For the rude endytyng off this story, / But every word ys wrytyn undyr correcion / Off them that laboure in this syens contynwally" (22–25), quoted in Wogan-Browne et al., *Idea of the Vernacular*, 52.

73. Ruth Evans, Andrew Taylor, Nicholas Watson, and Jocelyn Wogan-Browne, "The Notion of Vernacular Theory," 314–30, in Wogan-Browne et al., *Idea of the Vernacular*, at pp. 320–21. For the concept of *translatio studii et imperii*, see Rita Copeland, *Rhetoric, Hermeneutics, and Translation in the Middle Ages: Academic Traditions and Vernacular Texts* (Cambridge: Cambridge University Press, 1991 and 1995).

ne was ther spoken a word' (F 86)."[74] The knight speaks in a language both foreign to but comprehensible by the court;[75] he is "As wel in speche as in contenaunce" (94) that even Gawain could not correct him. Into this scene, the narrator inserts himself awkwardly, calling attention to his own inability in reproducing or translating the knight's language, which is either a foreign tongue or unfamiliar register:

> Al be that I kan nat sowne his stile,
> Ne kan nat clymben over so heigh a style,
> Yet seye I this, as to commune entente:
> Thus muche amounteth al that evere he mente,
> If it so be that I have it in mynde.
>
> (105–109)

The narrator states quite openly that he cannot reproduce or translate what the knight says; he is only able to give the sense of it. Thus, the narrator repeatedly asserts that only the barest sense, the roughest sketches of the beauty and eloquence, can be translated; his English translation cannot hope to replicate its sources. Yet the narrator appears too humble; his constant interjections about what he cannot tell (and then proceeds to tell) ring somewhat false. Whereas the narrator of a religious text, such as the *Prioress's Tale*, can imagine herself as an infant unable to speak and hand over all linguistic agency to God and Mary, similar (even if not as vehement) claims from this romance narrator seem overly dramatic, for the audience would never question the narrator's ability to translate the tale if he did not repeatedly emphasize his inability.

Even the brass horse points to the difficulties of translation. The first part of the tale draws to a close by focusing on the horse, the instrument of physical *translatio*. It is a miracle of science and technology, fully explained and never used. Its importance lies in the way in which this instrument of translation's function and design are translated to Cambyuskan. The description of the horse's operation has attracted some critical attention. Brian S. Lee has stated that the directions for its use are impossible to follow, calling them "the most muddled driving instructions in the history of transport."[76] Kathryn Lynch refutes this by arguing that the instructions couldn't be easier,

---

74. Sharon-Zisser, "*The Squire's Tale* and the Limits of Non-Mimetic Fiction," 381–82.
75. Ibid., 381.
76. Brian S. Lee, "The Question of Closure in Fragment V of *The Canterbury Tales*," *Yearbook of English Studies* 22 (1992): 190–200, at p. 194, quoted in Lynch, "East Meets West," 540.

noting that Cambyuskan understands the knight's instructions.[77] The mechanics of translation therefore are either terribly confusing or completely fathomable; one turns a pin here, another there, and the horse responds. This attention paid to how magical or miraculous translation happens, and the resulting confusion, is quite similar to vitae's explanations of how xenoglossia occurs. At first glance, xenoglossia may seem entirely understandable, yet it is often the focus of intense speculation and confusion (for example, where exactly does the miraculous translation occur, in the mouth of the speaker or the ears of the audience?). The particular device of translation appears to be completely understood by the king, but not implemented by him; the translation therefore ends with him, as the bridle is born away to the tower. The first half of the tale draws to a close with one last reference to the narrator's inability to describe or translate; "The hors vanysshed, I noot in what manere, / Out of hir sighte; ye gete namoore of me" (342–33), he states, even though he has just described the instructions.

The second part of the tale focuses on the opposite of the humble, incapable stance of the translator. Here what is presented is the desire for perfect equivalence, that of exact "word for word and sense for sense" translation. All claims of the inability to translate fall immediately away, and the impossible is made wholly possible. The subject becomes the example of perfect translation taking place between the king's daughter Canacee, the female falcon, and the reader; their is not an educated translation but rather a translation of feminine feeling and experience, of counsel and intimate conversation (a kind of romantic sapientia). In associating the realm of perfect equivalence with passive, receptive women, Chaucer genders miraculous translation as feminine.

This second half opens in Canacee's bedroom, which she shares with a number of waiting women. The setting moves from the feminine spaces of the bedroom to the park and back to the bedroom again. In contrast to the idea of translation presented in the first section, this section takes as its subject the idea of "true and perfect" translation or equivalence. This equivalence, however, is so jarring that we have a hard time accepting it, and rightly so, for with it Chaucer is interrogating the myth of word for word and sense for sense translation.

This section is unquestionably about translation. Accompanied by ten or twelve waiting women, Canacee takes a walk in the park bearing her magical ring with which she is able to understand the language of birds and be under-

---

77. "Enformed whan the kyng was of that kynght, / And hath conceyved in his wit aright / The manere and the forme of al this thyng" (335–37), quoted in Lynch, "East Meets West," 540.

stood by them in their own language. When the ring was first introduced, the knight described it thus:

> "Ther is no fowel that fleeth under the hevene
> That she ne shal wel understonde his stevene,
> And knowe his menyng openly and pleyn,
> And answere hym in his langage ageyn."
>
> (149–52)

The power of the ring is repeatedly emphasized by the narrator in the second part of the tale, and he reminds us in at least three places of its special ability: first, as the morning vapor rises as they begin their walk in the park: "And for the foweles that she herde synge. / For right anon she wiste what they mente / Right by hir song, and knew al hire entente" (398–400); second, after the bleeding falcon is found in the tree, when the narrator repeats the description of the ring:

> This faire kynges doghter, Canacee,
> That on hir fynger baar the queynte ryng,
> Thurgh which she understood wel every thyng
> That any fowel may in his leden seyn,
> And koude answeren hym in his ledene ageyn,
> Hath understonde what this faucon seyde.
>
> (432–37)

And third, once again the narrator reminds us that the bird is speaking in her own language with "Right in hir haukes ledene thus she seyde" (478).

The narrator repeatedly refers to the language of the exchange to underscore its miraculous qualities. The brass horse is a miracle of technology, created by man and operated by turning certain pins in certain directions; as a device of translation, it can be comprehended and perhaps mastered. But according to the courtiers, the fern-glass ring is either a miracle of the biblical age or of some sort of magic—it can transport its bearer to a state before the Fall of Babel, when all language was understood, or even to the Garden of Eden, when Adam knew the language of the animals. Once again, the narrator focuses much attention on the origins and nature of this aid to translation, only to confuse us and obscure its origins, as the townspeople are confused as well.

This kind of miracle of linguistic translation is only possible within the genres of romance or religion. If this were a religious tale, the miraculous translation of animal (or human) language could only be achieved through the gift of God. Whereas medieval saints experienced xenoglossia by means of God's grace, Canacee experiences bird *leden* by means of a mysterious ring. In saints' lives, a particular closeness with birds or even understanding bird language (or birds understanding human language) is not uncommon. For example, thirteenth-century legends of St. Francis of Assisi describe his preaching to the birds, which responded with joy at his words.[78] The hagiographer of Beatrice of Nazareth (d. 1268), a Flemish Cistercian nun and author of the mystical treatise *Van Seven manieren van heiliger minnen* (*The Seven Manners of Holy Love*), describes how wild birds would approach her, and the significance of their actions: "Also wild birds and small woodland fowl sometimes flew to her from their hiding places in the groves, and sat in her lap very tamely, fluttering up against her sweetly. By their novel and unusual joy in fluttering up to her they showed that this specially chosen servant of God was wholly lacking that harshness which little animals and birds of this kind naturally fear in other human beings."[79] *The Book of Margery Kempe* describes the "diuers tokenys in hir bodily heryng" (90.34–35) that she experiences regularly for approximately twenty-five years and which indicate the presence of the Holy Spirit; one of the ways is "þe voys of a lityl bryd whech is callyd a reedbrest þat song ful merily oftyn-tymes in hir right ere" (91.3–5). The sixteenth-century Joan of the Cross, when she received her miracle of tongues and was able to speak Arabic and Latin, was ordered to be shut away; while in her room, birds came to listen to her preaching.[80] The gift of speaking and being understood in an animal language is a kind of miracle of tongues, a harkening back to Eden, to the land of paradise where men and animals could speak together.[81]

In this way, the zooglossic Canacee is very much like a xenoglossic saint.

78. For animals in saints' lives, see also David Salter, *Holy and Noble Beasts: Encounters with Animals in Medieval Literature* (Cambridge: D. S. Brewer, 2001). Salter explores both hagiography and romance and argues that the treatment of animals in hagiography influences that in romance (8). To the biographers of St. Francis of Assisi, "the saint's 'love' of animals, and their affinity for him, was seen a sign that he had returned to the state of innocence and holiness enjoyed by Adam and Eve before the Fall" (7). Salter explains that scenes like this arise in saints' lives because Christ commanded men to preach to animal kingdom (Mark 16:15) (40).

79. *The Life of Beatrice of Nazareth, 1200–1268*, ed. and trans. Roger de Ganck, assisted by John Baptist Harbrouck, Cistercian Fathers Series 50 (Kalamazoo, MI: Cistercian Publications, 1991), 283.

80. Antonio Daca, *The Historie . . . of the Blessed Virgin, Sister Joane, 1625*, ed. D. M. Rogers. Vol. 335, English Recusant Literature, 1558–1640 (Yorkshire: Scholar Press, 1977), 151.

81. Salter emphasizes the similarities between animals in saints' lives and romances, including, for example, *Sir Orfeo*. Salter. *Holy and Noble Beasts*, 102–3.

Her experience in the Edenic garden, speaking with the falcon, evokes images of saints communing with birds. Her miraculous translation is also granted to understand a despairing female in pain and in need of counsel. In this way, her experience is very much like that of St. Lutgard, who aided a despairing woman in the convent by suddenly being able to speak and to understand French, or even Margery Kempe and the priest Wenslawe in Rome, who are granted the ability to understand one another so that the ostracized Margery can confess and discuss her spiritual dalliances. Similar to the linguistic gifts experienced by Margery and Wenslawe, or Lutgard and Clare of Montefalco and their female visitors, Canace's gift of bird tongues can enable the linguistic communion of two who share similar values and concerns.

In this case, however, it is not religious dalliance but rather romantic dalliance that Canacee and the falcon discuss. Although there are many similarities between Canacee and xenoglossic saints, there are also striking differences. First, this is not a saint's life but a romance; the emphasis is not on God's love but rather earthly love. Canacee's gift is not granted by a divine gift but rather by a ring that could have its source in either Old Testament knowledge or alchemical lore. It owes much to the tradition of understanding animal speech in romances, as we see in the *Lais of Marie de France* and a number of other romances in which knights, ladies, and falcons can communicate.[82]

Canacee is able to understand the falcon perfectly for two reasons: one is because of magic, the other because of her nature. Miraculous, perfect equivalence of language between bird and princess is possible not only because of the ring but also because of Canacee's noble feminine nature, which is full of compassion and *gentilnesse*. Indeed, the falcon will only explain her situation to Canacee because of her understanding "gentil herte," her romantic (rather than divinely given) *sapientia*: "I se wel that ye han of my distresse / Compassion, my faire Canacee, / Of verray wommanly benignytee / That Nature in youre principles hath set" (484–87). Indeed, Fyler asserts that "her gender is as important as her gentility: the falcon, appealing to Canacee's 'verray wommanly benignytee' (486), implies that a female human being can feel the sorrow of a female bird more readily than a male could."[83] It also appears that Canacee's female companions are equally compassionate and thus able to understand the falcon's plight, for although they presumably do not understand the falcon's speech, they too mourn for the bird: "Greet was the sorwe for the haukes harm / That Canacee and alle hir wommen made; / They nyste

82. For romances featuring talking birds, see Vincent DiMarco, "*The Squire's Tale*," *Sources and Analogues of the Canterbury Tales*, Correale and Hamel, 1:169–209, at pp. 180–82.

83. Fyler, "Domesticating the Exotic," 15.

hou they myghte the faucon glade" (632–34). Chaucer places the miraculous possibility of perfect translation in the realm of feminine language and understanding, making women the natural vehicles for such translation.

Canacee's innate understanding of the falcon's plight and, by extension, the plight of all female birds and women betrayed by men, is embodied by another example of successful translation as the tale draws to a close. When Canacee brings the falcon back to her bedroom, she creates another moment of translation; this time the falcon's story is rendered onto fabric, as Canacee has the story painted on the velvet covering:

> And al withoute, the mewe is peynted grene,
> In which were peynted alle thise false fowles,
> As ben thise tidyves, tercelettes, and owles;
> Right for despit were peynted hem bisyde,
> Pyes, on hem for to crie and chyde.
>
> (646–50)

The medium of fabric/embroidery/sewing becomes the canvas for Canacee's new translation of the falcon's story, a story that, with its presence next to the princess's bed, doubles as a warning to women about the duplicity of men. Canacee does not take the lesson to heart, unfortunately; another gift, the mirror, which exposes and translates men's duplicitous thoughts, is subtly invoked and dismissed at this moment, and we do not fail to see the veiled threat of incest that hangs over the end of the tale. If only Canacee would use the mirror and learn of her brother's intent; instead, the tale is hastily ended by the narrator, and the two contrasting forms of translation are left jarringly unresolved.

In sum, in the first half of the tale, the narrator presents exact translation as impossible, for his human efforts at translation cannot hope to approximate its authoritative source. In the second part of the tale, translation is entirely possible, and perfect equivalence is to be expected when facilitated by a magical object. But there is a problem in the second half, one that is exacerbated by the attention to translation in the first. This problem is that the translation seems "too" perfect. Chaucer makes bird speech look exactly like human speech and experience. In fact, the falcon sounds so human-like (indeed, she could be a maiden), that as audiences we are quite unnerved.

A number of significant and troubling questions are raised by the miraculous translation of the falcon's speech, particularly when the falcon describes granting her love to the false tercelet. The tercelet "Fil on his knees with so devout humblesse" (544) and declared his love to such an extent that she describes

> So ravysshed, as it semed, for the joye
> That nevere Jason ne Parys of Troye—
> Jason? certes, ne noon oother man
> Syn Lameth was, that alderfirst bigan
> To loven two, as written folk biforn—
> (547–51)

This passage is both humorous and worrisome, for as readers we must ask, how does a bird experience chivalric love in human terms?[84] How can the falcon compare her lover the tercelet to Trojan and biblical men and discuss stories that "written folk biforn"? What does she know of textual authorities? How does a bird fall on his knees? Furthermore, when, the falcon describes, "Ne were worthy unbokelen his galoche" (555), why would a bird speak of buckles on sandals? Indeed, the falcon seems too human here, for her language exactly mimics the realm of Canacee's language and experience, not that of a bird's.

Questions such as these have led critics to interpret the tale as a parody of romance, because we know logically that birds will never have knees and do not love as humans do. I believe, however, that our discomfort as readers also arises from the fact that the tale exposes and then erases several layers of translation at work. In the first half of the tale, we are repeatedly made aware of the difficulties of translation between human languages, as the narrator cannot hope to replicate in English what he has seen or heard of in another language and culture. In the second half, however, all problems with translation are ignored. In the "masculine realm" of the court, we are frustrated with the narrator for not translating certain moments, and we see his excessive attention to his linguistic inability as a weakness. In the second section, however, the narrator has forgotten his inabilities and has no trouble relating the story of the Canacee and the falcon; as we watch the translation of Canacee's human language and womanly experience into the falcon's bird language and vice versa, the narrator refuses to consider the ramifications of such an act of translation, and therefore we are left strangely sensitized to his insensitivity.

---

84. For a discussion of the Falcon's complaint, see Charles A. Owen, Jr., "The Falcon's Complaint in the *Squire's Tale*," *Rebels and Rivals: The Contestive Spirit in The Canterbury Tales*, ed. Susanna Greer Fein, David Raybin, and Peter C. Braeger, Studies in Medieval Culture 29 (Kalamazoo, MI: Medieval Institute, 1991), 173–88.

These questions have most often been interpreted by critics with recourse to genre. According to Fyler, the questions of interpretation raised by the falcon's speech can be explained in terms of the basic impulse of romance, that of "reintegration" or "abolishing the distance caused by alienating categories."[85] By examining how the Squire is not capable "of entering fully into an alien consciousness,"[86] we see how the foreign resists domestication: "When a young noble male European imagines the sentiments of a *gentil* female bird 'of fremde land' (429), as these are made evident in her colloquy with a Mongolian princess, we are assured that a basic impulse of romance, asserting and then overcoming distance, is being pushed to its furthest limits."[87]

As Taylor suggests, however, the ring actually does more than just translate language; it also translates thoughts and conceptions.[88] In this way, a bird's life and experience can be translated into human culture and language and vice versa. If Chaucer is asking us to consider these questions about birds, then he is surely asking us to consider a fundamental question about translation in general: can it reproduce an original in its word and sense, or must it necessarily rewrite and recast its sources? Chaucer is thus insisting that we look critically at two popular and opposing claims of the translator: to not be able to reproduce a source at all and to be able to reproduce it completely without change, both of which make us uncomfortable as readers. On the one hand, we are uncomfortable because the narrator keeps calling attention to his inability to equal his source, especially when we do not have the source with which to compare it. On the other hand, we are surprised by the easy translatability of human and bird language. Although we can easily imagine God overcoming differences of language for women whose experiences of faith are similar, it is harder to imagine the ring can overcome differences of human and bird experience, even with *gentilesse* as their common ground. While it may seem as if translators aim their rings at texts and these texts are magically transformed, in this tale Chaucer is exposing (and obscuring) the "pyns" and "gyns" of that process.

Conclusion

I have argued that in the *Canterbury Tales* Chaucer explores the varying positions or stances that a translator can claim in relation to his/her authoritative

85. Fyler, "Domesticating the Exotic," 21.
86. Ibid., 10.
87. Ibid., 13.
88. Taylor, "Chaucer's Strategies of Translation," 17.

sources, positions that are repeatedly feminized. In the *Prioress's Prologue*, the narrator abdicates any possible agency so that she may give up complete linguistic control to the Divine, to become a vessel through which language passes; the *Tale*, however, features a gift of restored speech that facilitates rote learning and represents those writers and translators who claim their traditional learning has been enhanced. In the *Man of Law's Tale*, the translator appears to be the rudderless ship on the sea at the mercy of her/his sources, scarcely able to steer, although she or he is secretly active. In the *Squire's Tale*, the translator has two choices: either she or he completely denies any ability to translate effectively and to replicate authoritative sources, or she or he completely ignores any translational difficulties and pretends that perfect equivalence is possible, leaving the audience to wonder just how cultural and linguistic differences can be surmounted in texts.

To think about the position of Chaucer's female characters, in relation to the xenoglossic women discussed in the earlier chapters, allows us to see how they are patterned in part on these hagiographic models. The Prioress presents herself as the blankest of slates, an infantilized babe whose words must be supplied by the Lord. Custance does not speak the language of Northumbria; nevertheless, she is understood by its inhabitants in a xenoglossic manner. Canacee understands bird language perfectly; her zooglossia, however, is similar to xenoglossia, for the falcon "speaks" in human courtly language. Yet these women are not holy saints, and their miraculous language must adapt to their more earthly or mundane situations.

It is also fruitful to see Chaucer's position as a hagiographer in relation to Kempe and other hagiographers who describe the miraculous language and understanding of their female subjects. Similar to other hagiographers discussed in this book, Chaucer imagines women who are models of piety and whose Latinity and access to language are different from his own. But does Chaucer see the linguistic ability or Latinity of his female characters as in any way *challenging* to masculine authority? It could be argued that one of the the boldest, most confident translators and interpreters of Latin Scripture in the *Canterbury Tales* is the Wife of Bath; she takes on masculine clerical authority and misquotes Scripture with either lustful naiveté or skillful manipulation, which is anything but miraculous. In addition, Chaucer offers the authoritative Prudence in the *Melibee*; she is a skilled translator of Latin scriptural, religious, and secular authorities, who, after much persuasion, guides her husband to a position of acceptance and forgiveness.[89] Thanks to Chaucer's care-

---

89. The source for Chaucer's tale is Renaud de Louens's French *Livre de Melibée et de Dame Prudence*, itself a translation and adaptation of Albertanus of Brescia's *Liber consolationis et consilii*. Benson, *Riverside Chaucer*, 923.

ful manipulation of his sources, it is not clear how we are to understand either of these women. Are we to laugh at or admire the Wife of Bath's manipulative scriptural translation? Are we meant to be deadened or inspired by Prudence's skillful quotation and weaving together of numerous authorities? *The Canterbury Tales* seems to be suggesting that women, depending on their motives, make either the very best or the very worst of translators.

In his essay, "Shortcut to Language Preparation: Radical Evangelicals, Missions, and the Gift of Tongues," Gary B. McGee explores nineteenth-century missionaries' expectations that the gift of tongues would facilitate their Christian evangelizing in foreign countries. According to McGee, the desire for the gift of tongues for missionary work arose with the New Scottish Revival Movement of the early 1830s, a charismatic movement in which a woman named Mary Campbell claimed that that she spoke miraculously both Turkish and the language of the Palau Island group to evangelize there.[1] McGee cites several examples of missionaries praying for tongues and describes how, in 1890, eight men and women set out from Topeka, Kansas, for Sierra Leone, "confident of biblical promises of healing and Pentecostal tongues," following Mark's promise that tongues will return. They soon realized, however, that they would need to learn the local dialect; the group returned to Kansas after several members who refused to take quinine died of malaria.[2]

In several respects, this acount is not so different from those first Franciscans who ventured into Germany without knowing any German, hoping that "God would provide" for them when all they knew was "Ja" and then meeting disastrous results. McGee cites a number of instances of ministry leaders advising missionaries to dedicate themselves to language learning because there would be no shortcuts; seven centuries earlier, Thomas Aquinas suggested

---

1. Gary B. McGee, "Shortcut to Language Preparation? Radical Evangelicals, Missions, and the Gift of Tongues," *International Bulletin of Missionary Research* 25 (2001): 118–23, at p. 119.

2. Ibid., 119.

that those studying foreign language for the sake of missionary work could approximate the gift of tongues through hard study.[3] One striking difference for these nineteenth-century missionaries, however, was the discussion that ensued when they returned, having been unsuccessful in their attempts at conversion. Many commentators openly criticized the missionaries' lack of preparation and were particularly angry with the preachers who had inspired them to trust in the gift instead of applying their efforts to language learning. If there was such an open discussion with those early Franciscans, it has not been recorded.

It is easy to understand the allure of xenoglossia. It promises that one can be an expert in a language without effort, to achieve a fluency of speech that most could never achieve, even after years of study. Xenoglossia posits that all languages are similar at a fundamental level and that they therefore can express the same concepts and nuances without difficulty. Basic translational issues are ignored. How would xenoglossia allow for a word to be translated from the source language when that word or concept does not exist in the target language? How would xenoglossia handle fundamental syntactical differences or differing registers of polite and informal address, for example?

Medieval accounts of xenoglossia suggest that they have at their root a popular medieval belief that all languages came from the same Adamic, pre-Babelian root, a form of Hebrew that existed before the fall of the tower of Babel divided the original language into many. The late medieval encyclopedia of knowledge *Sidrak and Bokkus*, which takes the form of a dialogue with question and response, asks in what language would a person think if he was deaf, blind, and mute from birth? The answer is that such a person would think in Hebrew, or the Adamic form of Hebrew.[4] A similar desire to uncover the "natural" language of mankind seems to have inspired Frederick Barbarossa in the thirteenth-century *Chronicle* of Salimbene de Adam. The Franciscan chronicler relates how Barbarosa experimented with infants to discover what language they would speak in if the wet-nurses were forbidden to speak to them: Hebrew ("the first language"), Latin, Greek, Arabic, or perhaps the tongues of their parents. The harsh experience resulted, however, in the death of the babies, because they were unable to survive "without the praise, fondling, playfulness, and happy expressions of their nurses."[5] Medieval experi-

3. *Summa Theologica*, Part I of Second Part, Q. 51, Art IV, in *Basic Writings of Saint Thomas Aquinas*, ed. Anton C. Pegis (New York: Random House, 1945), 2:392.

4. *Sidrak and Bokkus: A Parallel-Text Edition from Bodleian Library, MS Laud Misc. 559 and British Library, MS Lansdowne 793*, ed. T. L. Burton, Early English Text Society, o.s. 311, 312 (Oxford: Oxford University Press, 1998, 1999).

5. Salimbene de Adam, *The Chronicle of Salimbene de Adam*, ed. Joseph L. Baird, Guiseppe

ences of xenoglossia, therefore, may suggest the popular belief that all languages are a falling away from Hebrew (or an Adamic proto-Hebrew) and that they share fundamental similarities that allow for them to be translated so fluently.

However, medieval accounts of xenoglossia also emphasize the ability of the Divine to do what appears to be impossible to man. Xenoglossia, therefore, may suggest that languages were understood by medieval people as being fundamentally different from one another, and that the ability to smooth over or erase those differences is *only* possible with divine intervention. After all, medieval hagiographers go to some lengths to point out how xenoglossic experiences render the most diverse languages understandable; for example, as we recall from Chapter 1, St. Vincent Ferrer was said to be understood in languages as diverse as Breton and Hungarian. The "universal translator," therefore, is only possible with the "invisible translator," the Holy Ghost.

Indeed, the "universal translator" has long been a dream of science fiction; many plots make use of a device that conveniently translates between earthly and alien languages, no matter how different they are from one another. Douglas Adams parodies this common trope in his *Hitchhiker's Guide to the Galaxy*, which imagines a universal translator in the form of the Babel fish, a small fish that crawls into one's inner ear and creates wars by allowing everyone to understand each other.[6] More recently, the cartoon *Futurama*, which takes place in the thirty-first century, has also parodied the universal translator trope by imagining a useless device that translates all tongues into the long-dead language of French.[7]

The two most frequent questions I am asked about xenoglossia are, "Do you think it is a real experience?" and then, "If so, what do you think causes it?" As for it being "real," I can only report that many people claim that they

---

Baglivi, and John Robert Kane (Binghamton, NY: Medieval & Renaissance Texts & Studies, 1986), 352.

6. Douglas Adams, *The Hitchhiker's Guide to the Galaxy* (New York: Harmony, 1980), 42.

7. "Professor Hubert Farnsworth: [*Professor Farnsworth is showing Cubert, his clone, some of his inventions*] This is my Universal Translator. It could have been my greatest invention, but it translates everything into an incomprehensible dead language.

Cubert J. Farnsworth: [*into the translator's microphone*] Hello.
Universal Translator: Bonjour!
Professor Hubert Farnsworth: See? Lousy gibberish!

See *Independent Movie Database*, "Memorable Quotes from *Futurama*," http://www.imdb.com/title/tt0149460/quotes (accessed August 15, 2008).

have experienced a sudden ability to speak a foreign language and that they are unable to explain it logically. Anecdotal stories of xenoglossia abound; one woman, a former missionary who belonged to the Church of Jesus Christ of Latter-day Saints, recently described to me how after several months in France and without a strong command of the language, she suddenly spoke fluently about her faith, using terms she had never learned, with a woman experiencing a spiritual crisis.[8] Of course, it could be argued that the missionary had previously heard these words in conversation or had read them somewhere and did not consciously recall them. What is significant in her narration of the account, however, is how the returned missionary understood the experience to have provided for the other woman comforting words she needed to hear in a time of spiritual crisis.

The miraculous aside, the question of what causes xenoglossia can be approached from many perspectives. Stanley Burgess writes, "Buddhist doctrine explains xenolalia as a linguistic survivor from a prior existence. Jungian theory views glossolalia as an individual breakthrough from the collective unconscious"; it has also been attributed to stimulation of Broca's Area of the brain.[9] Certainly, many argue that xenoglossic people would have been exposed to the foreign language, perhaps informally, at some earlier point in their life. Anecdotal experiences related to me feature the subjects consuming alcohol and suddenly becoming fluent; the speakers therefore imagine themselves as "letting down barriers" and allowing language they have already been exposed to to surface.

Medieval miracles of xenoglossia, as they appear in the hagiographic record, are shaped by a number of forces. A medieval hagiographer composing or editing a life of a saint who lived many centuries before collects and compiles legends in the hope of creating a text that serves as a spiritual model for audiences to come. We can easily imagine how certain events become exaggerated in oral narratives; preaching to a large crowd soon becomes "50,000 listeners," for example. However, many of the accounts of xenoglossia are actually witnessed by historical figures who testify under oath what they saw and heard. We must therefore assume that these witnesses believed that they had observed xenoglossia. What explains this? Setting the miraculous aside, we can imagine that women and men regarded as blessed or holy, their communities, and their hagiographers were conditioned to look for the miraculous in everyday life and understood and inter-

---

8. My thanks to Amy Wilde Taylor for this account.

9. Stanley M. Burgess and Eduard M. van der Maas, eds., *The New International Dictionary of Pentecostal and Charismatic Movements*, rev. ed. (Grand Rapids, MI: Zondervan, 2002), 674.

preted the linguistic experiences as xenoglossic. Perhaps they saw something quite natural (conversations between people of similar languages who were communicating with each other at various levels of understanding) and understood the communication to be miraculous. Perhaps the subjects themselves or their community around them were unaware of or did not formally acknowledge their subjects' knowledge of that language because they had acquired it informally at some earlier point. It is also possible that the subject, community, or hagiographers purposefully underrepresented the subject's linguistic knowledge because they had a stake in representing her or his learning as miraculously gifted.

In this study, I have argued that xenoglossia is far more important to reputations of blessedness for medieval holy men and women than previously acknowledged by scholars. I have argued that men and women receive strikingly different experiences of xenoglossia; many more women receive miraculous gifts of Latin than vernacular gifts, and these are limited in scope when compared with men's. Most women's gifts emphasize their passivity; an exception to this is Bridget of Sweden, whose gift is used to ensure the accuracy of the translation of her visions, and whose gift asserts the importance of actual literary practice. Two late medieval English writers, Margery Kempe and Geoffrey Chaucer, adapt this hagiographic trope of women's miraculous translation into their work. For Margery, xenoglossia appears in her text and even influences her presentation of mundane translation; translation becomes an important way of proving God's favor and grace in the *Book*. Xenoglossia and miraculously mundane translation also allow Kempe and her scribe to control how Margery is represented, both to the internal audiences of the *Book* and to the wider external audiences. The literary author Chaucer adapts the tropes of women's xenoglossia in his *Canterbury Tales* to explore what it means to be a writer and translator of religious and secular texts. Women's xenoglossia is particularly appealing to him because of women's outwardly passive nature as a receptacle of language; their lack of learning allows him to assert lack of control while taking full control of his text.

I would like to conclude this project by offering several future directions of study. Certainly, more needs to be done on medieval xenoglossia in general and in particular women's miraculous literacy. I have not exhausted all the examples by any means, and each account of a linguistic gift calls for more detailed study into its individual cultural context. In addition, more attention needs to be given to examining how the tropes of xenoglossia are carried over into literature, not just Middle English texts but also other languages, including French and Italian. Manifestations of xenoglossia in the hagiographic record and literature in the early modern period also call for more attention.[10] Another fruitful area of study would be to explore how hagiographic and literary narratives of xenoglossia may have influenced spiritualist accounts in the early twentieth century.

---

10. A number of early modern studies mention xenoglossia, but the phenomena needs more study. For example, Luis Weckmann's *The Medieval Heritage of Mexico* (New York: Fordham University Press, 1992), notes that several early modern sources recount how friars received the gift of Indian languages to evangelize (262–63). The study refers to this gift as glossolalia; a more rigorous use of the terms in future studies, however, will help to expose the frequency of claims of xenoglossia in the hagiographic and historical record.

Selected Bibliography

PRIMARY SOURCES

Note: Specific bibliographic references for Latin vitae from the *Acta sanctorum* are included in the footnotes.

Acta et processus canonizacionis beate Birgitte. Edited by Isak Collijn. Samlingar utgivna av Svenska Fornskriftsällskapet, ser. 2, Lakinska skrifter 1. Uppsala: Almqvist & Wiksells Boktryckeri, 1924–31.

Acta sanctorum quotquot toto orbe coluntur. Antwerp and Brussels: Société des Bollandistes, 1643–1940.

Actus Beati Francisci et Sociorum Ejus. Edited by Paul Sabatier. Collection d'études et de documents 4. Paris: Librairie Fischbacher, 1902.

Agnes of Harcourt. "The Life of Isabelle of France." In *The Writings of Agnes of Harcourt: The Life of Isabelle of France and the Letter on Louis IX and Longchamp*, edited and translated by Sean L. Field. Notre Dame: University of Notre Dame Press, 2003.

An Alphabet of Tales: An English 15th Century Translation of the Alphabetum Narrationum of Etienne de Besançon. Edited by Mary Macleod Banks. Early English Text Society o.s. 126–127. London: Kegan Paul, Trench, Trübner, 1904–5; reprinted New York: Kraus Reprint Company, 1972.

Analecta Franciscana sive Chronica aliaque varia documenta ad historiam Fratrum Minorum spectantia. Edited by Patribus Collegii S. Bonaventurae. Vol. 10, *Legendae S. Francisci Assisiensis: saeculis XIII et XIV conscriptae*. Quaracchi, Florence: Ad Claras Aquas, 1926–1941.

Annales Minorum sue Trium Ordinum a S. Francisco Institutorum. Edited by Lucas Wadding. Vol. 11 of 25, Supplement 1–2. Rome: Typis Rochi Bernadò, 1731–1921.

Aquinas, Thomas. *Summa Theologiae*. Edited by Anthony Kenny. Vol. 22. New York: McGraw-Hill, 1964.

———. *Summa Theologica*. In *Basic Writings of Saint Thomas Aquinas*, edited by Anton C. Pegis. New York: Random House, 1945.

Augustine of Hippo. *Nicene and Post-Nicene Fathers, First Series*. Vol. 2, *Augustin: City of God, Christian Doctrine*. Edited by Philip Schaff. New York: Christian Literature Company, 1887; reprinted Peabody, MA: Hendrickson, 1995.

———. *Nicene and Post-Nicene Fathers, First Series*. Vol. 7, *Augustin: Homilies on the Gospel of John, Homilies on the First Epistle of John, Soliloquies*. Edited by Philip

Schaff. New York: Christian Literature Company, 1889; reprinted Peabody, MA: Hendrickson, 1995.

Berengario di Donadio. *The Life of Saint Clare of Montefalco*. Edited by John E. Rotelle. Translated by Matthew J. O'Connell. The Augustinian Series 9. Villanova, PA: Augustinian Press, 1999.

Berengario di San Africano [Donadio]. "Vita di S. Chiara da' Montefalco." Edited by M. Faloci Pulignani, 193–266. In *Archivo Storico per le Marche e per l'Umbria*, edited by M. Faloci Pulignani, G. Mazzatinti, and M. Santoni. Foligno, vol. 1, 1884, 557–625; vol. 2, 1885, 193–266.

Biblia Sacra iuxta Vulgatam Versionem. Edited by Bonifatius Fischer et al. Revised by Robertus Weber, 4th ed. Stuttgart: Deutsche Bibelgesellschaft, 1994.

Birgitta of Sweden: Life and Selected Revelations. Edited by Marguerite Tjader Harris. Translated by Albert Ryle Kezel. New York: Paulist Press, 1990.

St. Bonaventure. *Minor Life of St. Francis*. Translated by Benen Fahy. In *St. Francis of Assisi: Writings and Early Biographies*, ed. Habig, 789–831.

Boyd, Beverly, ed. *The Middle English Miracles of the Virgin*. San Marino, CA: Huntington Library, 1964.

Bridget of Sweden. *The Liber Celestis of St Bridget of Sweden: The Middle English Version in British Library MS Claudius B.i., Together with a Life of the Saint from the Same Manuscript*. Edited by Roger Ellis. Vol. 1. Early English Text Society o.s. 291. Oxford: Oxford University Press, 1987.

———. *Reuelaciones extrauagantes*. Edited by Lennart Hollman. Samlingar utgivna av Svenska Fornskriftsällskapet 2. Uppsala: Almqvist & Wiksells, 1956.

———. *Revelaciones, Book III*. Edited by Ann-Mari Jönsson. Samlingar utgivna av Svenska Fornskriftsällskapet, ser. 2, Latinska skrifter 7:3. Uppsala: Almqvist & Wiksells, 1998.

———. *Revelaciones, Book VI*. Edited by Birger Bergh. Samlingar utgivna av Svenska Fornskriftsällskapet 3, ser. 2, Latinska skrifter 7:7. Uppsala: Almqvist & Wiksells International, 1991.

Caesarius of Heisterbach. *The Dialogue on Miracles*. Translated by Henry von Essen Scott and C. C. Swinton Bland. 2 vols. London: G. Routledge & Sons, 1929.

Capgrave, John. *The Life of St. Norbert*. Edited by Cyril Lawrence Smetana. Studies and Texts 40. Toronto: Pontifical Institute of Mediaeval Studies, 1977.

Catherine of Siena. *Le Lettere di S. Caterina da Siena*. Edited by Niccolò Tommaseo, 4 vols.; Revised by Piero Misciattelli, 6 vols. Florence: C/E Giunt-G. Barbera, 1940.

———. *The Letters of Catherine of Siena*. Translated by Suzanne Noffke. Medieval and Renaissance Texts and Studies. 2 vols. Tempe: Arizona Center for Medieval and Renaissance Studies, 2001.

Chaucer, Geoffrey. *The Canterbury Tales*. In *The Riverside Chaucer*, edited by Larry D. Benson. 3rd ed. Boston: Houghton Mifflin, 1987.

Christina [Christine] of Stommeln. "Epistolae." In *Other Middle Ages: Witnesses at the Margins of Medieval Society*, edited by Michael Goodich, 164–68. Philadelphia: University of Pennsylvania Press, 1998.

Chrysostom, John. *Nicene and Post-Nicene Fathers, First Series*. Vol. 12, *Chrysostom: Homilies on the Epistles of Paul to the Corinthians*. Edited by Philip Schaff. New York: Christian Literature Company, 1889; reprinted Peabody, MA: Hendrickson, 1995.

Constantine of Orvieto. *Legenda Sancti Dominici*. Edited by D. H. C. Scheeben. Monumenta Ordinis Fratrum Praedicatorum Historica 16, 203–352. Rome, 1935. In *Saint Dominic: Biographical Documents*, edited and translated by Francis C. Lehner. Washington, D.C.: Thomist, 1964.

Correale, Robert and Mary Hamel, eds. *Sources and Analogues of Chaucer's Canterbury Tales*. 2 vols. Cambridge: D. S. Brewer, 2002–2005.

Daca, Antonio. *The Historie . . . of the Blessed Virgin, Sister Joane, 1625*. Edited by D. M. Rogers. English Recusant Literature, 1558–1640. Vol. 335. Yorkshire: Scholar Press, 1977.

Doble, G. H., and Simon D. Evans, ed. *Lives of the Welsh Saints*. Cardiff: University of Wales Press, 1971.

Elisabeth of Schönau: The Complete Works. Edited and translated by Anne L. Clark. New York: Paulist Press, 2000.

Evans, D. Simon, ed. *The Welsh Life of St. David*. Cardiff: University of Wales Press, 1988.

Floretum S. Francisci Assisiensis, Liber aureus qui italice dicitur I Fioretti di San Francesco. Edited by Paul Sabatier. Paris: Librairie Fischbacher, 1902.

Foxe, John. *The Acts and Monuments of John Foxe*. Edited by George Townsend. 3 vols. New York: AMS Press, 1965.

Gerardus de Frachet. *Vitae Fratrum Ordinis Praedicatorum*. Edited by Benedictus Reichert. Monumenta Ordinis Fratrum Praedicatorum Historica. Louvain: Typis E. Charpentier & J. Schoonjans, 1896.

Giordano of Giano. *Chronica Fratris Jordani*. In *Collection d'études et de documents sur l'histoire religieuse et littéraire du moyen âge*, edited by H. Boehmer, vol. 6. Paris: Librairie Fischbacher, 1908.

Goswin of Bossut. *Send Me God: The Lives of Ida the Compassionate of Nivelles, Nun of La Ramee, Arnulf, Lay Brother of Villers, and Abundus, Monk of Villers*. Edited and translated by Martinus Cawley. Medieval Women: Texts and Contexts 6. Turnhout: Brepols, 2003; University Park: Pennsylvania State University Press, 2006.

Gottfried of Disibodenberg and Theodoric of Echternach. *The Life of the Saintly Hildegard*. Edited and translated by Hugh Feiss. Toronto: Peregrina Publishing, 1996; reprinted 1999.

Gower, John. *The Complete Works of John Gower: The English Works*. Edited by G. C. Macaulay. Oxford: Clarendon, 1901; reprinted Gross Point, MI: Scholarly Press, 1968.

Gregersson, Birger, and Thomas Gascoigne. *The Life of Saint Birgitta*. Translated by Julia Bolton Holloway. Peregrina Translation Series 17. Toronto: Peregrina Publishing, 1991.

Gregory of Tours. *The History of the Franks*. Translated by O. M. Dalton. 2 vols. Oxford: Clarendon, 1927.

Gregory of Tours: Life of the Fathers. Translated by Edward James. 2nd ed. Liverpool: Liverpool University Press, 1991.

The Holy Bible: Translated from the Latin Vulgate, diligently compared with the Hebrew, Greek, and other editions in divers languages. The Old Testament first published by the English College at Douay, A.D. 1609, and the New Testament first published by the English College at Rheims, A.D. 1582. Rockford, IL: Tan Books, 1971.

Hugh of Floreffe. *The Life of Yvette of Huy*. Translated by Jo Ann McNamara. Toronto: Peregrina Press, 1999.

Ida of Louvain: Mediaeval Cistercian Nun. Translated by Martinus Cawley. Lafayette, OR: Guadalupe Translations, 1990.

Jacobus de Voragine. *The Golden Legend: Readings on the Saints.* 2 vols. Translated by William Granger Ryan. Princeton: Princeton University Press, 1993.

————. *Legenda aurea.* Edited by Giovanni Paolo Maggioni. 2nd ed. 2 vols. Tavarnuzze-Firenze: Sismel, Edizioni del Galluzzo, 1998.

John of Tynemouth. *Nova Legenda Anglie.* Edited by Carl Horstman. 2 vols. Oxford: Clarendon, 1901.

Kempe, Margery. *The Book of Margery Kempe.* Edited by Sanford Brown Meech with notes and appendices by Sanford Brown Meech and Hope Emily Allen. Early English Text Society o.s. 212. London: Oxford University Press, 1940; reprinted 1997.

The Legend of the Three Companions. Translated by Nesta de Robeck. In *St. Francis of Assisi: Writings and Early Biographies,* ed. Habig, 853–955.

The Life of Beatrice of Nazareth, 1200–1268. Edited and translated by Roger de Ganck, assisted by John Baptist Harbrouck. Cistercian Fathers Series 50. Kalamazoo, MI: Cistercian Publications, 1991.

The Life of Juliana of Mont Cornillon. Translated by Barbara Newman. Peregrina Translations Series 13, Matrologia Latina. Toronto: Peregrina Publishing, n.d.

"The Life of St. Umiltà, Abbess of the Vallombrosan Order in Florence." In *Consolation of the Blessed,* edited by Elizabeth Petroff, 121–150. New York: Alta Gaia Society, 1979.

"The Little Flowers of St. Francis." Translated by Raphael Brown. In *St. Francis of Assisi: Writings and Early Biographies,* ed. Habig, 1267–1530.

Lives of Ida of Nivelles, Lutgard, and Alice the Leper. Edited and translated by Martinus Cawley. Lafayette, OR: Guadalupe Translations, 1987.

"The Lyf of Seinte Cristin the Mervelous." Edited by C. Horstmann. In *Prosalegenden: Di Legenden des MS Douce 114. Anglia* 8 (1885): 102–96.

The New Oxford Annotated Bible: New Revised Standard Version. Edited by Michael D. Coogan. 3rd ed. New York: Oxford University Press, 2001.

————. *The New Oxford Annotated Bible with the Apocrypha: Revised Standard Version.* Expanded edition. Edited by Herbert G. May and Bruce M. Metzger. New York: Oxford University Press, 1977.

Nikephoros. *The Life of St Andrew the Fool.* Edited and translated by Lennart Rydén. 2 vols. Uppsala: Uppsala University, distributed by Stockholm: Almqvist & Wiksell International, 1995.

Peter Olofsson of Alvastra and Peter Olofsson of Skänninge. *Vita b. Brigide prioris Petri et magistri Petri.* In *Acta et processus canonizacionis beate Birgitte,* edited by Isak Collijn, 73–101. Translated by Albert Ryle Kezel in *Birgitta of Sweden: Life and Selected Revelations,* edited by Marguerite Tjader Harris, 71–98. New York: Paulist Press, 1990.

Philippine de Porcellet. *The Life of Saint Douceline, a Beguine of Provence.* Translated by Kathleen Garay and Madeleine Jeay. Woodbridge, Suffolk: D. S. Brewer, 2001.

Pierre de Reims et Perinne de la Roche et de Baume. *Les Vies de Sainte Colette Boylet de Corbie Réformatrice des Frères Mineurs des Clarisses (1381–1447).* Edited by Ubald d'Alençon. *Archives franciscaines* IV. Paris: A. Picard, 1911.

Il Processo di Canonizzazione di Chiara da Montefalco. Edited by Enrico Menestò. Quaderni del Centro per il Collegamento degli Studi Medievali e Umanistici nell'Università di Perugia 14. Perugia: Regione dell'Umbria, and Firenze: La Nuova Italia, 1984.

Raymond of Capua. *The Life of St Catherine of Siena*. Translated by George Lamb. New York: P. J. Kenedy & Sons, 1960.

Rhigyfarch. *Rhigyfarch's Life of St. David: The Basic Mid Twelfth-Century Latin Text.* Edited and translated by J. W. James. Cardiff: University of Wales Press, 1967.

Robertson, James Craigie, ed. *Materials for the History of Thomas Becket, Archbishop of Canterbury*. Vol. 2 of 7. Rolls Series 67. London: Longman; Trübner, 1876.

St. Francis of Assisi: Writings and Early Biographies; English Omnibus of the Sources for the Life of St. Francis. Edited by Marion A. Habig. 3rd ed. Chicago: Franciscan Herald Press, 1973.

Salimbene de Adam. *The Chronicle of Salimbene de Adam*. Edited by Joseph L. Baird, Guiseppe Baglivi, and John Robert Kane. Binghamton, NY: Medieval & Renaissance Texts & Studies, 1986.

Sancti Pachomii Vitae Graecae. Edited by François Halkin. Subsidia Hagiographica 19. Brussels: Société des Bollandistes, 1932.

Sidrak and Bokkus: A Parallel-Text Edition from Bodleian Library, MS Laud Misc. 559 and British Library, MS Lansdowne 793. Edited by T. L. Burton. Early English Text Society, o.s. 311, 312. Oxford: Oxford University Press, 1998, 1999.

Thomas of Cantimpré: The Collected Saints' Lives; Abbot John of Cantimpré, Christina the Astonishing, Margaret of Ypres, and Lutgard of Aywières. Edited by Barbara Newman. Translated by Margot H. King and Barbara Newman. Medieval Women: Texts and Contexts 19. Turnhout: Brepols, 2008.

———. *The Life of Christina the Astonishing*. Translated by Margot H. King and Barbara Newman. In Thomas of Cantimpré, *The Collected Saints' Lives*, 127–57.

———. *The Life of Lutgard of Aywières*. Translated by Margot H. King and Barbara Newman. In Thomas of Cantimpré, *The Collected Saints' Lives*, 211–96.

———. *The Life of Margaret of Ypres*. Translated by Margot H. King and Barbara Newman. In Thomas of Cantimpré, *The Collected Saints' Lives*, 163–206.

Thomas of Celano. *The Second Life of St. Francis*. Translated by Placid Hermann. In *St. Francis of Assisi: Writings and Early Biographies*, ed. Habig, 357–543.

Three Eleventh-Century Anglo-Latin Saints' Lives: Vita S. Birini, Vita et miracula S. Kenelmi and Vita S. Rumwoldi. Edited and translated by Rosalind C. Love. Oxford: Clarendon Press, 1996.

"Vita Margarete de Ypris." Edited by Gilles Meersseman, 106–30. Appendix of *Les Frères Prêcheurs at Mouvement dévot en Flandres au XIII siècle*. Archivum Fratrum Praedicatorum 18. Rome: Institutum historicum Fratrum Praedicatorum, 1948.

"Vita Sancti Goaris Auctore Wandalberto." In *Patrologia Latina*, edited by Jacques-Paul Migne, 639–54. Vol. 121 of 221 vols. Paris, 1844–1866.

SECONDARY SOURCES

Ambrisco, Alan S. " 'It lyth nat in my tonge': Occupatio and Otherness in the *Squire's Tale*." *Chaucer Review* 38 (2004): 205–28.

Anderson, Allan. *An Introduction to Pentecostalism: Global Charismatic Christianity*. Cambridge: Cambridge University Press, 2004.

Arnold, John H. "Margery's Trials: Heresy, Lollardy and Dissent." In *A Companion to The Book of Margery Kempe*, edited by John H. Arnold and Katherine J. Lewis, 75–93. Cambridge: D. S. Brewer, 2004.

Ashley, Kathleen M., and Pamela Sheingorn. *Interpreting Cultural Symbols: Saint Anne in Late Medieval Society*. Athens: University of Georgia Press, 1990.

Bardsley, Sandy. "Sin, Speech, and Scolding in Late Medieval England." In Fenster and Smail, *Fama*, 145–64.

Barratt, Alexandra. "Language and the Body in Thomas of Cantimpré's *Life* of Lutgard of Aywières." *Cistercian Studies Quarterly* 30 (1995): 339–47.

Bartlett, Anne Clark. *Male Authors, Female Readers: Representation and Subjectivity in Middle English Devotional Literature*. Ithaca: Cornell University Press, 1995.

———. "Miraculous Literacy and Textual Communities in Hildegard of Bingen's *Scivias*." *Mystics Quarterly* 18 (1992): 43–55.

Bassnett, Susan, and André Lefevere. "Introduction: Where Are We in Translation Studies?" In *Constructing Cultures: Essays on Literary Translation*, edited by Susan Bassnett and André Lefevere, 1–11. Topics in Translation 11. Clevedon: Multilingual Matters, 1998.

Beare, Frank W. "Speaking with Tongues: A Critical Survey of the New Testament Evidence." In Mills, *Speaking in Tongues*, 107–26. Reprinted from *Journal of Biblical Literature* 83 (1964): 229–46.

Beckwith, Sarah. "Margery Kempe's *Imitatio*." In *The Book of Margery Kempe: A New Translation, Contexts, Criticism*, edited and translated by Lynn Staley, 284–87. New York: W. W. Norton & Company, 2001; reprinted from *Christ's Body: Identity, Culture, and Society in Late Medieval Writings*, 80–83. London: Routledge, 1993.

———. "Problems of Authority in Late Medieval English Mysticism: Language, Agency, and Authority in *The Book of Margery Kempe*." *Exemplaria* 4 (1992): 171–99.

Bejczy, István P. "The *sacra infantia* in Medieval Hagiography." In Wood, *Church and Childhood*, 143–51.

Benson, C. David. *Chaucer's Drama of Style: Poetic Variety and Contrast in the Canterbury Tales*. Chapel Hill: University of North Carolina Press, 1986.

Benson, C. David, and Elizabeth A. Robertson, eds. *Chaucer's Religious Tales*. Cambridge: D. S. Brewer, 1990.

Berry, Craig. "Flying Sources: Classical Authority in Chaucer's *Squire's Tale*." *ELH* 68 (2001): 287–313.

Blamires, Alcuin. "Chaucer the Reactionary: Ideology and the *General Prologue* to *The Canterbury Tales*." *Review of English Studies* 51 (2000): 523–39.

———. "The Limits of Bible Study for Medieval Women." In *Women, the Book and the Godly: Selected Proceedings of the St. Hilda's Conference, 1993*, edited by Lesley Smith and Jane H. M. Taylor, 1:1–12. Cambridge: D. S. Brewer, 1995.

Block, Edward A. "Originality, Controlling Purpose and Craftsmanship in Chaucer's *Man of Law's Tale*." *PMLA* 68 (1953): 572–616.

Blumenfeld-Kosinski, Renate, and Timea Klara Szell, eds. *Images of Sainthood in Medieval Europe*. Ithaca: Cornell University Press, 1991.

Boenig, Robert. "*Alma Redemptoris Mater, Gaude Maria*, and the *Prioress's Tale*." *Notes and Queries* 46 (1999): 321–26.

———. "Chaucer and St. Kenelm." *Neophilologus* 84 (2000): 157–64.

Bornstein, Daniel E., and Roberto Rusconi, eds. *Women and Religion in Medieval and Renaissance Italy*. Translated by Margery J. Scheider. Chicago: University of Chicago Press, 1996.

Borst, Arno. *Der Turmbau von Babel: Geschichte der Meinungen über Ursprung und Vielfalt der Sprachen und Völker*. 4 vols. in 6. Stuttgart: A. Hiersemann, 1957–63.

Bowers, Terence N. "Margery Kempe as Traveler." *Studies in Philology* 97 (2000): 1–28.

Bozzano, Ernesto. *Polyglot Mediumship (Xenoglossy)*. Translated by Isabel Emerson. London: Rider, 1932.

Breeze, Andrew. "The Celtic Gospels in Chaucer's *Man of Law's Tale*." *Chaucer Review* 32 (1998): 335–38.

Broughton, Laurel. "The Prioress's Prologue and Tale." In *Sources and Analogues of Chaucer's Canterbury Tales*, edited by Robert Correale and Mary Hamel, 2:583–647. Cambridge: D. S. Brewer, 2005.

Burgess, Stanley M. "Medieval Examples of Charismatic Piety in the Roman Catholic Church." In *Perspectives on the New Pentecostalism*, edited by Russell P. Spittler, 14–26. Grand Rapids, MI: Baker Book House, 1976.

Burgess, Stanley M., and Eduard M. van der Maas, eds. *The New International Dictionary of Pentecostal and Charismatic Movements*. Rev. ed. Grand Rapids, MI: Zondervan, 2002.

Burrow, J. A. "A Maner Latyn Corrupt." *Medium Aevum* 30 (1961): 33–37.

Busenitz, Nathan. "The Gift of Tongues: Comparing the Church Fathers with Contemporary Pentecostalism." *The Master's Seminary Journal* 17 (2006): 61–78.

Caciola, Nancy. *Discerning Spirits: Divine and Demonic Possession in the Middle Ages*. Ithaca: Cornell University Press, 2003.

Cartledge, Mark J., ed. *Speaking in Tongues: Multi-Disciplinary Perspectives*. Studies in Pentecostal and Charasmatic Issues. Bletchley, UK and Waynesboro, GA: Paternoster Press, 2006.

Chaytor, H. J. *From Script to Print: An Introduction to Medieval Vernacular Literature*. Cambridge: Heffer, 1945.

Clark, Anne L. *Elisabeth of Schönau: A Twelfth-Century Visionary*. Philadelphia: University of Pennsylvania Press, 1992.

Clark, Roy Peter. "Wit and Witsunday in Chaucer's *Summoner's Tale*." *Annuale Mediaevale* 17 (1976): 48–57.

Cleve, Gunnel. "Margery Kempe: A Scandinavian Influence in Medieval England?" In *The Medieval Mystical Tradition in England: Exeter Symposium V, Papers Read at the Devon Centre, Dartington Hall, July 1992*, edited by Marion Glasscoe, 163–78. Cambridge: D. S. Brewer, 1992.

Coakley, John W. "Friars as Confidants of Holy Women in Medieval Dominican Hagiography." In Blumenfeld-Kosinski and Szell, *Images of Sainthood in Medieval Europe*, 222–46.

———. "A Marriage and Its Observer: Christine of Stommeln, the Heavenly Bridegroom, and Friar Peter of Dacia." In Mooney, *Gendered Voices*, 99–117, 229–35.

———. *Women, Men, and Spiritual Power: Female Saints and Their Male Collaborators*. New York: Columbia University Press, 2006.

Connolly, Seán. "Vita Prima Sanctae Brigitae: Background and Historical Value." *Journal of the Royal Society of Antiquaries of Ireland* 119 (1989): 5–49.

Cooney, Helen. "Wonder and Immanent Justice in the *Man of Law's Tale*." *Chaucer Review* 33 (1999): 264–87.

Cooper, Christine F. "'But algates therby was she understonde': Translating Custance in Chaucer's *Man of Law's Tale*." *Yearbook of English Studies* 36 (2006): 27–38.

———. "Miraculous Translation in *The Book of Margery Kempe*." *Studies in Philology* 101 (2004): 270–98.

Cooper, Helen. *The Canterbury Tales*. 2nd ed. Oxford Guides to Chaucer. Oxford: Oxford University Press, 1996.

Copeland, Rita. *Rhetoric, Hermeneutics, and Translation in the Middle Ages: Academic Traditions and Vernacular Texts*. Cambridge: Cambridge University Press, 1991 and 1995.

Correale, Robert. "Chaucer's Manuscript of Nicholas Trevet's *Les Cronicles*." *Chaucer Review* 25 (1991): 238–65.

Craun, Edwin D. *Lies, Slander, and Obscenity in Medieval English Literature: Pastoral Rhetoric and the Deviant Speaker*. Cambridge: Cambridge University Press, 1997.

Curtius, Ernst Robert. *European Literature and the Latin Middle Ages*. Translated by Willard R. Trask. New York: Pantheon, 1953.

Cutten, George Barton. *Speaking with Tongues, Historically and Psychologically Considered*. New Haven: Yale University Press, 1927.

Despres, Denise L. "Cultic Anti-Judaism and Chaucer's Litel Clergeon." *Modern Philology* 91 (1994): 413–27.

Dillon, Janette. "Holy Women and Their Confessors or Confessors and Their Holy Women? Margery Kempe and Continental Tradition." In Voaden, *Prophets Abroad*, 115–40.

———. "Margery Kempe's Sharp Confessor/s." *Leeds Studies in English* 27 (1996): 131–38.

Dinshaw, Carolyn. "The Law of Man and Its 'Abhomynacions.'" *Exemplaria* 1 (1989): 117–48.

Eco, Umberto. *The Search for the Perfect Language*. Translated by James Fentress. Oxford: Blackwell, 1995.

Edwards, Robert. *Ratio and Invention: A Study of Medieval Lyric and Narrative*. Nashville: Vanderbilt University Press, 1989.

Ellis, Roger. "'Flores ad fabricandam . . . coronam': An Investigation into the Uses of the *Revelations* of St Bridget of Sweden in Fifteenth-Century England." *Medium Aevum* 51 (1982): 163–86.

———. "Margery Kempe's Scribe and the Miraculous Books." In *Langland, the Mystics and the Medieval English Religious Tradition: Essays in Honour of S. S. Hussey*, edited by Helen Phillips, 161–75. Cambridge: D. S. Brewer, 1990.

———. "Translation." In *A Companion to Chaucer*, edited by Peter Brown, 443–58. Oxford: Blackwell, 2000.

Everts, Jenny. "Tongues or Languages? Contextual Consistency in the Translation of Acts 2." *Journal of Pentecostal Theology* 4 (1994): 71–80.

Facchinetti, Vittorino. *S. [San] Bernardino da Siena, mistico sole del secolo xv*. Milan: Casa Editrice S. Lega Eucaristica, 1933.

Fenster, Thelma S., and Daniel Lord Smail, eds. *Fama: The Politics of Talk and Reputation in Medieval Europe*. Ithaca: Cornell University Press, 2003.

Ferrante, Joan M. *To the Glory of her Sex: Women's Roles in the Composition of Medieval Texts*. Bloomington: Indiana University Press, 1997.

Field, Sean L. *Isabelle of France: Capetian Sanctity and Franciscan Identity in the Thirteenth Century*. Notre Dame: University of Notre Dame Press, 2006.

Finlayson, John. "Chaucer's *Summoner's Tale*: Flatulence, Blasphemy, and the Emperor's Clothes." *Studies in Philology* 104 (2007): 455–70.

Flournoy, Théodore. *From India to the Planet Mars: A Study of a Case of Somnambulism with Glossolalia*. New York: University Books, 1963; originally published New York: Harper and Brothers, 1900.

Ford, J. Massyngbaerde. "Toward a Theology of 'Speaking in Tongues.'" In Mills, *Speaking in Tongues*, 263–94.

Friedman, Albert B. "The Mysterious 'Greyn' in the *Prioress's Tale*." *Chaucer Review* 11 (1977): 328–33.

Furrow, Melissa. "Unscholarly Latinity and Margery Kempe." In *Studies in English Language and Literature: 'Doubt Wisely'; Papers in Honour of E. G. Stanley*, edited by M. J. Toswell and Elizabeth M. Tyler, 240–51. London: Routledge, 1996.

Fyler, John M. "Domesticating the Exotic in the *Squire's Tale*." *English Literary History* 55 (1988): 1–26.

Gaylord, Alan T. "The 'Miracle' of *Sir Thopas*." *Studies in the Age of Chaucer* 6 (1984): 65–84.

Gibson, Gail McMurray. "St. Margery: *The Book of Margery Kempe*." In Staley, *The Book of Margery Kempe: A New Translation, Contexts, Criticism*, 276–84. Originally published in Gibson, *The Theater of Devotion: East Anglian Drama and Society in the Late Middle Ages*, 47–66. Chicago: University of Chicago Press, 1989.

Gill, Katherine. "Women and the Production of Religious Literature in the Vernacular, 1300–1500." In *Creative Women in Medieval and Early Modern Italy: A Religious and Artistic Renaissance*, edited by E. Ann Matter and John Wayland Coakley, 64–104. Philadelphia: University of Pennsylvania Press, 1994.

Glenn, Cheryl. "Popular Literacy in the Middle Ages: *The Book of Margery Kempe*." In *Popular Literacy: Studies in Cultural Practices and Poetics*, edited by John Trimbur, 56–73. Pittsburgh: University of Pittsburgh Press, 2001.

Goff, James R., Jr. *Fields White unto Harvest: Charles F. Parham and the Missionary Origins of Pentecostalism*. Fayetteville: University of Arkansas Press, 1988.

Goodich, Michael E. *Miracles and Wonders: The Development of the Concept of Miracle, 1150–1350*. Aldershot, UK: Ashgate, 2007.

———. *Violence and Miracle in the Fourteenth Century: Private Grief and Public Salvation*. Chicago: University of Chicago Press, 1995.

Goodman, Anthony. *Margery Kempe and Her World*. London: Longman, 2002.

———. "The Piety of John Brunham's Daughter, of Lynn." In *Medieval Women: Dedicated and Presented to Rosalind M. T. Hill on the Occasion of Her Seventieth Birthday*, edited by Derek Baker, 347–58. Oxford: Blackwell, 1978.

von Görres, Joseph. *La Mystique Divine, Naturelle, et Diabolique*. Translated by C. Sainté-Foi. Paris: Poussielgue-Rusand. 1st ed., 1854–1855. 2nd ed., 1862. Originally published as *Die Christliche Mystik*, 4 vols. Regensburg: G. J. Manz, 1836–42; 2nd ed., 5 vols., 1879.

Gould, Graham. "Childhood in Eastern Patristic Thought: Some Problems of Theology and Theological Anthropology." In Wood, *Church and Childhood*, 39–52.

Grundmann, Herbert. "Litteratus-illiteratus. Der Wandel einer Bildungsnorm vom Altertum zum Mittelalter." *Archiv für Kulturgeschichte* 40 (1958): 1–65.

Guiley, Rosemary E., ed. *Harper's Encyclopedia of Mystical and Paranormal Experience*. San Francisco: HarperSanFrancisco, 1991.

Halkin, François, ed. *Manuscrits Grecs de Paris: Inventaire Hagiographique*. Subsidia Hagiographica 44. Brussels: Société des Bollandistes, 1968.

Hamilton, Marie Padgett. "Echoes of Childermas in the *Tale* of the Prioress." *Modern Language Review* 34 (1939): 1–8.

Hamilton, Michael Pollock, ed. *The Charismatic Movement*. Grand Rapids, MI: W. B. Eerdmans, 1975.

Harrisville, Roy. "Speaking in Tongues: A Lexicographical Study." *Catholic Bible Quarterly* 38 (1976): 35–48.

Haskell, Ann S. *Essays on Chaucer's Saints*. The Hague: Mouton, 1976.

Heene, Katrien. "'*De litterali et morali earum instruccione*': Women's Literacy in Thirteenth-Century Latin Agogic Texts." In Hemptinne and Góngora, *The Voice of Silence*, 144–66.

Heffernan, Carol. "Chaucer's *Squire's Tale*: The Poetics of Interlace or the 'Well of English Undefiled.'" *Chaucer Review* 32 (1997): 32–45.

Heltai, Pál. "Explication, Redundancy, Ellipsis and Translation." In *New Trends in Translation Studies, In Honour of Kinga Klaudy*, edited by Krisztina Károly and Ágota Fóris, 45–74. Budapest: Akadémiai Kiadó, 2005.

de Hemptinne, Thérèse de, and María Eugenia Góngora, eds. *The Voice of Silence: Women's Literacy in a Men's Church*. Medieval Church Studies 9. Turnhout: Brepols, 2004.

Henken, Elissa R. *Traditions of the Welsh Saints*. Cambridge: D. S. Brewer, 1987.

Hinnebusch, William A. *The History of the Dominican Order*. 2 vols. Staten Island, NY: Alba House, 1966–73.

Hinson, E. Glenn. "The Significance of Glossolalia in the History of Christianity." In Mills, *Speaking in Tongues*, 181–203.

Hirsch, John C. "Author and Scribe in *The Book of Margery Kempe*." *Medium Aevum* 44 (1975): 145–50.

Hopenwasser, Nanda. "The Human Burden of the Prophet: St. Birgitta's *Revelations* and *The Book of Margery Kempe*." *Medieval Perspectives* 8 (1993): 153–63.

Hopenwasser, Nanda, and Signe Wegener. "Vox Matris: The Influence of St. Birgitta's *Revelations* on *The Book of Margery Kempe*: St. Birgitta and Margery Kempe as Wives and Mothers." In *Crossing the Bridge: Comparative Essays on Medieval European and Heian Japanese Women Writers*, edited by Barbara Stevenson and Cynthia Ho, 61–85. New York: Palgrave, 2000.

Huber, Raphael M. *St. Anthony of Padua, Doctor of the Church Universal: A Critical Study of the Historical Sources of the Life, Sanctity, Learning, and Miracles of the Saint of Padua and Lisbon*. Milwaukee, WI: Bruce Publishing, 1948.

James, Edward. "Childhood and Youth in the Early Middle Ages." In *Youth in the Middle Ages*, edited by P. J. P Goldberg and Felicity Riddy, 11–23. Woodbridge, UK: York Medieval Press, 2004.

Johnson, William C., Jr. "Miracles in *The Man of Law's Tale*." *Bulletin of the Rocky Mountain Modern Language Association* 28 (1974): 57–65.

Jones, Sarah Rees, ed. *Learning and Literacy in Medieval England and Abroad*, Utrecht Studies in Medieval Literacy 3. Turnhout: Brepols, 2003.

Jotischky, Andrew. "The Mendicants as Missionaries and Travellers in the Near East in the Thirteenth and Fourteenth Centuries." In *Eastward Bound: Travel and Travellers, 1050–1500*, edited by Rosamund Allen, 88–106. Manchester: Manchester University Press, 2004.

Kamerick, Kathleen. "Art and Moral Vision in Angela of Foligno and Margery Kempe." *Mystics Quarterly* 21 (1995): 148–58.

Kienzle, Beverly Mayne, and Pamela J. Walker, eds. *Women Preachers and Prophets Through Two Millennia of Christianity*. Berkeley and Los Angeles: University of California Press, 1998.

Kolve, V. A. *Chaucer and the Imagery of Narrative: The First Five Canterbury Tales*. Stanford: Stanford University Press, 1984.

Kooper, E. S. "Inverted Images in Chaucer's *Tale of Sir Thopas*." *Studia Neophilologica* 56 (1984): 147–54.

Kordecki, Lesley. "Chaucer's *Squire's Tale*: Animal Discourse, Women, and Subjectivity." *Chaucer Review* 36 (2002): 277–97.

Krug, Rebecca. *Reading Families: Women's Literate Practice in Late Medieval England.* Ithaca: Cornell University Press, 2002.

Kuczynski, Michael P. "Don't Blame Me: The Metaethics of a Chaucerian Apology." *Chaucer Review* 37 (2003): 315–28.

Lee, Brian S. "The Question of Closure in Fragment V of *The Canterbury Tales.*" *Yearbook of English Studies* 22 (1992): 190–200.

Lee, Paul. *Nunneries, Learning, and Spirituality in Late Medieval English Society: The Dominican Priory of Dartford.* Woodbridge, UK: York Medieval Press, 2000; Rochester, NY: 2001.

Lefevere, André. "Translation: Its Genealogy in the West." In *Translation, History, and Culture*, edited by Susan Bassnett and André Lefevere, 1–15. London: Pinter, 1990.

Lett, Didier. *L'enfant des miracles: Enfance et société au Moyen Âge (XIIᵉ–XIIIᵉ siècle).* Paris: Aubier, 1997.

Levitan, Alan. "The Parody of Pentecost in Chaucer's *Summoner's Tale.*" *University of Toronto Quarterly* 40 (1971): 236–46.

Levy, Bernard S. "Biblical Parody in the *Summoner's Tale.*" *Tennessee Studies in Literature* 11 (1966): 45–60.

Lewis, Gertrud Jaron. *By Women, for Women, About Women: The Sister-Books of Fourteenth-Century Germany.* Studies and Texts 125. Toronto: Pontifical Institute of Mediaeval Studies, 1996.

Lochrie, Karma. *Margery Kempe and Translations of the Flesh.* Philadelphia: University of Pennsylvania Press, 1991.

Lodge, Sir Oliver. "Discussion of Professor Richet's Case of Automatic Writing in a Language Unknown to the Writer." *Proceedings of the Society for Psychical Research* 19 (1905–1907): 195–204.

Lombard, Émile. *De la Glossolalie chez les premiers chrétiens et des phénomènes similaires, étude d'exégèse et de psychologie.* Lausanne: G. Bridel, 1910.

Long, Lynne, ed. *Translation and Religion: Holy Untranslatable?* Clevedon: Multilingual Matters, 2005.

Lynch, Kathryn L. "East Meets West in Chaucer's *Squire's* and *Franklin's Tales.*" *Speculum* 70 (1995): 530–51.

———. "Storytelling, Exchange, and Constancy: East and West in Chaucer's *Man of Law's Tale.*" *Chaucer Review* 33 (1999): 409–22.

Macchia, Frank D. "Babel and the Tongues of Pentecost: Reversal or Fulfillment?—A Theological Perspective." In Cartledge, *Speaking in Tongues*, 34–51.

Machan, Tim William. "Chaucer as Translator." In *The Medieval Translator: The Theory and Practice of Translation in the Middle Ages*, edited by Roger Ellis and assisted by Jocelyn Price, Stephen Medcalf, and Peter Meredith, 55–67. Cambridge: Brewer, 1989.

Mandonnet, Pierre. *St. Dominic and His Work.* Translated by Mary Benedicta Larkin. St. Louis: B. Herder, 1944.

McAvoy, Liz Herbert. *Authority and the Female Body in the Writings of Julian of Norwich and Margery Kempe.* Studies in Medieval Mysticism 5. Cambridge: D. S. Brewer, 2004.

McEntire, Sandra J. "The Dialogics of Margery Kempe and Her *Book.*" *Mystics Quarterly* 26 (2000): 179–97.

McGee, Gary B. "Shortcut to Language Preparation? Radical Evangelicals, Missions, and the Gift of Tongues." *International Bulletin of Missionary Research* 25 (2001): 118–23.

McSheffrey, Shannon. "Literacy and the Gender Gap in the Late Middle Ages: Women and Reading in Lollard Communities." In *Women, the Book and the Godly: Selected Proceedings of the St Hilda's Conference, 1993*, edited by Lesley Smith and Jane H. M. Taylor, 157–70. Woodbridge, UK: D. S. Brewer, 1995.

Meens, Rob. "Children and Confession." In Wood, *The Church and Childhood*, 53–65.

Melville, Herman. *Moby-Dick; or, the White Whale*. Everyman's Library Classics. New York: Alfred A. Knopf, 1991; originally published New York: Harper, 1851.

Menestò, Enrico. "The Apostolic Canonization Proceedings of Clare of Montefalco, 1318–1319." In *Women and Religion in Medieval and Renaissance Italy*, edited by Daniel Bornstein and Roberto Rusconi, translated by Margery J. Scheider, 104–29. Chicago: University of Chicago Press, 1996.

Mills, Watson E. *Glossolalia: A Bibliography*. Studies in the Bible and Early Christianity 6. New York: Edwin Mellen Press, 1985.

———. "Glossolalia: A Survey of the Literature." In Mills, *Speaking in Tongues*, 13–31.

———, ed. *Speaking in Tongues: A Guide to Research on Glossolalia*. Grand Rapids, MI: W. B. Eerdmans, 1986.

Minnis, A. J. *Medieval Theory of Authorship: Scholastic Literary Attitudes in the Later Middle Ages*. Philadelphia: University of Pennsylvania Press, 1988.

Mitchell, Rosamund, and Florence Myles. *Second Language Learning Theories*. London: Arnold, 1998.

Mooney, Catherine M. "Authority and Inspiration in the *Vitae* and Sermons of Humility of Faenza." In *Medieval Monastic Preaching*, edited by Carolyn Muessig, 123–43. Brill's Studies in Intellectual History 90. Leiden: Brill, 1998.

———, ed. *Gendered Voices: Medieval Saints and Their Interpreters*. Philadelphia: University of Pennsylvania Press, 1999.

Moorman, John. *A History of the Franciscan Order, from Its Origins to the Year 1517*. Oxford: Clarendon, 1968.

Mormando, Franco. "Signs of the Apocalypse in Late Medieval Italy: The Popular Preaching of Bernardino of Siena." Edited by Paul Maurice Clogan. *Medievalia et Humanistica: Studies in Medieval and Renaissance Culture* 24 (1997): 95–122.

Morris, Bridget. *St Birgitta of Sweden*. Studies in Mysticism 1. Woodbridge, UK: Boydell, 1999.

Morrison, Susan Signe. "Don't Ask, Don't Tell: The Wife of Bath and Vernacular Translations." *Exemplaria* 8 (1996): 97–123.

Morse, Mary. "Seeing and Hearing: Margery Kempe and the *mise-en-page*." *Studia Mystica* 20 (1999): 15–42.

Mosiman, Eddison. *Das Zungenreden, geschichtlich und psychologisch untersucht*. Tübingen: J. C. B. Mohr, 1911.

Muessig, Carolyn. "Prophecy and Song: Teaching and Preaching by Medieval Women." In Kienzle and Walker, *Women Preachers and Prophets Through Two Millennia of Christianity*, 146–58.

Mulder-Bakker, Anneke B., ed. *Seeing and Knowing: Women and Learning in Medieval Europe, 1200–1550*. Medieval Women: Texts and Contexts 11. Turnhout: Brepols, 2004.

Munday, Jeremy. *Introducing Translation Studies: Theories and Applications*. London: Routledge, 2001.

Newman, Barbara. "Devout Women and Demoniacs in the World of Thomas of Cantimpré." In *New Trends in Feminine Spirituality: The Holy Women of Liège and Their Impact*, edited by Juliette Dor, Leslie Johnson, and Jocelyn Wogan-Browne, 35–60. Turnhout: Brepols, 1999.

———. "Hildegard and Her Hagiographers: The Remaking of Female Sainthood." In Mooney, *Gendered Voices*, 16–34, 195–202.

———. "Possessed by the Spirit: Devout Women, Demoniacs, and the Apostolic Life in the Thirteenth Century." *Speculum* 73 (1998): 733–70.

———. *Sister of Wisdom: St. Hildegard's Theology of the Feminine*. Berkeley and Los Angeles: University of California Press, 1987.

———. "What Did It Mean to Say 'I Saw'? The Clash Between Theory and Practice in Medieval Visionary Culture." *Speculum* 80 (2005): 1–43.

Nicholson, Peter. "Chaucer Borrows from Gower: The Sources of the *Man of Law's Tale*." In *Chaucer and Gower: Difference, Mutuality, Exchange*, edited by R. F. Yeager, 85–99. English Literary Monograph Series 51. Victoria, Canada: English Literary Studies, University of Victoria, 1991.

———. "*The Man of Law's Tale*: What Chaucer Really Owed to Gower." *Chaucer Review* 26 (1991): 153–74.

Olson, Glending. "The End of the *Summoner's Tale* and the Uses of Pentecost." *Studies in the Age of Chaucer* 21 (1999): 209–45.

———. "Geoffrey Chaucer." In *The Cambridge History of Medieval English Literature*, edited by David Wallace, 566–88. Cambridge: Cambridge University Press, 1999.

Olson, Linda, and Kathryn Kerby-Fulton, eds. *Voices in Dialogue: Reading Women in the Middle Ages*. Notre Dame: University of Notre Dame Press, 2005.

O'Malley, J. Michael, and Anna Uhl Chamot. *Learning Strategies in Second Language Acquisition*. Cambridge: Cambridge University Press, 1990.

Orth, William. "The Problem of the Performative in Chaucer's Prioress Sequence." *Chaucer Review* 42 (2007): 196–210.

Owen, Charles A., Jr. "The Falcon's Complaint in the *Squire's Tale*." In *Rebels and Rivals: The Contestive Spirit in The Canterbury Tales*, edited by Susanna Greer Fein, David Raybin, and Peter C. Braeger, 173–88. Studies in Medieval Culture 29. Kalamazoo, MI: Medieval Institute, 1991.

Patai, Raphael. "Exorcism and Xenoglossia among the Safed Kabbalists." *Journal of American Folklore* 91 (1978): 823–833.

Patterson, Lee. "'The Living Witnesses of Our Redemption': Martyrdom and Imitation in Chaucer's *Prioress's Tale*." *Journal of Medieval and Early Modern Studies* 31 (2001): 507–560.

Paull, Michael. "The Influence of the Saint's Legend Genre in the *Man of Law's Tale*." *Chaucer Review* 5 (1971): 179–94.

Pearsall, Derek. "Chaucer's Religious Tales: A Question of Genre." In Benson and Robertson, *Chaucer's Religious Tale*, 11–19.

Petroff, Elizabeth, ed. *Consolation of the Blessed*. New York: Alta Gaia Society, 1979.

Power, Eileen Edna. *Medieval English Nunneries, c. 1275–1535*. Cambridge: Cambridge University Press, 1922.

Poythress, Vern S. "The Nature of Corinthian Glossolalia: Possible Options." *Westminster Theological Journal* 40 (1977): 130–35.

Raybin, David. "Custance and History: Woman as Outsider in Chaucer's *Man of Law's Tale*." *Studies in the Age of Chaucer* 12 (1990): 65–84.

von Reuter, Florizel. *The Consoling Angel*. London: [s.n.], 1930.

————. *Psychical Experiences of a Musician (in Search of Truth)*. London: Simpkin, Marshall, and the Psychic Press, 1928.

Richards, Marie. "Community and Poverty in the Reformed Order of St. Clare in the Fifteenth Century." *Journal of Religious History* 19 (1995): 10–25.

Richet, Charles. "Xenoglossie: L'Écriture automatique en langues étrangères." *Proceedings of the Society for Psychical Research* 19 (1905–1907): 162–94.

Riddy, Felicity. "Text and Self in *The Book of Margery Kempe*." In Olson and Kerby-Fulton, *Voices in Dialogue*, 435–53.

Robertson, Elizabeth. "The 'Elvyssh' Power of Constance: Christian Feminism in Geoffrey Chaucer's *The Man of Law's Tale*." *Studies in the Age of Chaucer* 23 (2001): 143–80.

Rollo, David. *Glamorous Sorcery: Magic and Literacy in the High Middle Ages*. Medieval Cultures 25. Minneapolis: University of Minnesota Press, 2000.

Sahlin, Claire L. *Birgitta of Sweden and the Voice of Prophecy*. Studies in Medieval Mysticism 3. Woodbridge, UK: Boydell, 2001.

————. "Submission, Role Reversals, and Partnerships: Birgitta and Her Clerical Associates." *Birgittiana* 3 (1997): 9–41.

Salih, Sarah. *Versions of Virginity in Late Medieval England*. Woodbridge, UK: D. S. Brewer, 2001.

Salter, David. *Holy and Noble Beasts: Encounters with Animals in Medieval Literature*. Cambridge: D. S. Brewer, 2001.

Sanok, Catherine. *Her Life Historical: Exemplarity and Female Saints' Lives in Late Medieval England*. Philadelphia: University of Pennsylvania Press, 2007.

Scase, Wendy. "St. Anne and the Education of the Virgin: Literary and Artistic Traditions and their Implications." In *England in the Fourteenth Century: Proceedings of the 1991 Harlaxton Symposium*, edited by Nicholas Rogers, 81–96. Harlaxton Medieval Studies 3. Stamford, CT: P. Watkins, 1993.

Schibanoff, Susan. "Worlds Apart: Orientalism, Antifeminism, and Heresy in Chaucer's *Man of Law's Tale*." *Exemplaria* 8 (1996): 59–96.

Schnapp, Jeffrey T. "Virgin Words: Hildegard of Bingen's *Lingua Ignota* and the Development of Imaginary Languages Ancient to Modern." *Exemplaria* 3 (1991): 267–98.

Scott, Karen. "Mystical Death, Bodily Death: Catherine of Siena and Raymond of Capua on the Mystic's Encounter with God." In Mooney, *Gendered Voices*, 136–67, 238–44.

Shahar, Shulamith. *Childhood in the Middle Ages*. London: Routledge, 1990.

Sharon-Zisser, Shirley. "*The Squire's Tale* and the Limits of Non-Mimetic Fiction." *Chaucer Review* 26 (1992): 377–94.

Sheingorn, Pamela. "'The Wise Mother': The Image of St. Anne Teaching the Virgin Mary." In *Gendering the Master Narrative: Women and Power in the Middle Ages*, edited by Mary C. Erler and Maryanne Kowaleski, 105–34. Ithaca: Cornell University Press, 2003. Reprinted from "'The Wise Mother': The Image of St. Anne Teaching the Virgin Mary." *Gesta* 32 (1993): 69–80.

Shoaf, R. A. "'Unwemmed Custance': Circulation, Property, and Incest in the *Man of Law's Tale*." *Exemplaria* 2 (1990): 287–302.

Sikorska, Liliana. "Between Penance and Purgatory: Margery Kempe's *Pélegrinage de la vie Humaine* and the Idea of Salvaging Journeys." In *Beowulf and Beyond*, edited by Hans Sauer and Renate Bauer, 235–57. Frankfurt: Peter Lang, 2007.

Simons, Walter. "'Staining the Speech of Things Divine': The Uses of Literacy in

Medieval Beguine Communities." In Hemptinne and Góngora, *The Voice of Silence*, 85–110.

Smith, Lesley, and Jane H. M. Taylor, eds. *Women, The Book and the Godly: Selected Proceedings of the St Hilda's Conference, 1993.* Vol. 1. Cambridge: D. S. Brewer, 1995.

Smoller, Laura A. "Miracle, Memory, and Meaning in the Canonization of Vincent Ferrer, 1453–1454." *Speculum* 73 (1998): 429–54.

Somerset, Fiona. "'As just as is a squyre': The Politics of 'Lewed Translacion' in Chaucer's *Summoner's Tale*." *Studies in the Age of Chaucer* 21 (1999): 187–207.

Spearing, A. C. "*The Book of Margery Kempe*: Or, the Diary of a Nobody." *Southern Review* 38 (2002): 625–35.

———. "Narrative Voice: The Case of Chaucer's *Man of Law's Tale*." *New Literary History* 32 (2001): 715–46.

Staley, Lynn, ed. and trans. *The Book of Margery Kempe: A New Translation, Contexts, Criticism.* New York: W. W. Norton & Company, 2001.

———. *Margery Kempe's Dissenting Fictions.* University Park: Pennsylvania State University Press, 1994.

Stelten, Leo F. *Dictionary of Ecclesiastical Latin.* Peabody, MA: Hendrickson, 1995.

Stevenson, Ian. *Unlearned Language: New Studies in Xenoglossy.* Charlottesville: University Press of Virginia, 1984.

———. *Xenoglossy: A Review and Report of a Case.* Charlottesville: University Press of Virginia, 1974.

Stock, Brian. *The Implications of Literacy: Written Language and Models of Interpretation in the Eleventh and Twelfth Centuries.* Princeton: Princeton University Press, 1983.

Stokes, Charity Scott. "Margery Kempe: Her Life and the Early History of Her Book." *Mystics Quarterly* 25 (1999): 9–67.

Suydam, Mary A. "Beguine Textuality: Sacred Performances." In Suydam and Ziegler, *Performance and Transformation*, 169–210.

Suydam, Mary A., and Joanna E. Ziegler, eds. *Performance and Transformation: New Approaches to Late Medieval Spirituality.* Basingstoke: Macmillan, 1999; New York: St. Martin's Press, 1999.

Sweetman, Robert. "Christine of Saint-Trond's Preaching Apostolate: Thomas of Cantimpré's Hagiographical Method Revisited." *Vox Benedictina* 9 (1992): 66–97.

———. "Thomas of Cantimpré, *Mulieres Religiosae*, and Purgatorial Piety: Hagiographical *Vitae* and the Beguine 'Voice.'" In *A Distinct Voice: Medieval Studies in Honor of Leonard E. Boyle, O.P.*, edited by Jacqueline Brown and William P. Stoneman, 606–28. Notre Dame: University of Notre Dame Press, 1997.

Tarvers, Josephine K. "The Alleged Illiteracy of Margery Kempe: A Reconsideration of the Evidence." *Medieval Perspectives* 11 (1996): 113–24.

Tatlock, J. S. P. "Caradoc of Llancarfan." *Speculum* 13 (1938): 139–52.

Taylor, David G. K. "St. Ephraim's Influence on the Greeks." *Hugoye: Journal of Syriac Studies* 1.2 (1998). http://syrcom.cua.edu/Hugoye/Vol1No2/HV1N2Taylor.html.

Taylor, Paul Beekman. "Chaucer's Strategies of Translation." *Chaucer Yearbook* 4 (1997): 1–19.

Townsend, David, and Andew Taylor, eds. *The Tongue of the Fathers: Gender and Ideology in Twelfth-Century Latin.* Philadelphia: University of Pennsylvania Press, 1998.

Trembinski, Donna. "*Non Alter Christus*: Early Dominican Lives of Saint Francis." *Franciscan Studies* 63 (2005): 69–105.

Valone, Carolyn. "The Pentecost: Image and Experience in Late Sixteenth-Century Rome." *Sixteenth Century Journal* 24 (1993): 801–28.

Van Dam, Raymond. *Saints and Their Miracles in Late Antique Gaul.* Princeton: Princeton University Press, 1993.

Vauchez, André. *Sainthood in the Later Middle Ages.* Translated by Jean Birrell. Cambridge: Cambridge University Press, 1997.

Venuti, Lawrence. *The Scandals of Translation: Towards an Ethics of Difference.* London: Routledge, 1998.

———. *The Translation Studies Reader.* New York: Routledge, 2000.

———. *The Translator's Invisibility: A History of Translation.* London: Routledge, 1995.

Voaden, Rosalynn. "God's Almighty Hand: Women Co-Writing the Book." In Smith and Taylor, *Women, the Book, and the Godly,* 55–65.

———. *God's Words, Women's Voices: The Discernment of Spirits in the Writings of Late-Medieval Women Visionaries.* Suffolk, UK: York Medieval Press, 1999.

———, ed. *Prophets Abroad: The Reception of Continental Holy Women in Late-Medieval England.* Cambridge: D. S. Brewer, 1996.

Wacker, Grant. *Heaven Below: Early Pentecostals and American Culture.* Cambridge: Harvard University Press, 2001.

Warren, Nancy Bradley. "Monastic Politics: St Colette of Corbie, Franciscan Reform, and the House of Burgundy." In *New Medieval Literatures* V, edited by Rita Copeland, David Lawton, and Wendy Scase, 203–228. Oxford: Oxford University Press, 2002.

Wasyliw, Patricia Healy. "The Pious Infant: Developments in Popular Piety During the High Middle Ages." In *Lay Sanctity, Medieval and Modern: A Search for Models,* edited by Ann W. Astell, 105–15. Notre Dame: University of Notre Dame Press, 2000.

Watson, Nicholas. "Censorship and Cultural Change in Late-Medieval England: Vernacular Theology, the Oxford Translation Debate, and Arundel's Constitutions of 1409." *Speculum* 70 (1995): 822–64.

———. "The Making of *The Book of Margery Kempe.*" In Olson and Kerby-Fulton, *Voices in Dialogue,* 395–434.

———. *Richard Rolle and the Invention of Authority.* Cambridge Studies in Medieval Literature 13. Cambridge: Cambridge University Press, 1991.

Watt, Diane. "Faith in the Landscape: Overseas Pilgrimages in *The Book of Margery Kempe.*" In *A Place to Believe In: Locating Medieval Landscapes,* edited by Clare A. Lees and Gillian R. Overing, 170–87. University Park: Pennsylvania State University Press, 2006.

———. *Secretaries of God: Women Prophets in Late Medieval and Early Modern England.* Cambridge: D. S. Brewer, 1997.

Weckmann, Luis. *The Medieval Heritage of Mexico.* New York: Fordham University Press, 1992.

Weinstein, Donald, and Rudolph M. Bell. *Saints and Society: The Two Worlds of Western Christendom, 1000–1700.* Chicago: University of Chicago Press, 1982.

Welliver, Kenneth Bruce. *Pentecost and the Early Church: Patristic Interpretation of Acts 2.* Ph.D. diss., Yale University, 1961.

White, Andrew Dickson. *A History of the Warfare of Science with Theology in Christendom.* 2 vols. New York: D. Appleton and Company, 1898.

Whymant, A. Neville J. *Psychic Adventures in New York.* London: Morley & M. Kennerley, Jr., 1931.

William, George H., and Edith Waldvogel. "A History of Speaking in Tongues and Related Gifts." In *The Charismatic Movement*, edited by Michael Pollock Hamilton, 61–113. Grand Rapids, MI: W. B. Eerdmans, 1975.

Williams, Cyril G. "Glossolalia as a Religious Phenomenon: 'Tongues' at Corinth and Pentecost." *Religion* 5 (1975): 16–32.

Wogan-Browne, Jocelyn, Nicholas Watson, Andrew Taylor, and Ruth Evans, eds. *The Idea of the Vernacular: An Anthology of Middle English Literary Theory, 1280–1520*. University Park: Pennsylvania State University Press, 1999.

Wood, Diana, ed. *The Church and Childhood: Papers Read at the 1993 Summer Meeting and the 1994 Winter Meeting of the Ecclesiastical History Society*. Studies in Church History 31. Oxford: Blackwell, 1994.

Wood, Frederic Herbert. *This Egyptian Miracle: or, the Restoration of the Lost Speech of Ancient Egypt by Supernormal Means*. Philadelphia: David McKay, 1939.

Wright, Michael J. "What They Said to Margery Kempe: Narrative Reliability in Her Book." *Neophilologus* 79 (1995): 497–508.

Yoshikawa, Naoë Kukita. "The Jerusalem Pilgrimage: The Centre of the Structure of the *Book of Margery Kempe*." *English Studies* 86 (2005): 193–205.

———. "Veneration of Virgin Martyrs in Margery Kempe's Meditation: Influence of the Sarum Liturgy and Hagiography." In *Writing Religious Women: Female Spiritual and Textual Practices in Late Medieval England*, edited by Denis Renevey and Christiania Whitehead, 177–95. Toronto: University of Toronto Press, 2000.

Zeiman, Katherine. "Reading, Singing, and Understanding: Constructions of the Literacy of Women Religious in Late Medieval England." In Jones, *Learning and Literacy in Medieval England and Abroad*, 97–120.

Zerhusen, Bob. "The Problem of Tongues in 1 Cor 14: A Reexamination." *Biblical Theology Bulletin* 27 (1997): 139–52.

Index